SPELLING

Fourth Edition

THE EASY WAY

Joseph Mersand
Former Associate Professor of Education
York College of the City University of New York

Francis Griffith
Former Emeritus Professor of Education
Hofstra University,
Hempstead, New York

Kathryn O'D. Griffith
Former Chair, Speech Department
George Washington High School,
New York City

BARRON'S

Acknowledgments

The authors wish to express their thanks to Margaret C. Chandler, James W. Connolly, Paul Connolly, Bidabee Gloster, Estelle J. Mersand, Laura and Robert Pagano, Gladys D. Roche, David Sharp, Carol Sullivan, and Jeremiah J. Sullivan for their assistance in preparing and editing the manuscript over the course of three editions.

In addition, contributions to this fourth edition by Linda Diamond are gratefully acknowledged.

© Copyright 2006 by Barron's Educational Series, Inc.
Prior editions © copyright 1996, 1988, 1982 by Barron's Educational Series, Inc.

All inquiries should be addressed to:
Barron's Educational Series, Inc.
250 Wireless Boulevard
Hauppauge, New York 11788
www.barronseduc.com

Library of Congress Catalog Card No. 2005057072

ISBN-13: 978-0-7641-3410-4
ISBN-10: 0-7641-3410-8

Library of Congress Cataloging in Publication Data
Mersand, Joseph E., 1907–1981
    Spelling the easy way / Joseph Mersand, Francis Griffith,
  Kathryn O'D. Griffith.—4th ed.
      p.   cm.
    ISBN-13: 978-0-7641-3410-4
    ISBN-10: 0-7641-3410-8
    1. English language—Orthography and spelling. [1. English language—Spelling.]
  I. Griffith, Francis J. II. Griffith, Kathryn O'D. III. Title

  PE1145.2.M39   2006
  428.1'3—dc22   2005057072

PRINTED IN THE UNITED STATES OF AMERICA
9 8 7 6 5 4 3

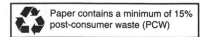 Paper contains a minimum of 15% post-consumer waste (PCW)

CONTENTS

INTRODUCTION

Does spelling count? Asked to write anything in school, the first thing students like to ask a teacher is: "Does spelling count?" or "Are you going to take off for spelling?" The answer is likely to be a vigorous "Yes!" and the truth is, spelling often counts A LOT.

Why? Well, for one reason—certainly not the best—it counts for the same reason **cloths** do. People judge by appearances, and spelling still **seams** to be evidence of ignorance. **Its** embarrassing to misspell words regularly. Spelling may not be **awl** that counts, but it's **wholly** in many people's minds.

But, you may think, I work at a computer—with a spell-check program! It spells for me. And indeed, a computer program COULD have checked for you that *embarrassed* has two *r*'s and two *s*'s and that *misspell* was not misspelled! But the previous paragraph *does* have five mistakes in it. You probably noticed them in **boldface** (and maybe wondered, "Was I wise to buy this book?") The five are (1) the misuse of *cloths* for *clothes*, (2) *seams* for *seems*, (3) the rather obvious *awl* for *all*, and (4) that familiar nuisance: *its* or *it's*. (It should have been *it's*, a contraction of *it is*.) Finally, (5) which is correct? Is it *wholly* or *holy*? (We meant to say that good spelling is a sacred concern to some people, not that their concern is *wholly* a matter of attitude.)

A computer's spell-checker couldn't tell you which is correct. In fact, a spell-checker couldn't identify ANY of these problems, since all five words are properly spelled, if misused, above. Nor could a dictionary tell you how to spell *awl* unless you knew how to use one (a dictionary, that is, not the pointed tool used for making holes (not **wholes**) in wood and leather). (See Chapters 3 and 4 on using a dictionary, and Chapter 19 on Homonyms and Homophones.)

Another good reason to become a good speller is to enjoy the fascination of words themselves: of homophones, for example—words that sound the same but differ in origin, spelling, and meaning (*seams* and *seems* or *awl* and *all*). Or of etymologies—the word *embarrassed* comes ultimately from the Latin *imbarrare,* to put in bars. It is embarrassing to be in jail. The word *spell* itself, for a second example, derives from Old French *espelir*, meaning to read out; to puzzle out or comprehend something letter by letter. (See Chapters 7, 8, 9, and 20 on prefixes, suffixes, and families of words with common parts.)

The best reasons for reading this book, then, are (1) to avoid embarrassment that comes from misspelled words that create impressions of which we are not even aware, and (2) to come under the spell of words—to enjoy the rich pleasure that comes from knowing the history and geography of words, and the science of their construction.

Why Choose This Speller?

Since Noah Webster published his first speller in 1783, many have appeared on the market. What distinguishes this book, we believe, are the following features:

- **Principles of Spelling:** *Spelling the Easy Way* promises no quick fix. Yes, it offers an invaluable **10,000 Word Ready Reference Spelling List**, but a list is not a substitute for the principles of good spelling one needs to learn in order to avoid always looking up words on lists.

- **Stimulating Information:** *Spelling the Easy Way* assumes we learn best what interests us most. It appeals not only to self-discipline but also to the curiosity, pleasure, and satisfaction that knowledge of language provides.
- **Exercises, Tests, and More Exercises:** *Spelling the Easy Way* contains many exercises and tests to strengthen and challenge your skill. Practice does *not* make perfect; it only makes permanent. Testing yourself further assures you good habits of correct spelling.
- **Clear, Comprehensive Organization:** *Spelling the Easy Way*'s fully detailed Table of Contents and spacious layout make it easy to find and use what you need—a guide to hyphenation (Chapter 15), a reminder about capitalization (Chapter 17), or hints on abbreviating (Chapter 18).
- **Demons and Superdemons:** "The One Hundred Pests" (Chapter 21), and the computer and medical terms in Chapters 22 and 23 make *Spelling the Easy Way* both practical and enjoyable to use.

We wish you pleasure in the work before you. Spelling is surely not all that counts, in school or out, but it *does* count!

PRETEST

The first step to becoming a better speller is to discover your strengths and weaknesses. To do that, take the Spelling Pretest before you attempt the instruction that follows it. Use the Answer Key to check your answers and to find the correct spellings. See whether you understand why your answer was incorrect. As you progress through the book, you will find all of the rules discussed.

Spelling Pretest

Directions: Circle the letter of the incorrectly spelled word in each group.

1. A. efficient
   B. patience
   C. recieve
   D. audience

2. A. equally
   B. authorities
   C. definitely
   D. actualy

3. A. acustomed
   B. illegible
   C. grammar
   D. appearance

4. A. children
   B. analyses
   C. sheeps
   D. pianos

5. A. carried
   B. beautyful
   C. iciness
   D. angrily

6. A. dont
   B. could
   C. you're
   D. she's

7. A. A.M.
   B. Jr
   C. assn.
   D. Capt.

8. A. thirty-one
   B. when-ever
   C. far-fetched
   D. much-needed

9. A. exceed
   B. recede
   C. proced
   D. succeed

10. A. irrelevant
    B. disolve
    C. misjudge
    D. irrelevant

11. A. prescribe
    B. persist
    C. propose
    D. perpare

12. A. eligible
    B. legible
    C. permissable
    D. intelligible

13. A. drizzel
    B. swivel
    C. brutal
    D. quarrel

14. A. governor
    B. inventer
    C. editor
    D. passenger

15. A. guidance
    B. violence
    C. pleasant
    D. importence

16. A. loveing
    B. owing
    C. becoming
    D. using

17. A. intensity
    B. poreous
    C. sincerity
    D. extremety

18. A. completeness
    B. likeness
    C. vagueness
    D. coarsness

19. A. duly
    B. wholly
    C. truley
    D. awfully

20. A. spinner
    B. omitting
    C. begining
    D. conferring

21. A. inferring
    B. refering
    C. permitting
    D. occurring

22. A. precede
    B. preceede
    C. accede
    D. concede

23. A. superseede
    B. exceed
    C. succeed
    D. proceed

24. A. its
    B. were
    C. theyre
    D. we'll

25. A. produce
    B. perceive
    C. personnel
    D. perpose

26. A. principal
    B. prinsiple
    C. principle
    D. principles

27. A. certain
    B. extravagant
    C. probuble
    D. dictionary

28. A. liquify
    B. plague
    C. cellar
    D. counselor

29. A. picnicing
    B. trafficking
    C. engaging
    D. colicky

30. A. completeness
    B. amusement
    C. rudness
    D. arrangement

31. A. reversible
    B. collectible
    C. navigable
    D. admissable

32. A. reducable
    B. eligible
    C. readable
    D. permissible

33. A. comprehensible
    B. digestable
    C. combustible
    D. convertible

34. A. divisible
    B. legible
    C. deductable
    D. eatable

35. A. comfortable
    B. accountible
    C. favorable
    D. preventable

36. A. usually
    B. equally
    C. logically
    D. practicaly

37. A. couragous
    B. adventurous
    C. outrageous
    D. analagous

38. A. quarrel
    B. personal
    C. funnal
    D. annual

39. A. regel
    B. legal
    C. arrival
    D. denial

40. A. model
    B. trowal
    C. kernel
    D. cancel

41. A. kisses
    B. buses
    C. losses
    D. clases

42. A. children
    B. women
    C. thiefs
    D. lives

43. A. chiefes
    B. beliefs
    C. shoes
    D. roofs

44. A. vetoes
    B. volcanoes
    C. solos
    D. heros

45. A. lives
    B. knives
    C. leaves
    D. loafs

46. A. solos
    B. pianos
    C. altoes
    D. sopranos

47. A. sisters-in-law
    B. handfuls
    C. cupfuls
    D. mother-in-laws

48. A. oxes
    B. feet
    C. deer
    D. sheep

49. A. louses
    B. women
    C. men
    D. geese

50. A. wield
    B. veil
    C. sieze
    D. grieve

Pretest Answer Key

Use this chart to check your answers. Total the number of your correct responses at the bottom of the chart. Then read the recommendations that follow.

Item	Answer	Correct Spelling	Item	Answer	Correct Spelling
1.	C.	receive	26.	B.	principle
2.	D.	actually	27.	C.	probable
3.	A.	accustomed	28.	A.	liquefy
4.	C.	sheep	29.	A.	picnicking
5.	B.	beautiful	30.	C.	rudeness
6.	A.	don't	31.	D.	admissible
7.	B.	Jr.	32.	A.	reducible
8.	B.	whenever	33.	B.	digestible
9.	C.	proceed	34.	D.	deductible
10.	B.	dissolve	35.	B.	accountable
11.	D.	prepare	36.	D.	practically
12.	C.	permissible	37.	A.	courageous
13.	A.	drizzle	38.	C.	funnel
14.	B.	inventor	39.	A.	regal
15.	D.	importance	40.	B.	trowel
16.	A.	loving	41.	D.	classes
17.	B.	porous	42.	C.	thieves
18.	D.	coarseness	43.	A.	chiefs
19.	C.	truly	44.	D.	heroes
20.	C.	beginning	45.	D.	loaves
21.	B.	referring	46.	C.	altos
22.	B.	precede	47.	D.	mothers-in-law
23.	A.	supersede	48.	A.	oxen
24.	C.	they're	49.	A.	lice
25.	D.	propose	50.	C.	seize

To discover the spelling areas in which you need improvement, check your score.

1. Total your number of correct answers out of the possible 50 answers. You should have 90 to 95 percent correct, or about 48 correct answers.
2. If your score is below 95 percent, pay special attention to the spelling lessons that review the rules and explanations.

THE IMPORTANCE OF SPELLING

Chapter 1

WHY BOTHER TO SPELL CORRECTLY?

We forgive ourselves poor spelling much more readily than we do mistakes in grammar. Perhaps the reason is that others can readily hear our grammar: "Each person is doing their job." or "We was dumbfounded!" But they need to see our spelling to detect its error. Once we write, however, we may realize a half-dozen good reasons why we should be careful to spell correctly:

1. Others aren't tolerant of poor spelling. Some readers may be quick to judge you, even if they misspell other words themselves.
2. Misteaks can be distracting. Truthfully, were you or were you not so strongly distracted by that *misteaks* that you cannot really recall the sentence in which it appeared?
3. Misspelling is not an act of creative expression, at least not after the "invented spelling" stage of childhood. Art is creative. Spelling is conventional, a way of providing easy passage through a society's language. Yes, poets sometimes play with spelling, as they do with every other part of language, but a word is a word, not a woid, even in Brooklyn.
4. Spelling mistakes, some cynics believe, earn teachers a living. It is definitely not how the business world makes its living, however. Where "time is money," words had better be spelled correctly.
5. Misspelling masks misunderstanding. Words that sound or look alike nevertheless mean different things. When we confuse *affect* (influence) and *effect* (accomplish) or *fair* and *fare* or (the classic homophone) *to*, *too*, and *two*, we confuse meaning, not just letters.
6. We often spell with our ears, transcribing what we hear. What we pronounce correctly, we are more likely to spell correctly. The reverse is also true; what we spell correctly, we are more likely to pronounce correctly. Spelling and speaking improve together.

Misspelling can suggest to others that we confuse similar things, think imprecisely, are too lazy or negligent to consult a dictionary, or do not read, write, or speak with care. Worse, it can undermine our self-confidence, convincing us that we are less able than we are.

Computerized spell-check programs may help, but they are no substitute for learning. Spell-checkers know only what they've been told. They cannot tell *gorilla* (the animal) from *guerrilla* (a member of an irregular army); *council* from *counsel*; *born* from *borne*; or *canvas* (the cloth) from *canvass* (poll voters). While a computer may know *Beethoven*, it probably can't spell *Tchaikovsky*. It's still up to us to know the difference—or learn it.

(And learning to spell *Tchaikovsky* may take some guessing at the first few letters, and some persistence.)

Today, only a reactionary would contest the value or resist the use of a spell-checker as a line of first resistance to misspellings in a text. However, even spell-checkers omit many words; spell-checkers never tell us when we have used a right word in the wrong place (*their* for *there*, for example), and constantly correcting mistakes takes time that avoiding them would have saved.

And, finally, perhaps the best reason to study spelling is to learn language, which grows "curiouser and curiouser," as the Mad Hatter told Alice in Wonderland, the more we know of it.

Nothing is more curious than the spelling of many English words, and so the next chapter begins to explain: "Why Is Spelling So Difficult?"

Chapter 2

WHY IS SPELLING SO DIFFICULT?

Nearly everybody has difficulty with spelling. Foreign-born speakers have trouble learning English because they see no relationship between the way words are spelled and the way they are pronounced. Native-born speakers of English have trouble for the same reason.

In other languages, words are more often spelled as they are pronounced. If you did not know Italian and came across the Italian word, *inglese*, meaning English, you might pronounce it *ing-gleez*. In Italian, however, the word is pronounced *een-glay-say* because in that language there are no silent vowels such as the silent *e* in English.

There are thousands of English words in which some vowels and consonants are not pronounced. English spelling and pronunciation are often unrelated.

Why?

Linguistic Change

To find the answer we must take a brief look at the development of the English language.

About the middle of the fifth century, three tribes, the Angles, Saxons, and Jutes, who inhabited a section of the North Sea shore that is now Germany and Denmark, invaded Britain, drove the inhabitants into Wales, and established their own kingdoms. They spoke a language that was basically German. Today it is referred to as Old English or Anglo-Saxon.

In 1066 A.D. the Normans, who lived in northwestern France, invaded and conquered Britain. They imposed their language and culture on the conquered land. The common people began to speak a dialect which was a mixture of Anglo-Saxon and Norman French. This dialect is called Middle English.

The most important author to write in this new dialect was Geoffrey Chaucer whose famous book, *The Canterbury Tales*, written about 1387, is still read with enjoyment today.

Chaucer and his contemporaries spelled words as they were pronounced. A final *e* was pronounced like the *a* in *about*; for instance, *nonne* (nun) was pronounced *non-nuh*. All consonants and vowels were pronounced.

Pronunciation began to change about Chaucer's time and continued to change for almost two hundred years, until about 1550. One reason for the change was the French influence because England held large possessions in France. There were other reasons for the shift in pronunciation that we do not fully understand.

At this time printing was introduced into England. The most famous printer of the period, William Caxton, preserved Chaucer's Middle English spelling. Those who came after him followed his example even though most words were no longer pronounced as they had been in Chaucer's time. Pronunciation changed but spelling remained the same. English spelling was no longer phonetic. Print had preserved the visual look of words, even as their sounds continued to evolve with social usage.

The Modern English period began about 1550. From that time until today pronunciation has continued to change, but spelling has remained relatively fixed. There have been spelling changes, of course, but the rate of change has slowed down, though the mass media can rapidly accelerate public acceptance of *thruway*, for example, or even *cold slaw* (which is, more properly, *cole slaw*, German for *sliced cabbage*). What becomes proper in a country as vigorously democratic as the United States is finally determined more by publicly accepted usage than by academic fiat.

Does this mean that there are no spelling rules? Not at all. There are basic rules, each with exceptions to be sure, but the exceptions are not so numerous as you might think. You can learn these rules with a little effort. By learning them you will greatly improve your spelling ability. In succeeding chapters these rules are stated and explained.

Our Confusing Alphabet

Our alphabet is another cause of spelling difficulties.

A single letter may stand for several different sounds. For example, the letter *a* represents six different sounds and the letter *s* four.

Single Letters with Several Sounds	
A	**S**
p*a*t (ă)	*s*ea (s)
b*a*ke (ā)	no*s*e (z)
c*a*re (â)	*s*ure (sh)
f*a*ther (ä)	plea*s*ure (zh)
*a*ll (a)	
*a*bout (ə)	

At the same time one sound may be represented by several different letters or combinations of letters. For example, the sound of *ā* may be spelled as follows.

Single Sounds Represented by Several Letters
ā Sound
ay — *as in* say
a — *as in* page
ai — *as in* maid
au — *as in* gauge
e — *as in* beta
ey — *as in* obey
ei — *as in* weigh

The *-ough* words show how many different pronunciations may result from identical spelling.

-*OUGH* Has Many Sounds	
Word	**Sound**
thro*ugh*	(oo)
ro*ugh*	(uff)
co*ugh*	(awf)
pl*ough*	(ow)
thor*ough*	(oh)
hicc*ough*	(up)

To show to what extremes one may go in the strangeness of English spelling, consider the word *potato*. Using some of the unusual combinations in English it is possible to spell the word thus: *ghoughpteighbteau*.

Here is the key:

gh	as pronounced in hiccou*gh*
ough	as pronounced in th*ough*
pt	as pronounced in *pt*omaine
eigh	as pronounced in w*eigh*
bt	as pronounced in de*bt*
eau	as pronounced in b*eau*

gh/ough/pt/eigh/bt/eau
(potato)

Try to discover why the word *fish* can be spelled *ghoti*.

Homonyms and Homophones

Words spelled and pronounced alike but differing in meaning are called *homonyms*.

Homonyms	
Same Spelling, Same Pronunciation, Different Meaning	
pool (a body of water)	pool (a game)
fair (light-colored)	fair (a market)
bug (insect)	bug (virus) bug (secretly record)
bank (embankment)	bank (place where money is kept)
mouse (rodent)	mouse (computer component)
long (lengthy)	long (yearn for)
surf (ride a wave)	surf (scan the Internet)
fire (flames)	fire (discharge from work)
run (campaign)	run (jog)

The English language is filled with homonyms. The next time you look up a word in the dictionary, notice how many different definitions are listed. But first, look up *run* and you will find quite a few homonyms.

Words pronounced alike but differing in spelling, derivation, and meaning are called *homophones*.

Homophones

Different Spelling, Same Pronunciation, Different Meaning

air	heir	
ate	eight	
be	bee	
beat	beet	
berth	birth	
compliment (praise)	complement (that which completes)	
sum	some	
their	there	their
aisle	I'll	isle
won	one	
flower	flour	
wait	weight	
weather	whether	
allowed	aloud	
week	weak	
knew	new	
blue	blew	
bow	bough	

More Confusing Word Pairs

Same Spelling, Different Punctuatioin, Different Meaning

wind (breeze)	wind (turn, as with a clock)
invalid (not valid)	invalid (disabled person)

The abundance of homonyms and homophones in English is a source of difficulty, especially to students for whom English is a second language.

Regional Pronunciations

In some regions of our country some words are pronounced differently from common usage. For example, creek is pronounced *crik*; sauce, *sass*; film, *filum*; and draw, *drawr*.

Since we tend to spell words as we hear them pronounced, these and similar regional pronunciations cause spelling difficulties. We must be able to discern dialectal pronunciations to avoid spelling errors.

Remember!

- **Pronunciation has changed rapidly since Modern English began, but spelling has remained relatively stable. As a result, spelling and pronunciation do not always correspond.**
- **A single alphabetic symbol may stand for several different sounds, and one sound may be represented by more than one symbol.**
- **There are hundreds of homonyms and homophones in our language.**
- **Regional pronunciations may be a source of spelling errors.**

These characteristics of English do not sufficiently explain why misspelling is so widespread. Other factors enter that will be discussed in subsequent pages.

Chapter 3

WHY WE MISSPELL

We betray our characteristics and feelings in many ways, for example, by the way we behave, speak, sit, and listen. A keen observer like the fictional Sherlock Holmes can learn much about a person by noticing little things.

Mistakes in spelling tell others many things about us. Some of them we may not want people to know. But once the misspelled word is on paper, there is no recall. We have to suffer the consequences, be they social ostracism, failure to get that position or raise, or loss of respect from the reader.

Consider the fate of the secretary in Arnold Bennett's delightful comedy, *The Stepmother*.

Christine:	Dismiss me, madam?
Gardner:	Cora, can you be so cruel?
Mrs. Prout:	Alas, yes! She has committed the secretarial sin which is beyond forgiveness. She has misspelt.
Gardner:	Impossible!

Mispronunciation

We have a tendency to spell words as we hear them. If a word is not pronounced correctly, it will be misspelled. Spelling errors may result from listening to the poor enunciation of others or they may result from our own mispronunciations.

Listen for syllables, but remeber that you cannot always trust your ear. Common pronunciation often combines syllables, making it more difficult to spell by ear. For instance, some people pronounce every syllable in the word *incidentally*; many of us, however, cut out a syllable from the spoken word, so it sounds like *incidently*.

Here are some words in which syllables or letters are commonly omitted. The correct number of syllables is indicated in parentheses.

Words with Syllables Commonly Omitted

Correct Word	Common Pronunciation
in·ter·est·ing (4)	in·tres·ting (3)
priv·i·lege (3)	priv·lege (2)
hy·gi·en·ic (4)	hy·genic (2)
lic·o·rice (3)	lick·rice (2)
di·a·mond (3)	di·mond (2)
mack·er·el (3)	mack·rel (2)
sar·sa·pa·ril·la (5)	sars·pa·ril·la (4)
lab·o·ra·to·ry (5)	la·bra·to·ry (4)

When practicing spelling aloud, break the word into syllables. Spell by syllables. You will find this method helpful.

Sometimes when we pronounce a word incorrectly we add a syllable where it does not belong, omit a sound, or substitute one sound for another. The following is a list of words that are commonly mispronounced. The correct pronunciation and spelling is in the left column. The common mispronunciation and subsequent misspelling is in the right column. Do you make these mistakes?

Words Commonly Mispronounced

Correct Word	Mispronounced Word
athletic	athaletic
asked	ast
February	Febuary
government	goverment
kindergarten	kindergarden
library	libery
strictly	strickly

If you have a habit of slurring consonants, omitting syllables, or running syllables together like a verbal accordion player, you make it difficult for your listeners to understand what you are saying. You create an unfavorable impression and raise a barrier to your social and professional success. One way of improving your speech habits is by listening attentively to individuals who speak clearly.

Hasty Reading

The tremendous amount of reading material we encounter—from the daily newspaper, to books and magazines, to mail (both virtual and paper), to the countless pages that might interest us on the Internet—causes us to be *skimmers* more often than *readers*. While skimming is often necessary, careful reading, at times, is important as well.

There is a limit to the speed with which you can read. If you go beyond that limit, words become indistinct, blurred, and meaningless. If you boast about finishing the latest novel in two hours, the chances are you misspell many words because you do not have a clear picture of them. You can rarely read more than fifty pages an hour and derive the full benefit of the reading.

Check up on yourself You will discover that many words that you first met in print, you misspell in your personal writings because you raced over them instead of forming a clear picture of the words in your mind.

This is not to deny the value of rapid reading for a specific purpose, which is called *skimming*. When you are not particularly interested in getting every idea and fact from the printed page but only some statistic or date or personal name, it would be a waste of time to read every word slowly. A rapid glance at the entire page will give you the answer you are seeking. However, to read for ideas, beauty of style, or for a detailed explanation requires slow, careful reading.

Suggestion! _____

After writing a letter or report, read it over carefully. You may find errors committed in haste. Correct them before your letter or report leaves your hands.

Infrequent Reading

People who read extensively and carefully are usually good spellers. They have learned to spell by reading. Almost unconsciously, they observe the spelling of the words they read.

On the other hand, poor spellers usually do not have the reading habit. They limit their reading to newspaper headlines or an occasional magazine article.

Read widely, every day if possible. Reading is an excellent means of improving your spelling.

Faulty Observation

A story is told of Toscanini, the great conductor, that illustrates his phenomenal power of observation. He conducted entirely from memory; once he committed to memory the entire score of Respighi's *Pines of Rome* in twenty-four hours. A certain bassoon player wanted to be excused from a rehearsal because his bassoon needed some repairing. One of the keys would not play the note.

"What note doesn't play?" asked the maestro.

"B-flat," answered the bassoon-player.

"Never mind. Stay for the rehearsal. There are no B-flats for the bassoon parts in tonight's program."

That is careful observation. Infinite pains, hours of concentration, and nerve-wracking study went into such perfect knowledge. How many of us will take those pains. How many of us care to observe.

The fault of poor observation is with most of us. The reason is our inertia. Careful observation is too much trouble. By failing to note the correct spelling at first, we fall into the habit of misspelling many words.

Many people, when they are doubtful about the spelling of a word, write it down two or three times. The incorrect forms do not *appear* right. They have a mental picture of the correct word. When they write the correct form, something clicks within them. They recognize they have it right.

You will notice that those who have observed carefully have formed such a vivid picture of the word that they can recall it when they want.

Failure to Consult the Dictionary

There are more than 800,000 words in the English language. Probably no one knows how to spell all of them. Misspellings occur because some words are rare and unusual.

But the spelling of most words is easy because spelling follows established rules. If in doubt, don't guess. Consult the dictionary.

Keep a dictionary at hand when you write or bookmark a good online dictionary on your computer. Check on the spelling of unusual words or those words that give you trouble.

Develop the dictionary habit!

Remember!

Misspellings occur because of:

- **Mispronunciations**
- **Hasty reading**
- **Infrequent reading**
- **Faulty observation**
- **Failure to consult the dictionary**

Careful observation pays and pays well.

Chapter 4

HOW TO BECOME A GOOD SPELLER

Aristotle, the great Greek philosopher, was tutor to the future king, Alexander the Great. One day they were doing a lesson in mathematics that required many calculations. Alexander, always impatient, suddenly threw aside his work and exclaimed:

"Why must I go through all these little steps? Why can't I get the answer immediately? I'm the future king!" "There is no royal road to knowledge," answered his tutor.

There is no royal road to knowledge. There is no short cut to any branch of learning, and that is especially true for spelling. We had trouble with spelling in America long before Noah Webster published his famous speller. Nobody was ever born a perfect speller. Spellers are *made*, not born. Everyone can become a good speller by following certain steps. There are some who had to learn the spelling of every word they met painfully and slowly. That was a waste of nervous energy. Time and nerve-power will be conserved, and success will be assured if you will follow the steps below. This is a prescription for good spelling that has rarely failed.

Learn the Rules and Develop Memory Devices

1. Learn and apply the rules of spelling.
2. Try to discover little devices of your own that will help you remember the spelling of words that have no rules. Such devices are called *mnemonics*, and are as old as ancient Greece. (The word comes from Mnemosyne, the Greek goddess of memory and mother of the Muses.) For more about *mnemonics*, see Chapter 5.

EXAMPLE:
PRINCIP*AL* VS. PRINCIP*LE*
Principal: the head of a school or the main thing
Principle: a rule or a truth

One simple device will remove forever the confusion between these two words:

A princip*le* is a ru*le*. Both of these end in *-le*. Now you have the whole secret. If it means a ru*le*, spell it with the *-le*.

The other meaning must be spelled princi*pal*. You may remember it another way if your principal was a *pal* to you. And there you have the second sure way of remembering these two spelling demons.

EXAMPLE:

STATION*ARY* VS. STATION*ERY*

Stationary: immobile
Stationery: materials for writing

These two have been fighting on our literary battleground ever since we can remember. You think you have the correct spelling when suddenly the other one butts in and then you're lost again.

How can you be certain? Easily. Take a let*ter*; yes, a let*ter*. That's what stationery is used for, and you'll notice that let*ter* ends in *-er*. Now station*ery* ends in *-ery*.

The other word means st*a*nding still. Think of the *a* in st*a*nding and you'll remember the *-ary* in station*ary*.

EXAMPLE:

SEP*A*RATE

The word sep*a*rate has long been a trouble spot.

Think of the word p*art*. When you sep-*ar*-ate, you take things ap-*art*. That will tell you to be sure to spell the word with *ar*.

You may use these three devices, but the best of these tricks are the ones you think up yourself. When you discover a way to spell a word that has always given you trouble, you will never forget the spelling.

Remember!

Form your own memory devices.

Consult the Dictionary

Form the habit of consulting a dictionary when you are confronted with any spelling difficulty. When a word bothers you and no rule or device will help, look it up while the question is fresh in your mind.

A dictionary will provide the correct spelling, pronunciation, and meaning. It will show the difference between *capital* and *capitol*, *strait* and *straight*, and *formerly* and *formally*.

The recommendation made in the previous chapter about consulting the dictionary bears repetition. Keep a dictionary on your desk or bookmarked online.

Be sure that your dictionary is up to date. Language is always changing, and what once was two words may become hyphenated and, ultimately, come together as one word. Even the most recent dictionaries may differ on whether *townhouse* is acceptable yet as one word. As you can see, you won't want to check your 1988 dictionary for the most accurate answer as to whether a word is hyphenated.

The language is growing nearly at the speed of technology; as technology grows, so do the words that define it. Many new words also find their way into the dictionary because of common usage. Even misuse can ultimately create a word in the dictionary. In the last printing of this book, *alright* was listed as an incorrect word, a mistaken way of writing *all right*. However, the word was widely used and defended, and *alright* is now listed in the dictionary.

Using a Dictionary for Pronunciation and Spelling

Learning to spell will also help your pronunciation. Learn to pronounce a word, as you check its correct spelling, with the help of a dictionary.

Good dictionaries include:

1. A *phonetic spelling* of each word immediately following each main entry, which is often in **boldface**. For example, **grovel** ('gröv-əl): "to creep with the face to the ground." A phonetic spelling translates the printed sight of a word into its spoken sounds. The phonetic spelling and main entry also divide each word into syllables, and use primary and secondary stress marks to show emphasis in pronunciation (e.g., ham′ bur′ ger).
2. An *abbreviated pronunciation key* is also usually printed at the bottom of each page, for the convenience of the reader, or sometimes across the bottom of each pair of facing pages. This key illustrates the sound of each symbol in the phonetic spelling through a short word.
3. A *full Pronunciation Key* that includes all the phonetic symbols used, in the front of the dictionary. Phonetic symbols represent every possible sound of speech that individual letters in the alphabet can represent visually within the many words of a written language. The symbol for each key sound is also illustrated in a key word. Familiarize yourself with the location of this Pronunciation Key in your own dictionary.

Using a dictionary, you learn to pronounce the word through its phonetic spelling. For example, **epitome** is pronounced ĭ-pit′-a-mē. The curved and straight lines above ĭ and ē in the phonetic spelling, called *diacritical* marks, indicate that the vowel is pronounced briefly (˘) or held for a longer sound (¯). The stress mark indicates that the second syllable is emphasized.

A good dictionary is a treasure house of information on language, often containing introductory essays on the history of the language, on spelling and grammar, on dialects, and on usage. (A good dictionary will also contain usage notes within its definitions of those words that are growing, dying, or changing their meaning or social acceptability, because words are living things.) Anyone who becomes familiar with a dictionary, as one lexicographer has written, "will take a positive pleasure in reading, not merely consulting, the dictionary."

Exercise

In the space provided, copy the phonetic spelling of each of the following words from a dictionary, including separation of syllables and diacritical and stress markings.

_____   1. supercilious

_____   2. humor

_____   3. liquid

_____   4. intricacy

_____   5. intimidate

_____   6. naive

_____   7. gubernatorial

_____   8. farcical

_____   9. decadence

_____   10. review

Remember!

Consult the Dictionary.

Make Your Own Spelling List

Make a list of your difficult words. Try to use these as often as the opportunity presents itself. Mark Twain said, "Use a new word correctly three times, and it's yours." Use a word that has given *you* trouble three times correctly and you should not have any dfficulty. The important thing is to use it *correctly*. Misspelling a word a number of times only fixes the misspelling more firmly. "Practice makes perfect." But that should really be "Practice makes permanent." If we always make the same mistake, no amount of practice will do anything to improve our knowledge. Remember to use it correctly the first time.

Listen Attentively

Develop the art of listening carefully. Many people whose hearing shows no organic defect are poor listeners. They do not pay attention and, consequently, they don't really hear what is being said. Terms like *government, security, conservation* are heard repeatedly. Do you hear *gover-n-ment* or *guvment*? *Scurity* or security? *Consivation* or *conservation*?

It is true that sometimes the speaker's enunciation is not perfect. That does not excuse the listener, however. If a word does not seem quite clear to you, you owe it to yourself to consult the dictionary.

Remember!

- **Learn the rules and the exceptions.**
- **Consult the dictionary if you are in doubt.**
- **Make your own spelling list.**
- **Listen attentively.**

What has just been said are general instructions. Below are the steps you are to follow in learning any particular word that has given you trouble. Don't take short cuts. Follow the instructions to the letter!

Method for Learning to Spell Any Hard Word!

1. *Look* at your word. *Pronounce* each syllable carefully. For example,

in·de·pen·dent

2. *Close your eyes* or turn away and form a picture of the word in your mind. If the letters are not clearly before you, look at the word again, until you see it with your eyes closed.
3. *Pronounce* the word and write it at the same time. If you are not sure, try to picture the word. Be certain that you write it correctly the first time.
4. *Write* the word a second time as used in a sentence.
5. The next day write the word as someone else reads it to you.

Chapter 5

MNEMONICS

Clever students and teachers create words to make important lists easier to recall. Anyone who has ever struggled to remember the names of the five Great Lakes must be grateful to the creator of HOMES—*H*uron, *O*ntario, *M*ichigan, *E*rie, and *S*uperior.

In Greek mythology, the goddess *Mnemosyne* (nē-ʹmŏ-sĭ-nē) was the personification of memory. The nine Muses (goddesses of poetry, music, dance, etc.) were the children of Mnemosyne and *Zeus*. Whatever her place in mythology, Mnemosyne's name has been carried over into our word, *mnemonics*—a system to enhance or develop the memory.

Focusing on Words Frequently Misspelled

Throughout this book, attention has been called to ways of remembering how to deal with words that are frequently misspelled. Here are some useful suggestions for helping avoid the common mistakes made with such words:

- Never be*lie*ve a *lie*.
- You might shriek "eee!" in a c*e*m*e*t*e*ry, to recall that it contains three *e*'s.
- Your princi*pal* is your *pal* (hopefully).
- Bad gram*mar* will *mar* your composition.
- A *comple*ment is something that makes perfect or *comple*tes, while a compl*i*ment is an adm*i*ring remark.
- We use station*ery* to write a lett*er*, but a st*a*nding object is station*a*ry.
- A *villa*in may live in a *villa*.
- There's a *rat* in sep*a*rate.
- Call your professor "Prof." (one *f*)
- Super*sede* is the only English word ending in *sede*.
- Pro*ceed* to ex*ceed* and suc*ceed* (the only English words ending in *ceed*).
- *Full* is the only English word ending in *full*.
- Stala*g*mites grow from the *g*round up, while stala*c*tites grow from the *c*eiling down.

Acronyms in Mnemonics

An *acronym* is a word that is formed from the first letters of a name (NATO for North Atlantic Treaty Organization) or by combining initial letters or parts of a series of words, as *sonar* (for *s*ound, *na*vigation, and *r*anging). In the field of mnemonics, acronyms are indispensable in helping us to remember lists, progressions, numbers, sequences, etc.

For example, think of an opera in which a diva is about to suffer a *stab* wound. We remember the quartet of voices: *s* = *s*oprano, *t* = *t*enor, *a* = *a*lto, *b* = *b*ass. And which of us does not recall the lines on a music staff from *"every good boy does fine"*?

Perhaps when you are a *Jeopardy* contestant, you might remember to ask "What is UCAN?" in answer to the only place in the United States where four states touch—*U*tah, *C*olorado, *A*rizona, *N*ew Mexico.

Here are some other acronyms that people have thought up to assist their ability to recall:

- PWELGAS for the Seven Deadly Sins: *P*ride, *W*rath, *E*nvy, *L*ust, *G*luttony, *A*varice, *S*loth.
- ROYGBIV for the colors of the spectrum: *R*ed, *O*range, *Y*ellow, *G*reen, *B*lue, *I*ndigo, *V*iolet. (Some prefer *"R*ichard *o*f *Y*ork *g*ave *b*attle *i*n *v*ain.")

Acronyms . . . Plus

Other wordsmiths have prepared easily remembered lines of prose or poetry to assist in recall, such as:

- *"M*y *v*ery *e*ager *m*other *j*ust *s*erved *u*s *n*ine *p*ickles" helps us to remember the planets in their order away from the sun: *M*ercury, *V*enus, *E*arth, *M*ars, *J*upiter, *S*aturn, *U*ranus, *N*eptune, *P*luto.
- Medical students who were required to memorize the twelve cranial nerves, have long learned this ditty:

> *O*n *o*ld *O*lympia's *t*owering *t*op,
> *A F*inn *a*nd *G*erman *v*ault *a*nd *h*op.

The first letters are the key to the nerves: *o*lfactory, *o*ptic, *o*culomotor, *t*rochlear, *t*rigeminal, *a*bducens, *f*acial, *a*uditory, *g*lossopharyngeal, *v*agus, *a*ccessory, *h*ypoglossal.
- Mathematicians have a way to tick off the 21 numbers in pi:

> Pie.
> I wish I could remember pi.
> Eureka cried the great inventor
> Christmas pudding; Christmas pie
> Is the problem's very center.

By counting the number of letters in each word, we discover the transcendental number that represents the ratio of the circumference to the diameter of a circle: 3.14158265358979323846.

- The four hydrocarbons (*m*ethane, *e*thane, *p*ropane, *b*utane) are immortalized in "*M*ary *e*ats *p*eanut *b*utter."

Mnemonics and the Telephone

A young executive, moving out of state, had trouble remembering her new telephone number until she realized that mnemonics could help. Her problem vanished once she began to call MY PHONE (697-4663).

Corporations and individual entrepreneurs with 800-numbers have cleverly requested mnemonics that spell out their often hard-to-remember telephone numbers. As a result, you will find the following listings in your Yellow Pages:

> BAD BACK (223-2225)—chiropractor
> GET CASH (438-2274)—loan company
> DESK TOP (337-5867)—computer sales
> NEW HAIR (639-4247)—hair replacement
> ASPHALT (227-4258)—paving company

Does your own telephone number lend itself to an easily remembered word? Try to create five catchy telephone numbers that businesses might appropriate.

Exercise 1

Compile a list of other mnemonic devices or make up ten of your own.

Exercise 2

Try to invent mnemonics to avoid such misspellings as athelete (*athlete*), excercise (*exercise*), occassion (*occasion*), preforming (*performing*), priviledge (*privilege*), similiar (*similar*), *and others.*

Exercise 3

Government, business, science, technology, and education make use of acronyms regularly. Do you know what the following stand for?

1. MOMA
2. NASDAQ
3. NATO
4. ASPCA
5. NAFTA
6. NASA
7. HDTV
8. WHO

RULES FOR SPELLING

Chapter 6

BETTER SPELLING BY EAR

Know the Rules!

It is possible, of course, to consult your dictionary every time you are in doubt about the spelling of a word. The knowledge of a few helpful rules, however, will make it unnecessary for you to waste precious time in consulting the dictionary on every occasion when you are in doubt. As is true of almost all rules in English grammar, there are some exceptions to the rules in spelling, too. It is, therefore, necessary to master the exceptions as well as the rules. Study the rules, do the exercises, and try using some of the words you have studied as soon as possible.

Spell by Pronunciation

It has been mentioned before that an impression conveyed by several senses will remain longer in the mind than one coming through only one sense organ. Most human beings are visual-minded. They form an eye-impression of the things they learn. Some people (musicians especially) are ear-minded. You may discover that you are ear-minded by employing the following spelling devices.

Although English has been rightly accused of not being spelled exactly as it sounds, the fact remains that thousands of words *are spelled* precisely as they are pronounced. If you pronounce these words correctly when you are in doubt about them, you will find no difficulty in spelling them.

You must first understand something about *syllables* and *syllabication*. The late E. L. Thorndike of Columbia University in his *Century Junior Dictionary* defined a syllable as "part of a word pronounced as a unit consisting of a vowel alone or with one or more consonants."

do — word of one syllable
dough·nut — word of two syllables
syl·la·ble — word of three syllables

Divide a Word into Syllables

Rule 1

Begin **a syllable with a consonant when the consonant is between two vowels and the flrst vowel is** *long*.

EXAMPLE:
   ro·man·tic

The consonant *m* begins the second syllable because the vowel *o* is long.
The long vowels are pronounced exactly as they are pronounced when you recite the alphabet.

$$\bar{a} - as\ in\ \text{hay}$$
$$\bar{e} - as\ in\ \text{bee}$$
$$\bar{i} - as\ in\ \text{kite}$$
$$\bar{o} - as\ in\ \text{note}$$
$$\bar{u} - as\ in\ \text{mute}$$

Other examples of Rule 1 are:

Mo·hawk   ro·tate   na·ture

Rule 2

End **a syllable with a consonant when the consonant is between two vowels and the first vowel is** *short*.

EXAMPLE:
   hab·it

The consonant *b* ends the first syllable because it is between two vowels and the first vowel is short.
The short vowels are present in this line:

patter, petter, pitter, potter, putter

Syllables with short vowels:

a — *as in* fash·ion, tap·es·try
e — *as in* nec·es·sa·ry
i — *as in* crit·i·cism
o — *as in* prom·i·nent
u — *as in* sub·urb

Other examples of Rule 2 are:

proph·et   pun·ish   ex·ec·u·tive

Rule 3

Adjoining consonants most often separate into syllables.

EXAMPLES:
mur·mur   can·dy   ex·pense

Rule 4

Double consonants are not divided when a sufrix is added.

EXAMPLES:
mill·er   hiss·ing

These rules should help you also in dividing words at the end of a line. Study the syllabication of the following words that are associated with the automobile:

per·for·mance
gas·o·line
man·u·fac·ture
pneu·mat·ic
se·dan

It was one of the principles of the government of Ancient Rome to "divide and conquer." The same rule might apply for long words. Divide them into their component syllables and you can conquer them.

Spell as You Pronounce Syllable by Syllable

Many words appear difficult to spell until we pronounce them carefully. They fall naturally into simple syllables and their difficulty disappears.

Method!

1. **Pronounce the word slowly.**
2. **Spell it aloud *by syllables*.**
3. **Pronounce it slowly twice more, writing as you do so.**
4. **Pronounce it quickly in a sentence, writing the whole sentence.**

Each of the following words will lose its terror if you use this method.

ac·com·mo·date	ar·tic·u·late
mag·nif·i·cent	priv·i·lege
mag·a·zine	dis·ap·pear

Exercise 1

Divide the following words into syllables.

_____   1. bonanza

_____   2. repent

_____   3. fatigue

_____   4. punishment

_____   5. ordeal

_____   6. rummage

_____   7. missing

_____   8. gasoline

_____   9. excavate

_____   10. tyrannical

Pay Attention to Troublesome Words

In this section are lists of words that have had their thousands of victims. Have someone dictate these words to you. Spell them. Then compare your spelling with those in the book. The ones you have spelled correctly, you need no longer bother with. Your misspelled words, you must examine. What errors did you make? Practice the words until you can spell them correctly without of thinking twice about them.

Difficult "A" Words

Each of the following words has *a* trouble. People forget the existence of *a* and substitute another letter:

captain	certain	calendar
finally	grammar	illegal
maintain	plain	criminal
preparations	probable	dictionary
separate	straight	liberal
usually	villain	justifiable
balance	equivalent	equally
performance	salary	congressional
actually	extravagant	professional
village	capital	temperature
partially	principal	similar

Difficult "E" Words

Each of the words below has an *e* difficulty. Writers frequently forget the *e* and use another letter incorrectly.

apparently	competent	conscience
dependent	coherent	audience
prominent	current	correspondence
machinery	efficient	existence
independent	experience	magnificent
stationery	opponent	patience
privileges	permanent	superintendent
luncheon	cafeteria	description

Difficult "I" Words

In the following words, the *i*'s have it:

acquainted
compliment
criticized
participle
quantities
physical
articles

auxiliary
definite
sympathized
peculiar
quiet
individual

business
exhibition
until
principle
respectively
hosiery
anticipate

Difficult "O" Words

Do you omit these *o*'s? In the words below, the letter *o* comes in for much abuse and neglect. Be kind to these words:

attorney
conspicuous
favorable
notorious
society
odor
colonel
colors
humorist
precious
surgeon

authorize
conqueror
memorial
organization
strenuously
aviator
accustomed
favorite
memory
proprietor

competitors
editor
minor
senator
tailor
capitol
authority
interior
motorist
successor

Double Letter Problems

Concentrate on the double letters in these words. They are the cause of many common errors:

accommodate
beginning
embarrass
necessary
recommend
across
dissatisfaction
disappeared
disappointed
illegible
occasion
opposite

agreed
committee
loose
parallel
speech
baggage
affirmative
chauffeur
immigrant
possession
misspell

agreeable
guaranteed
proceed
succeed
assistance
appearance
appropriate
disapproved
interrupted
Mediterranean
professor

Letters Not "Seen"

It used to be said of children that they should be seen and not heard. These words have letters that are often not seen when writing. Don't omit them:

gover*n*ment   prom*p*tly   February
inde*b*ted   pamp*h*let   ple*d*ged
                              condem*n*

Exercise 2

Some of the following words are spelled correctly and some are misspelled. Put a check on the blank if a word is spelled correctly. Rewrite it correctly if it is misspelled.

_____	1. grammar
_____	2. seperate
_____	3. usally
_____	4. village
_____	5. calender
_____	6. existence
_____	7. description
_____	8. untill
_____	9. attorney
_____	10. senator
_____	11. odor
_____	12. accomodate
_____	13. proffessor
_____	14. goverment
_____	15. promptly
_____	16. accross
_____	17. ilegible
_____	18. equivelent
_____	19. precious
_____	20. accustomed

Reversal Problems

A common type of misspelling occurs when letters are interchanged. For example, *l* and *v* are often reversed in *relevant* so that the word is misspelled *revelant*. This type of error is called *metathesis*. Observe the correct spelling of the following ten words:

Correct	**Incorrect**
cava*l*ry	calvary
child*ren*	childern
hund*red*	hunderd
jew*el*ry	jewlery
lar*ynx*	larnyx
mod*ern*	modren
patt*ern*	pattren
*per*spiration	prespiration
rel*ev*ant	revelant
west*ern*	westren

Exercise 3

Fill in the missing letters:

1. hund __ __ d
2. mod __ __ n
3. p __ __ spiration
4. west __ __ n
5. re __ e __ ant
6. ca __ a __ ry
7. child __ __ n
8. jew __ __ __ y
9. lar __ __ x
10. patt __ __ n

Chapter 7

SOME SPECIAL PROBLEMS

IE and *EI*

The *Saturday Review of Literature* once published the following story:

> A neophyte copy editor in a large advertising agency was slowly going out of his mind because his copy chief was constantly taking a small slip of paper from his breast pocket, looking at it, leering, then putting it back. After watching this for months he managed one day, when the copy chief was taking a nap, to steal the secret paper from the jacket in back of the chief's chair. He opened the slip of paper with trembling hands.
>
> It read.
>
> "*I* before *E* except after *C*"[1]

You may be rel*ie*ved when you rec*ei*ve this information. Although a great deal of misch*ie*f has been caused by people who were confused about the use of *ie* or *ei*, there is a simple rule that will take care of all cases. Learn this rule!

Rule

Put i before e,
Except after c,
Or when sounded like *a*,
As in *neighbor* and *weigh*;
And except *seize* and *seizure*
And also *leisure*,
Weird, height, and *either*,
Forfeit and *neither*.

---

[1]Reprinted by permission of *Saturday Review of Literature*.

IE

Examine the list below. Notice that in no case does a *c* precede the *ie*.
    Now examine the additional list.

achieve	belief	fiend	grief	interview
aggrieve	believe	fierce	grievance	mischievous
alien	besiege	fiery	grieve	piece
chief	brief	friend	mischief	piety
niece	lieu	mien	pierce	priest
quiet	piebald	pied	reprieve	retrieve
review	relief	relieve	shriek	thievery
siege	series	shield	thief	yield
view	wield	sieve	handkerchief	
befriend	field	frontier	hygiene	

Exercise 1

Study the list above carefully; notice that never does a c precede the ie. *Any other letter in the alphabet may do so, but not the c. Write each word once, one word to a line; pronounce it; then write it once in a sentence; follow this scheme.*

Word	*Pronounce*	*Sentence*
achieve	a chēē v	I hope to achieve my goal.

Exercise 2

When you feel certain that you know the preceding words, copy and fill in the missing letters in the following:

1. aggr __ __ ve
2. br __ __ f
3. fr __ __ nd
4. gr __ __ ve
5. front __ __r
6. misch __ __ f
7. sh __ __ ld
8. shr __ __ k
9. w __ __ ld
10. spec __ __ s

11. rel __ __ ve

12. l __ __ sure

13. handkerch __ __ f

14. rec __ __ pt

15. s __ __ ze

16. perc __ __ ve

17. gr __ __ f

18. n __ __ ce

19. conc __ __ ve

EI

Now we can master the other combinations. Study the following chart:

Handling *EI*		
EL follows C	**EL because the sound is ā as in HAY**	**special cases**
dec*ei*t	fr*ei*ght	*ei*ther
perc*ei*ve	v*ei*l	h*ei*ght
rec*ei*ve	n*ei*gh	l*ei*sure
		forf*ei*t
		n*ei*ther
		s*ei*ze
		w*ei*rd
		s*ei*zure

EXAMPLE:
EI follows C

Read this list carefully and notice that in each case the *ei* follows *c*.

*cei*ling	dec*ei*tful
con*cei*t	de*cei*ve
con*cei*ted	re*cei*pt
con*cei*ve	re*cei*ve

EXAMPLE:
EI Sounds as Ā

The following list has the *ei* because it sounds like ā in *bay*.

reign	vein
sleigh	weigh
surveillance	weight
veil	

EXAMPLES:
Special Cases

1. The final *feit* is pronounced *fit*.

   forfeit
   counterfeit
   surfeit

2. These are pronounced ī as *kite*. Be sure to put the *e* in.

   height
   sleight

3. A few words have *cie*, but in all cases the *c* is pronounced as *sh*.

ancient	glacier
conscience	proficient
deficient	species
efficient	sufficient

Exercise 3

Have the following passage read aloud to you. Ask the reader to stress the italicized words and to pause for you to write those words. Then, study those that were difficult or that you misspelled.

A *thief* was planning to *deceive* the clerk with a *counterfeit* bill. He saw a *surveillance* camera, but his *conceit* made him *believe* he could never be caught. He knew the clerk would be in trouble if the bill was discovered, leaving *receipts* short at the end of the day. The clerk was so *friendly*, the thief's *conscience* made him *forfeit* his plan.

-SEDE, -CEED, and -CEDE

Because various letters are pronounced alike in English, difficulties in spelling arise. Originally the letter *c* was pronounced as a *k*. We know that, because the old Romans of 2,000 years ago sounded it that way. They had a word *centum*, which means "one hundred." Today, when a student in high school studies Latin, he says *kentum* (like kennel). But this same word in Italian is pronounced *chento* (cento); in French it is *saunt* (cent). Because it came into English from the French back in the days of the Norman conquest of 1066, our word *cent* is really one-hundredth part of something and is pronounced *sent*. This similarity of pronunciation between *c* and *s* is responsible for the confusion in spelling words ending in *-cede*, *-ceed*, and *-sede*.

-SEDE

You should never forget the single word ending in *-sede*. It is *supersede*.

-CEED

You can easily remember all the words in *-ceed*. There are only three:

proc*eed*   exc*eed*   succ*eed*

If you want a little device to aid your memory with these words, think of boxer. First, he is a *pro*-fessional. When he is past his prime, he is an *ex*-fighter; then he has a *suc*-cessor.

-CEDE

All the other words in this class end in *-cede*. Some are:

accede	recede
precede	secede
concede	

Remember! _____

The ending -CEDE is more common than -SEDE or -CEED. Memorize the few words that end in -SEDE or -CEED. All other words end in -CEDE.

Exercise 4

Have the following passage read aloud to you. Ask the reader to stress the italicized words and to pause for you to write those words. Then, study those that were difficult or that you misspelled.

Without practice, the spelling rules you learn will *recede* in your memory. But if you *proceed*, you will *succeed*. You may even *exceed* your expectations. Your confidence will *supersede* any fears you have about misspellings.

Chapter 8

PREFIXES

This chapter contains only one rule. The rule is simple and easily learned. It will help you avoid many misspellings. It has to do with prefixes.

A prefix is one or more syllables attached to the beginning of a word. Prefixes, as those below, change the meaning of words to which they are attached.

$$dis + \text{agree} = \text{disagree}$$
$$il + \text{logical} = \text{illogical}$$
$$un + \text{kind} = \text{unkind}$$
$$mis + \text{spell} = \text{misspell}$$
$$super + \text{vision} = \text{supervision}$$

A List of Common Prefixes

Here is a list of some common prefixes. Become familiar with them to discover the meaning and spelling of words that are new to you.

Common Prefixes

Prefix	Meaning	Examples
a-	on, in	abed
		afire
	not, without	asexual
		achromatic (without color)
ab-	away, from	abject
		abduct
ante-	before	anteroom (a room before another)
		antecedent (a preceding event)
anti-	against	antiseptic (against poisoning)
		anti-noise (against noise)
circum-	around	circumscribe (to write around)
		circumnavigate (to sail around)
		circumlocution (act of talking around a topic rather than directly)

Prefix	Meaning	Examples
com-, con-	with, together	concelebrate (to celebrate together)
		commingle (to combine)
de-	down	descend
		demote (to put down)
dis-	apart	dismember (to tear from limb to limb)
		dissolve (to fall apart in a liquid)
		disarm (to separate a soldier from his weapons)
hyper-	above, beyond	hyperactive
		hypercritical
hypo-	under, beneath	hypothesis (an assumption under consideration)
il-, im-,	not	illogical
in-, ir-		immoral
		indisposed
		irrelevant
inter-	among, between	interview
		intercollegiate
		international
intra-	within	intracoastal
		intravenous (with a vein)
		intramural (within the walls)
mis-	wrongly, unfavorably	misjudge
		misunderstand
		misappropriate
non-	not	nonsense
		noncombatant
		nonconformist
over-	excessive	overcharge
		overcoat
per-	through	permeate (to penetrate)
		perspire
		persevere
post-	behind, after	postmortem (after death)
		postpone
		postgraduate
pre-	before	precede
		precipitate
		predecessor
		prevent
pro-	forward, instead of	procession
		provide (to look forward)
		promote
		provisions
re-	back, again, against	refer (to bring back to the previous question)
		retaliate (to fight back)
		retract (to take back)
		repel (to hurl back)

Prefix	Meaning	Examples
sub-	under	subway
		subtract
super-	above	superintendent
		superficial
		superstructure
trans-	across	transcontinental
		transfer
		transplant
		translucent (permitting the passage of light)
un-	not	unnatural
		unnoticeable
		unoccupied

Adding a Prefix

Armed with a knowledge of these prefixes, you are now ready for the spelling rule relating to them.

Rule

When you add a prefix, do *not* change the spelling of either the preflx or the original word.

EXAMPLES:

$$dis + \text{appear} = \text{disappear}$$
$$inter + \text{action} = \text{interaction}$$
$$in + \text{eligible} = \text{ineligible}$$
$$hyper + \text{sensitive} = \text{hypersensitive}$$
$$un + \text{tie} = \text{untie}$$

Simple, isn't it? Yet with this easy rule, you can correctly spell thousands of words.

Caution!

Most errors occur when a prefix ends with the same letter with which the word begins. For example:

$$un + \text{natural} = \text{unnatural} \ (not \ \text{unatural})$$
$$dis + \text{satisfied} = \text{dissatisfied} \ (not \ \text{disatisfied})$$
$$mis + \text{step} = \text{misstep} \ (not \ \text{mistep})$$

Remember, when you add a prefix, do *not* change the spelling of either the prefix or the original word.

Exercise 1

How many s's in:

_____ 1. di ___(?)___ olve

_____ 2. di ___(?)___ imilar

_____ 3. mi ___(?)___ pell

_____ 4. di ___(?)___ appear

_____ 5. mi ___(?)___ take

Exercise 2

Try your skill in building your own words. Take, for example, scribe, *meaning a writer.*

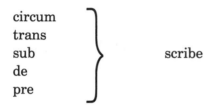

circum
trans
sub   }   scribe
de
pre

Give the meaning of each.

Exercise 3

By adding the proper Latin prefixes to the following italicized words, spell the new formations correctly. Some require changing the word form.

EXAMPLES:
not *satisfied*   *dissatisfied*
not *legible*   *illegible*

_____ 1. A *step* wrongly taken

_____ 2. not to *understand*

_____ 3. not *similar*

_____ 4. to *start* again and again

_____ 5. below the *standard*

_____ 6. above the speed of *sound*

_____ 7. before the time of *Columbus*

        _____ 8. against *imperialism*

        _____ 9. *navigates* around the globe

        _____ 10. after an *operation*

Pay Attention to *PER-*, *PRE-*, *PRO-*

Some difficulties with the spelling of prefixes may be due to carelessness in pronunciation. Thus, if you don't pronounce *prescription* properly, you may not spell the prefix with *pre*. The reverse error may come with a word like *per*spiration, in which the initial *per* may be misspelled.

    Knowing the meaning of certain prefixes, as indicated earlier in this chapter, will help you to both know the meaning of the word and its spelling.

PER-, *PRE-*, *PRO-*

PER- means "through"	
Word	**Meaning**
permeate	to penetrate through and through
perforate	to pierce through
perpetual	through the years
persist	to continue through a project
persecute	to follow through
perspective	to see through

PRE- means "before"	
Word	**Meaning**
precocious	to develop earlier
prefer	to place before
prepare	to make ready beforehand
prejudice	a judgment before the evidence is in
prescribe	to write before

PRO- means "forward"	
Word	**Meaning**
propose	to place before a group
prophesy	something stated before it happens
proceed	to move forward
proclaim	to shout before
produce	to bring forth
prognosis	to forecast the probable outcome of a disease

Exercise 4

Underline the correct spelling of the pairs of words in the following sentences.

1. The protesting students felt they had been (persecuted, presecuted).

2. Let us (preceed, proceed) with the trial.

3. This young bright child was obviously (precocious, percocious).

4. We must look at world affairs in the proper (perspective, prospective).

5. The patient asked the doctor to (proscribe, prescribe) something for his cough.

6. The illness was diagnosed as a (perforated, proferated) ulcer.

7. It costs a great deal to (perduce, produce) a musical comedy.

8. We must (persist, presist) in our efforts to find ways to peace.

9. Searching for the truth requires (perpetual, prepetual) effort.

10. Let us (propose, perpose) a toast.

Chapter 9
CONFUSING SUFFIXES

A suffix is one or more syllables attached to the end of a word.

EXAMPLES:

desire + *able* = desirable
move + *ing* = moving
kind + *ly* = kindly
mean + *ness* = meanness
fame + *ous* = famous

Words Ending in -*ABLE*, -*IBLE*

These suffixes are troublesome. When you are able to add them correctly, you are well on your way to becoming a good speller.

Rule 1

The ending -ABLE is more common than -IBLE. If in doubt, use -ABLE and you have more than a fair chance of being correct.

-*ABLE*

1. Our most familiar words add -ABLE to form the adjective.

comfort + *able* = comfortable
drink + *able* = drinkable
laugh + *able* = laughable
read + *able* = readable
unthink + *able* = unthinkable

2. A noun ending in -ATION will have an adjective ending in -ABLE.

abomination   navigation
abomin*able*   navig*able*

-IBLE

1. Words ending in *-ible* are often preceded by a double SS before the -IBLE.

acce*ss*ible   permi*ss*ible
admi*ss*ible   transmi*ss*ible
compre*ss*ible

2. Words ending in *-ible* often have a noun form ending in *-ion*. Drop the -ION and add -IBLE.

permission
permiss*ible*

Examine the following words that are all formed the same way:

admission	expansion	extension
admiss*ible*	expans*ible*	extens*ible*
compression	reversion	corruption
compress*ible*	revers*ible*	corrupt*ible*
permission	coercion	division
permiss*ible*	coerc*ible*	divis*ible*
transmission	comprehension	perception
transmiss*ible*	comprehens*ible*	percept*ible*
combustion	digestion	reprehension
combust*ible*	digest*ible*	reprehens*ible*
destruction	collection	conversion
destruct*ible*	collect*ible*	convert*ible*

3. Use -IBLE to keep the soft sound of *g* or *c*. The word *tangent* has the adjective *tangible* because an *-able* would change the pronunciation of *g* from its present *j* sound to the sound of *g* in *gum*. Other words in this class are:

dedu*c*ible	produ*c*ible	incorri*g*ible
condu*c*ible	corri*g*ible	iras*c*ible
eli*g*ible	ineli*g*ible	le*g*ible
intelli*g*ible	invin*c*ible	

Remember!

Be sure that you know all the reasons for adding *-ible*.

1. **It follows double *ss* and comes from a noun ending in *-sion* (permission/ permissible).**
2. **It comes from a noun ending in *-ion* (coercion/coercible).**
3. **It keeps the *c* or *g* soft (deducible, eligible).**

Exercise 1

Here is a list of words. Add -able or -ible.

account	depend	market
avoid	detest	perish
comfort	discount	return
companion	fashion	review
credit	favor	season

Did you add -able to each of these? Then you were 100% correct. Now add -able or -ible to the roots of these words:

HINT: consol-*a*-tion   consol-*able*

commendation
admiration
conformation
appreciation
consideration

Did you add -able to the roots of each of these words? You were 100% correct. Remember, a noun ending in -ation will have an adjective in -able. As a final task, add the endings -able, or -ible to the roots of the following words.

HINT: demonstr-*ation*   demonstr-*able*

derivation	exportation	notation
duration	habitation	refutation
estimation	imagination	separation
execration	irritation	taxation
	lamentation	toleration

You should add -able to the roots of each of the words.

Exercise 2

Have someone dictate the following passage that contains many words ending in the suffixes -ible or -able.

The prosecuting attorney protested that the evidence by the defendant about his *taxable* income was *inadmissible*. In the first place, it was not easily *accessible*. In the second place, although the evidence was originally *acceptable* in a lower court, the decisions in such courts are *reversible*.

The defendant's attorney objected that such reasoning was *unsupportable* and *intolerable* and that it was *reprehensible* on his opponent's part to bring up such a claim. The tension was increasing *perceptibly*. If this continued, the defending attorney might have to be ejected *forcibly*, or be *eligible* for disbarment. However, it took some time for the atmosphere to be cleared and the case proceeded to its *inevitable* conclusion.

The Adverbial Suffix -*LY*

Rule 2

In forming adverbs from adjectives ending in -*al*, simply add -*ly* to the original word.

adjective + *ly* = adverb

EXAMPLE:
   verbal + *ly* = verbally

Exercise 3

Form the adverbs of the following adjectives:

_____   1. accidental

_____   2. critical

_____   3. elemental

_____   4. equal

_____   5. exceptional

_____   6. final

_____   7. general (adj.)

_____   8. incidental

_____ 9. intentional

_____ 10. ironical

_____ 11. logical

_____ 12. mathematical

_____ 13. practical

_____ 14. professional

_____ 15. real

_____ 16. typical

_____ 17. usual

_____ 18. verbal

_____ 19. global

Words Ending in -*OUS*

-*OUS* After a Consonant

Rule 3

When adding -*ous* to a noun ending in a consonant, do *not* change the spelling of the noun.

		-*OUS* After a Consonant		
Noun		**Suffix**		**Adjective**
danger	+	*ous*	=	dangerous
hazard	+	*ous*	=	hazardous
humor	+	*ous*	=	humorous
libel	+	*ous*	=	libelous
marvel	+	*ous*	=	marvelous
moment	+	*ous*	=	momentous
mountain	+	*ous*	=	mountainous
murder	+	*ous*	=	murderous
peril	+	*ous*	=	perilous
poison	+	*ous*	=	poisonous
riot	+	*ous*	=	riotous
slander	+	*ous*	=	slanderous

Caution!

Nouns ending in *-f* change the *f* to *v* when *-ous* is added.

EXAMPLES:

grief + *ous* = grievous (*not* grievious)
mischief + *ous* = mischievous (*not* mischievious)

Remember!

Most nouns ending in *-y* drop the *y* and add *e* before *-ous*, but these words are not very common. An exception to this rule is joyous.

EXAMPLES:

beauty + *ous* = beauteous
duty + ous = duteous
pity + *ous* = piteous
plenty + *ous* = plenteous
joy + *ous* = joyous

-OUS After a Vowel

Rule 4

When adding *-ous* to a noun ending in *-e*, drop the *e*.

EXAMPLES:

adventure + *ous* = adventurous
analogue + *ous* = analogous
desire + *ous* = desirous

Note!

Occasionally the final *-e* is left before *-ous* to retain the same pronunciation of the last letter.

EXAMPLES:

courage + *ous* = courageous
advantage + *ous* = advantageous
outrage + *ous* = outrageous

Exercise 4

Write the correct adjectives of the following nouns by adding the suffix -ous.

_____ 1. advantage

_____ 2. courage

_____ 3. peril

_____ 4. mountain

_____ 5. beauty

_____ 6. desire

_____ 7. mischief

_____ 8. adventure

_____ 9. bounty

_____ 10. danger

_____ 11. grief

_____ 12. humor

_____ 13. outrage

_____ 14. libel

_____ 15. poison

Troublesome Affixes *-AL, -EL, -LE*

The endings, *-al*, *-el*, and *-le* are called affixes. They are added to the end of words and are a source of many spelling difficulties because they are pronounced in approximately the same way.

Although there are no hard-and-fast rules governing their use, here are some guidelines that will help you correctly spell most of the words in which they occur.

The Affix -*AL*

Rule 5

The affix -*al* is added to nouns and adjectives only. The affix -*al* means *of*, *belonging to*, *pertaining to*, or *appropriate to*.

If you remember these meanings, you will scarcely make a mistake.

EXAMPLES:
personal — *of* the person
autumnal — *belonging* to autumn
royal — *pertaining* to a king
nautical — *appropriate* to ships

Common Words Ending in -*AL*				
Adjectives			**Nouns**	
additional	general	original	acquittal	proposal
adverbial	jovial	oval	arrival	recital
annual	legal	penal	betrayal	refusal
brutal	logical	personal	capital	rival
classical	magical	regal	denial	signal
clerical	mechanical	several		
comical	medical	trivial		
fatal	neutral			
fiscal	normal			

Caution!

Do not confuse *capital*, a city, with *capitol*, a building.

The Affix -*EL*

The affix -*el* originally diminished the meaning of a word to which it was attached. For example, tunnel once meant a small barrel or tun, and chapel meant a small church. Nowadays the original significance of -*el* is forgotten.

If you remember that -*el* is used less frequently than -*al* and if you memorize the spelling of the common words below, you will greatly reduce the possibility of misspelling words in which it appears.

Common Words Ending in -EL			
bushel	jewel	novel	satchel
cancel	kennel	nickel	shovel
channel	kernel	panel	swivel
flannel	model	parcel	travel
funnel	morsel	quarrel	trowel

The Affix -*LE*

The affix -*le* is used far more frequently than -*al* or -*el*. This method will help you to remember the words that end in -*le*.

1. Examine the following list carefully.
2. Form a mental image of each word.
3. Pronounce each word aloud, then write it down. Underline the *le* after you complete writing the word.
4. Pronounce the word again.

When you perform these steps, you are seeing, feeling, and hearing. In other words you are employing three senses to help you remember the correct spelling.

Note!

The affixes -*el* and -*le* are never used to make adjectives from nouns. *Nickel* and *little* are adjectives but they were not formed by adding an affix to a noun.

Common Words Ending in -LE

able	dribble	muscle	settle
ample	drizzle	muzzle	shuffle
angle	fable	myrtle	shackle
article	fickle	needle	shuttle
ankle	fiddle	nestle	sizzle
baffle	frizzle	nibble	sparkle
battle	gable	nuzzle	sprinkle
beetle	gentle	paddle	squabble
bottle	giggle	peaceable	strangle
brittle	gristle	people	subtle
buckle	grizzle	pestle	tackle
bundle	handle	pickle	thimble
bungle	huddle	possible	thistle
cattle	humble	prattle	treble
chuckle	hurdle	principle	tremble
circle	jangle	puzzle	trestle
couple	jingle	raffle	trickle
cripple	juggle	riddle	trifle
castle	jungle	ruffle	triple
corpuscle	knuckle	scribble	trouble
dangle	mantle	scruple	turtle
dazzle	miracle	scuffle	twinkle
double	muffle	scuttle	

Exercise 5

Select the word in each pair that is correctly spelled, and write it in the blank.

_____ 1. a. brutel   b. brutal

_____ 2. a. proposal   b. proposale

_____ 3. a. flannel   b. flannal

_____ 4. a. dangle   b. dangel

_____ 5. a. drizzel   b. drizzle

_____ 6. a. corpuscle   b. corpuscel

_____ 7. a. fatal   b. fatel

_____ 8. a. swivle   b. swivel

_____ 9. a. tripel   b. triple

_____ 10. a. signel   b. signal

_____	11. a. battle	b. battel
_____	12. a. quarrle	b. quarrel
_____	13. a. riddel	b. riddle
_____	14. a. mechanicle	b. mechanical
_____	15. a. angal	b. angle
_____	16. a. rival	b. rivle
_____	17. a. jewel	b. jewal
_____	18. a. nickel	b. nickle
_____	19. a. girdel	b. girdle
_____	20. a. tragicle	b. tragical
_____	21. a. thimble	b. thimbel
_____	22. a. capital	b. capitle
_____	23. a. knuckel	b. knuckle
_____	24. a. parcle	b. parcel
_____	25. a. regel	b. regal

Words Ending in *-ER* or *-OR*

The suffixes *-er* and *-or* mean *one who* or *that which*. For example, a *visitor* is *one who visits* and an *indicator* is *that which indicates.*

When should you use *-er* and when should you use *-or*?

Caution! _____

Although there are many words with these suffixes, there is no rule governing their use.

The lack of rule, however, need not disturb you. Simply remember that most words end in *-or*. Then study the list of *-er* words (page 56) and pay attention to those you use most often.

Common Words Ending in -OR, -ER				
-OR			**-ER**	
actor	counselor	operator	advertiser	manager
administrator	editor	radiator	beginner	manufacturer
author	educator	refrigerator	bookkeeper	passenger
aviator	elevator	senator	computer	printer
bachelor	escalator	spectator	consumer	purchaser
collector	governor	sponsor	employer	receiver
commentator	indicator	supervisor	farmer	scanner
conductor	inventor		interpreter	treasurer
contractor	investigator		laborer	writer

Words Ending in -AR

A relatively small number of words end in -ar. The most common are listed below. If you study the list, this ending should never cause you trouble.

Common Words Ending in -AR			
beggar	dollar	grammar	familiar
calendar	regular	peculiar	liar
collar	singular	similar	

Notice!

Distinguish between *hangar*, a shelter for housing airplanes, and *hanger*, which hangs clothes.

Exercise 6

Add the suffix -or, -er, or -ar to each of the following words:

1. begg ___ ___
2. receiv ___ ___
3. conduct ___ ___
4. passeng ___ ___
5. govern ___ ___
6. scann ___ ___
7. operat ___ ___
8. doll ___ ___
9. supervis ___ ___
10. operat ___ ___

Words Ending in *-ANCE, -ENCE*

There are no simple ways of learning when to add *-ance* or *-ence*. It is best to study each of the following lists, using the words as often as possible until you habitually spell them correctly.

Common *-ANCE, -ANCY, -ANT* Words			
abundant	descendant	important	preponderant
abundance	elegance	inheritance	remembrance
acquaintance	elegant	irrelevancy	repentance
appearance	endurance	irrelevant	repentant
assistance	entrance	lieutenant	restaurant
assistant	entrant	maintenance	sergeant
balance	grievance	nuisance	significance
brilliance	guidance	observance	significant
brilliant	hindrance	observant	stimulant
clearance	ignorance	pendant	tenancy
countenance	ignorant	perseverance	tenant
defendant	importance	pleasant	tolerance

Common *-ENCE, -ENCY, -ENT* Words

absence	diligence	occurrence
absent	diligent	opponent
abstinence	divergence	patent
abstinent	divergent	patience
adherence	efficiency	patient
adherent	efficient	penitence
antecedent	eminence	penitent
apparent	eminent	permanence
audience	essence (essential)	permanent
coherence	equivalent	persistence
coherent	excellence	persistent
coincidence	excellent	pestilence
concurrence	existence	precedence
concurrent	existent	preference
conference	experience	presence
confidence	government	present
confident	impertinence	prominence
conscience	impertinent	prominent
consequence	imprudence	providence
consequent	imprudent	provident
competence	independence	reference
competent	independent	repellent
compliment (praise)	indulgence	reverence
convenience	indulgent	reverent
convenient	inference	residence
correspondence	influence (influential)	resident
correspondent	insistence	sentence
deference (deferential)	insolence	sufficient
dependence	insolent	superintendent
dependent	intelligence	tendency
difference	intelligent	violence
different	intermittent	violent
diffidence	magnificence	
diffident	magnificent	

Words Ending in -*ENSE*

There are only a few words ending in *-ense*.

Words Ending in -*ENSE*
defense
expense
immense
offense *or* offence
pretense *or* pretence
suspense

Exercise 7

Insert a *or* e *in the space indicated for the following words:*

1. complim ___ nt
2. remembr ___ nce
3. consist ___ nt
4. superintend ___ nt
5. depend ___ nt
6. exist ___ nce
7. descend ___ nt
8. acquaint ___ nce
9. griev ___ nce
10. perman ___ nt
11. magnific ___ nt
12. brilli ___ nce
13. compl ___ mentary
14. conveni ___ nce
15. abund ___ nce
16. guid ___ nce
17. consci ___ nce
18. coincid ___ nce
19. appar ___ nt
20. consequ ___ ntial

Words Ending in -*ARY*, -*ERY*

There are more than 300 words ending in -*ary*. There are fewer commonly used words ending in -*ery*.

Common Words Ending in -*ERY*
---

bribery
machinery
cemetery
stationery
bakery

Perhaps it may help you to remember that in cemetery only *e*'s are used. Recall that station*ery* is used to write a lett*er*.

Common Words Ending in -*ARY*
---

auxiliary	honorary	secretary
boundary	imaginary	secondary
centenary	infirmary	tertiary
dictionary	involuntary	tributary
elementary	library	vocabulary
evolutionary	revolutionary	

Exercise 8

Select the word in each pair that is correctly spelled, and write it in the blank.

_____	1. a. boundery	b. boundary
_____	2. a. revolutionary	b. revolutionery
_____	3. a. cemetary	b. cemetery
_____	4. a. imaginery	b. imaginary
_____	5. a. tributery	b. tributary
_____	6. a. corollary	b. corollery
_____	7. a. coronery	b. coronary
_____	8. a. solitary	b. solitery
_____	9. a. militery	b. military
_____	10. a. infirmary	b. infirmery

Words Ending in *-ISE*, *-IZE*

There are no hard and fast rules to differentiate between the words ending in *-ise* and *-ize*. Perhaps the best procedure would be to master the list of *-ise* words and then remember that all others are spelled *-ize*.

Common Words Ending in -ISE, -IZE

-ISE

advertise (advertisement)	enterprise
advise	exercise
adviser	franchise
arise	merchandise
chastise (chastisement)	revise (revision)
compromise	supervise (supervision)
demise	surmise
despise	surprise
disguise	reprise (reprisal)

-IZE

agonize	idolization
antagonize	itemize
authorize (authorization)	legitimatize
burglarize	localize
capsize	modernize
centralize	neutralize
characterize (characterization)	ostracize
demoralize	patronize
dramatize	pulverize
emphasize (but emphasis)	realize
familiarize	recognize
fertilize	specialize
generalize	symbolize
generalization	tantalize
humanize	terrorize
hypnotize	visualize

Note!

There are only two common words ending in *-YZE*:

analyze   **paralyze**

Exercise 9

Add the suffix -ise or -ize to each of the following stems.

1. agon _____
2. chast _____
3. exerc _____
4. surpr _____
5. visual _____
6. superv _____
7. modern _____
8. enterpr _____
9. fertil _____
10. general _____

Chapter 10

PLURALS OF NOUNS

Regular Plurals

Rule 1

Most English nouns add -*S* to form the plural.

EXAMPLES:

cat + *s* = cats
hat + *s* = hats
house + *s* = houses

Nouns Endings in a Sibilant Sound

Rule 2

Nouns ending in a sibilant sound (-*s*, -*ss*, -*sh*, soft -*ch*, -*x*, or -*z*) add -*ES* to form the plural.

Nouns Ending in a Sibilant Sound Add -*ES* for Plural	
Sibilant Sound	**Plural Nouns**
-*S*	bus + *es* = buses
	gas + *es* = gases
-*SS*	kiss + *es* = kisses
	loss + *es* = losses
	pass + *es* = passes
	class + *es* = classes
	mass + *es* = masses
	business + *es* = businesses
-*SH*	parish + *es* = parishes
-*CH*	church + *es* = churches
	lunch + *es* = lunches
	bunch + *es* = bunches
	punch + *es* = punches
-*X*	box + *es* = boxes
	tax + *es* = taxes
-*Z*	buzz + *es* = buzzes
	quartz + *es* = quartzes

Nouns Ending in Long $\bar{O}$

A number of nouns ending in long $\bar{o}$ add -*ES* for the plural. Learn this entire list.

Nouns Ending in Long $\bar{O}$ with -*ES* Plural		
buffalo*es*	echo*es*	potato*es*
calico*es*	embargo*es*	tomato*es*
cargo*es*	hero*es*	torpedo*es*
desperado*es*	mosquito*es*	volcano*es*
domino*es*	motto*es*	

A few nouns ending in $\bar{o}$, add only an -*S*. Remember them by groups.

Nouns Ending in Long $\bar{O}$ with -*S* Plural		
Music	**Miscellaneous**	**Circular Appearance**
alto*s* ⎫	bronco*s*	dynamo*s*
soprano*s* ⎬ all are borrowed	studio*s*	cameo*s*
contralto*s* ⎬ from Italian	tattoo*s*	silo*s*
piano*s* ⎬	torso*s*	
solo*s* ⎭		

Nouns Ending in -*F* or -*FE*

Rule 3

Certain nouns ending in -*f* or -*fe* form the plural by changing *f* to *v* and adding -*S* or -*ES*.

Nouns Changing Final *F* or -*FE* to -*V* and Adding -*S* or -*ES* for Plural

Common Nouns

calf	→	calves
elf	→	elves
knife	→	knives
leaf	→	leaves
life	→	lives
loaf	→	loaves
thief	→	thieves
wife	→	wives
wolf	→	wolves

All of the words above except *calf* may be learned in groups according to the sound of the vowel before the *f*.

Nouns with $\overline{ee}$ Sound

leaf	→	leaves
thief	→	thieves

Nouns with $\bar{\imath}$ Sound

knife	→	knives
life	→	lives
wife	→	wives

Nouns with *el* Sound

elf	→	elves
self	→	selves
shelf	→	shelves

Nouns Ending in -F and Adding Only -S for Plural

-IEF

belief	→	beliefs
brief	→	briefs
chief	→	chiefs
grief	→	griefs
handkerchief	→	handkerchiefs

-OOF

hoof	→	hoofs (rarely hooves)
proof	→	proofs
roof	→	roofs

-RF

dwarf	→	dwarfs
scarf	→	scarfs (or scarves)
turf	→	turfs
wharf	→	wharfs (or wharves)

Exercise 1

Write plurals for the following words:

_____   1. reproof

_____   2. reprieve

_____   3. sieve

_____   4. halo

_____   5. gulf

_____   6. chief

_____   7. albino

_____   8. shelf

_____   9. puff

_____   10. muff

_____   11. slough

_____   12. basso

_____   13. mambo

_____   14. surf

_____   15. trough

_____ 16. stiletto

_____ 17. sheaf

_____ 18. radio

_____ 19. calf

_____ 20. loaf

Nouns Ending in -*Y*

Rule 4

Words ending in *y* preceded by a *vowel* form their plural by adding -*S*.

Ending in -*Y*, Preceded by a Vowel, Adding -*S* for Plural

day	→	days
boy	→	boys
monkey	→	monkeys
valley	→	valleys
volley	→	volleys

Exercise 2

Write the plurals of these words:

_____ 1. holiday

_____ 2. alley

_____ 3. attorney

_____ 4. buoy

_____ 5. chimney

_____ 6. donkey

_____ 7. journey

_____ 8. key

_____ 9. pulley

_____ 10. turkey

Rule 5

When the final *-y* is preceded by a *consonant* or *qu*, the *-y* changes to *i* and *-ES* is added to form the plural.

<table>
<thead>
<tr><th colspan="3">Words Ending in -Y, Preceded by a Consonant, or qu,
Changing -Y to -I and Adding -ES for Plural</th></tr>
</thead>
<tbody>
<tr><td>academy</td><td>→</td><td>academies</td></tr>
<tr><td>ally</td><td>→</td><td>allies</td></tr>
<tr><td>army</td><td>→</td><td>armies</td></tr>
<tr><td>caddy</td><td>→</td><td>caddies</td></tr>
<tr><td>cry</td><td>→</td><td>cries</td></tr>
<tr><td>soliloquy</td><td>→</td><td>soliloquies</td></tr>
</tbody>
</table>

Special Situations

Compound Nouns

Rule 6

Compound nouns add *-S* or *-ES* to only the principal word to form the plural.

EXAMPLES:
In the *in-law* series, the principal word is son, brother, etc.

brothers-in-law
mothers-in-law

Notice!

A few compound words are practically single words and add the *-S* at the end. This explains such cases as

spoonfuls	**cupfuls**
bowlfuls	**handfuls**

Old English Plurals

A long time ago the English language had quite a list of words whose plurals ended not in *-S* but in *-EN*. Only a few are left today, but they never give any trouble because they are learned in the very early grades of school. Other variations follow:

Old English Plurals		
General Words		
child	→	child*ren*
ox	→	ox*en*
foot	→	f*ee*t
tooth	→	t*ee*th
goose	→	g*ee*se
deer	→	deer
sheep	→	sheep
swine	→	swine
Animals		
louse	→	l*i*ce
mouse	→	m*i*ce
The Sexes		
man	→	m*e*n
woman	→	wom*e*n

Names of People

Rule 7

As a general rule, add *S* to form the plural of names of people.

EXAMPLES:
All the Johns in the school
All the Jennys in this class

Letters, Signs, Figures

Rule 8

Letters, signs, and figures form their plural by adding 'S.

EXAMPLES:
Cross your t's.
Mind your P's and Q's.
Underline the 3's in the line.
IQ's

Foreign Words

Foreign words act differently when their plurals are formed. Many English words are derived from Latin and Greek; study their unique plurals below.

1. Many Latin words ending in *-us* form their plural by changing the *us* to *i*. The most familiar of such words are

Latin Words Changing Final -*US* to *I* for Plural		
alumnus	→	alumn*i*
fungus	→	fung*i*
radius	→	radi*i*
bacillus	→	bacill*i*
terminus	→	termin*i*

2. Some Latin words ending in *-um* change to *a* to form the plural. A familiar word to us is *datum, data*.

Latin Words Changing Final -*UM* to -*A* for Plural		
medium	→	media
addendum	→	addenda
bacterium	→	bacteria
curriculum	→	curricula
maximum	→	maxima
memorandum	→	memoranda
minimum	→	minima
stratum	→	strata

3. **Greek** has a group of nouns ending in *-is* singular, *-es* plural. A familiar case is *crisis*, *crises*.

Greek Words Changing *-IS* to *-ES* for Plural		
analysis	→	analyses
antithesis	→	antitheses (opposite)
axis	→	axes (center)
ellipsis	→	ellipses
hypothesis	→	hypotheses (assumption)
oasis	→	oases
parenthesis	→	parentheses
synopsis	→	synopses

4. The Greek language has given us a few words ending in *-on* singular, *-a* plural. These are from the ancient Greeks.

Greek Plurals		
automaton	→	automata (mechanical figures working by themselves)
criterion	→	criteria (standard of judgment)

5. From the **French** have come these plurals:

French Plurals		
beau	→	beaux (or beaus)
tableau	→	tableaux (or tableaus)
chateau	→	chateaux
portmanteau	→	portmanteaux (or portmanteaus)

6. These familiar words are all **Italian** plural forms:

Italian Plurals
spaghetti
confetti
banditti
ravioli

Exercise 3

Plurals of nouns.
Form the plurals of the following nouns:

_____	1. t
_____	2. deer
_____	3. anniversary
_____	4. wife
_____	5. kerchief
_____	6. 4
_____	7. court-martial
_____	8. lieutenant colonel
_____	9. bay
_____	10. tray
_____	11. flurry
_____	12. sulky
_____	13. surrey
_____	14. inequity
_____	15. satellite
_____	16. functionary
_____	17. avocado
_____	18. dynamo

Exercise 4

Have someone dictate the following passage containing many singular nouns for which you will write the plurals.

Brenda's mother sent her to the store to purchase some *grocery* _____ for the long weekend. Among the *thing* _____ on the list were: *tomato* _____ , *potato* _____ , and *avocado* _____ . She also asked for several *quart* _____ of milk, several *piece* _____ of cake, and a pound of caramel-filled *chocolate* _____ .

After making these and several other *purchase* _____ , Brenda started to return home. On the way, she met her friend Nancy who was one of the best *soprano* _____ in the school choir. Brenda herself was usually placed among the *alto* _____ . After wandering up and down several narrow *alley* _____ , she found a bundle of *key* _____ which she had lost several *day* _____ before.

Chapter 11

THE FINAL -Y

Notice these words:

Singular		Plural
abb(ey)	→	abbeys
journ(ey)	→	journeys
monk(ey)	→	monkeys

The -Y Preceded by a Vowel

Rule 1

The final -Y following a *vowel* remains Y when suffixes are added.

These suffixes may be:

1. The letter -S to form the plural.

EXAMPLES:

$$attorney + s = attorneys$$
$$chimney + s = chimneys$$
$$donkey + s = donkeys$$
$$medley + s = medleys$$
$$pulley + s = pulleys$$
$$trolley + s = trolleys$$
$$valley + s = valleys$$
$$volley + s = volleys$$

2. The suffix *-ING* or *-ED*

EXAMPLES:

allay + *ed* = allay*ed*
annoy + *ed* = annoy*ed*
buy *not applicable; irregular part tense: bought*
allay + *ing* = allay*ing*
annoy + *ing* = annoy*ing*
buy + *ing* = buy*ing*

3. The suffix *-ER* meaning *one who*

EXAMPLES:

buy + *er* = buy*er*
employ + *er* = employ*er*

4. The suffix *-ANCE*

EXAMPLE:

convey + *ance* = convey*ance*

5. The suffix *-AL*

EXAMPLE:

portray + *al* = portray*al*

Exercise 1

Spell the following words correctly.

_____ 1. *tourney* in plural

_____ 2. The past tense of *allay*

_____ 3. The past tense of *volley*

_____ 4. *alley* in plural

_____ 5. Past tense of *survey*

_____ 6. Present participle of *portray*

_____ 7. Past tense of *journey*

_____ 8. Past tense of *relay*

_____ 9. Plural of *delay*

_____ 10. Past tense of *parlay*

The -*Y* Preceded, by a Consonant

Rule 2

When a *consonant* precedes the -*Y*, the *Y* changes to *I* when suffixes are added.

Kinds of suffixes:

1. The plural of the noun formed with -*ES*.

   EXAMPLES:

ally + *es*	= all*ies*
enemy + *es*	= enem*ies*
salary + *es*	= salar*ies*
tragedy + *es*	= traged*ies*

2. The verb form with *he*, *she*, or *it*, formed by adding -*ES*, or -*ED*.

   EXAMPLES:

carry + *es*	= carr*ies*
dignify + *es*	= dignif*ies*
marry + *es*	= marr*ies*
carry + *ed*	= carr*ied*
dignify + *ed*	= dignif*ied*

3. Making an adjective by adding -*FUL*.

   EXAMPLES:

beauty + *ful*	= beaut*iful*
mercy + *ful*	= merc*iful*
pity + *ful*	= pit*iful*

4. Making a noun by adding -*NESS*.

   EXAMPLES:

busy + *ness*	= bus*iness*
cozy + *ness*	= coz*iness*
icy + *ness*	= ic*iness*

5. Making an adverb by adding *-LY*.

   EXAMPLES:

   airy + *ly*   = air*ily*
   angry + *ly*   = angr*ily*
   busy + *ly*   = bus*ily*
   clumsy + *ly*   = clums*ily*

Caution!

There is only one case in which the *Y* is retained. This is before *-ING*.

   EXAMPLES:

   carry + *ing*   = carry*ing*
   copy + *ing*   = copy*ing*

Exercise 2

In the space to the left put the letter C *if the spelling is correct. If it is incorrect, write the proper spelling.*

_____   1. merciful

_____   2. beautiful

_____   3. cozily

_____   4. attornies

_____   5. valleys

_____   6. surveyor

_____   7. portraying

_____   8. pitying

_____   9. busied

_____   10. icyly

Exercise 3

Write the correct spelling of the following words all of which end in final Y before adding a suffix.

_____	1. pretty + ness
_____	2. petty + ness
_____	3. steady + ing
_____	4. ready + ed
_____	5. bully + s
_____	6. airy + ness
_____	7. pity + ed
_____	8. tally + ing
_____	9. buy + er
_____	10. duty + ful
_____	11. ready + ness
_____	12. carry + ed
_____	13. hurry + ing
_____	14. copy + er
_____	15. sloppy + ness
_____	16. lively + hood

Remember!

When adding the present participle (-*ing*) to verbs ending in -Y, do not change the Y.

EXAMPLES:

Word	+ *ING*		Present Participle
accompany	+ ing	=	accompanying
bury	+ ing	=	burying
hurry	+ ing	=	hurrying
study	+ ing	=	studying
worry	+ ing	=	worrying

Chapter 12

THE FINAL -*E*

DyEing or *Dying?*

One *E* can make a world of difference.

English has five *vowels*: A, E, I, O, U. The other letters are called *consonants*. Very often a consonant or group of consonants is added to a word and we get a second word. For example, let us consider the letters *-ry*. Add these to the following nouns (names of persons, places, acts, or things).

chemist	— one who analyzes things
chemis*try*	— the science of matter
forest	— the collection of trees
forest*ry*	— the study of care of forests
mimic	— one who imitates another
mimic*ry*	— the art of imitation

You see that no change occurs in spelling. You simply add the final element to a familiar word and you get a second word of a different meaning.

There are many endings of this character. If you remember that they do not change the spelling of the original word, you will find that they are really old friends with new attachments.

Exercise 1

Write the following words correctly by adding the suffix indicated:

_____ 1. pleasant + ry

_____ 2. artist + ry

_____ 3. portrait + ure

_____ 4. clock + wise

_____ 5. rocket + ry

_____ 6. jewel + ry

_____   7. nation + ality

_____   8. person + ality

_____   9. dialectic + al

_____   10. practical + ity

Few writers have any trouble in spelling words with added parts such as those described. But when a silent -*E* occurs at the end of a word, problems arise. When should you retain the silent -*E* and when should you drop it?

Dropping the Final -*E*

Rule 1

Drop the final -*E* before a suffix beginning with a *vowel* (*a, e, i, o, u*).

Suffixes Beginning with a Vowel	
-able	-ence
-ed	-ance
-er	-ing
-est	-ous
-ity	

How to handle these suffixes.

1. Dropping the final *e* before -*ER*.

    EXAMPLES:
    large + *er* = lar*ger*
    love + *er* = lo*ver*
    live + *er* = li*ver*

2. Dropping the final *e* before -*EST*.

    EXAMPLES:
    large + *est* = larg*est*
    brave + *est* = brav*est*

3. Dropping the final *e* before *-ABLE*.

   EXAMPLES:
   move + *able* = mov*able*
   love + *able* = lov*able*
   imagine + *able* = imagin*able*
   advise + *able* = advis*able*
   desire + *able* = desir*able*

4. Dropping the final *e* before *-ING*.

   EXAMPLES:
   come+ *ing* = com*ing*
   receive + *ing* = receiv*ing*
   ache + *ing* = ach*ing*

Note! _____

When *-ing* is ADDED to words ending in *-ie*, the *-e* is dropped and the *i* changed to *y* to prevent two *i*'s from coming together.

$$\textbf{die} + \textbf{\textit{ing}} = \textbf{dy\textit{ing}}$$
$$\textbf{lie} + \textbf{\textit{ing}} = \textbf{ly\textit{ing}}$$

Since many mistakes are made with the *-ing* words, the following list is provided. It contains some of your most useful words.

Handling *-ING*		
whine	argue	advise
whin*ing*	argu*ing*	advis*ing*
write	surprise	dine
writ*ing*	surpris*ing*	din*ing*
shine	owe	lose
shin*ing*	ow*ing*	los*ing*
oblige	purchase	fascinate
oblig*ing*	purchas*ing*	fascinat*ing*
judge	pursue	become
judg*ing*	pursu*ing*	becom*ing*
choose	tie	use
choos*ing*	ty*ing*	us*ing*

5. Dropping final *e* before *-OUS*.

>   **EXAMPLE:**
>
>   The suffix *-ous* is frequently added to a verb to make an adjective that always has the meaning, *full of.*
>
>   desire + *ous* = desir*ous*

>   **EXAMPLE:**
>
>   Sometimes the suffix *-ous* is added to a noun. Again an adjective results also meaning, *full of.*
>
>   pore + *ous* = por*ous* full of pores

6. Dropping final *e* before *-ITY*.

>   **EXAMPLE:**
>
>   The suffix *-ity* may be added to an adjective to form a noun. The final *E* before the suffix disappears.
>
>   extreme + *ity* = extrem*ity*

The same thing happens with these words:

Handling -*ITY*		
austere	extreme	sincere
auster*ity*	extrem*ity*	sincer*ity*
dense	facile	immense
dens*ity*	facil*ity*	immens*ity*
opportune	grave	intense
opportun*ity*	grav*ity*	intens*ity*
scarce	passive	rare
scarc*ity*	passiv*ity*	rar*ity*

Exercise 2

Form new words by spelling the following:

_____   1. revere + ing

_____   2. love + ly

_____   3. purchase + able

_____   4. extreme + ly

_____   5. pleasure + able

_____   6. large + ly

_____   7. nudge + ed

_____   8. state + ed

_____   9. fete + ed

_____   10. fine + ed

_____   11. dive + ing

_____   12. shove + ed

_____   13. devise + ing

_____   14. deceive + ed

_____   15. relieve + ing

_____   16. procrastinate + ing

_____   17. imagine + ed

_____   18. besiege + ed

_____   19. receive + ing

Caution! _____

Verbs ending in *oe* (canoe) retain the -*E* to preserve the pronunciation.

canoeing   hoeing

Dye* and *singe* retain the -*E* to differentiate the word from *die* and *sing

dyeing (one's hair)   dying (absence of life)
singeing (burning)   singing (a song)

Exercise 3

Form the present participle (+ -ing) and the past participle (+ -ed) of the following verbs.

Word	Present Participle	Past Participle
1. benefit		
2. commit		
3. lure		
4. refer		
5. pine		
6. elevate		
7. propel		
8. fit		
9. recur		
10. remit		
11. open		
12. club		
13. plunge		
14. singe		
15. pursue		
16. scare		
17. throb		
18. trot		
19. use		
20. whip		

Retaining the Final -*E*

Rule 2

The final -*E* is retained when the suffix begins with a *consonant*.

Suffixes Beginning with a Consonant

-ness   -ful
-ment   -less

How to handle these suffixes.

1. Adding the suffix -*NESS*.
   Examine the following words that all belong in this class:

Handling -*NESS*

complete	genuine	acute
complete*ness*	genuine*ness*	acute*ness*
expensive	large	appropriate
expensive*ness*	large*ness*	appropriate*ness*
coarse	fierce	vague
coarse*ness*	fierce*ness*	vague*ness*
like	polite	remote
like*ness*	polite*ness*	remote*ness*
rude	wide	
rude*ness*	wide*ness*	

2. Adding the suffix -*MENT*.
   Examine the following words that are all formed the same way:

Handling -*MENT*

---

amuse	enforce	advance
amuse*ment*	enforce*ment*	advance*ment*
arrange	engage	advertise
arrange*ment*	engage*ment*	advertise*ment*
commence	excite	amaze
commence*ment*	excite*ment*	amaze*ment*
move	require	manage
move*ment*	require*ment*	manage*ment*
discourage	achieve	
discourage*ment*	achieve*ment*	

Note! _____

***Abridgement*, *acknowledgement*, and *judgement* are usually spelled *abridgment*, *acknowledgment*, and *judgment*.**

---

3. Adding the suffix -*FUL*.
   The following words belong to this division:

Handling -*FUL*

---

care	grace	remorse
care*ful*	grace*ful*	remorse*ful*
revenge	disgrace	hate
revenge*ful*	disgrace*ful*	hate*ful*
taste	resource	shame
taste*ful*	resource*ful*	shame*ful*

4. Adding the suffix *-LESS*.
   Again the silent *E* is preserved because the suffix begins with the consonant *l*.

Handling *-LESS*

age	tongue	taste
age*less*	tongue*less*	taste*less*
care	noise	voice
care*less*	noise*less*	voice*less*
shame	sense	name
shame*less*	sense*less*	name*less*
change	shape	use
change*less*	shape*less*	use*less*
grace	cease	
grace*less*	cease*less*	
guide	smoke	
guide*less*	smoke*less*	

Caution!

Some exceptions.
- *Due, true, whole,* **drop the** *-E* **before** *-LY—duly, truly, wholly.*
- **Some words ending in** *-E,* **drop the** *-E* **before** *-MENT* **or** *-FUL. Argument* **is an instance, as is** *awful* **(from awe).**

Unusual Situations

Rule 3

Some words retain the final *-E* **regardless of the suffix in order to retain pronunciation.**

1. When the word ends in double -*EE*, the final -*E* is not dropped. This happens in order to retain the same pronunciation.

   EXAMPLES:
   agree
   agree*able*
   agree*ing*
   agree*ment*

2. Words ending in -*OE* retain the final -*E*.

   EXAMPLES:

canoe	shoe	hoe	woe
canoe*ing*	shoe*maker*	hoe*ing*	woe*ful*
	shoe*string*		woe*begone*
	shoe*ing*		

3. Words ending in -*CE* or -*GE* will retain the final -*E* before a suffix beginning with a vowel. This is necessary to keep the soft pronunciation.

   EXAMPLES:

notice	change	outrage
notice*able*	change*able*	outrage*ous*
service	courage	advantage
service*able*	courage*ous*	advantage*ous*

Rule 4

Certain words would lose their hard pronunciation of certain consonants unless a -*K* is added before a suffix beginning with *E*, *I*, or *Y* (used as vowel).

EXAMPLES:
mimic + *ing* = *mimicing*, which would not be pronounced with the hard *c* (= to *k*). Hence the *k* is inserted between the final *c* and the beginning vowel of the suffix. Note the following.

colic	→	colic*ky*		
frolic	→	frolic*king*	→	frolic*ked*
mimic	→	mimic*king*	→	mimic*ked*
panic	→	panic*king*	→	panic*ked*
picnic	→	picnic*king*	→	picnic*ked*
traffic	→	traffic*king*	→	traffic*ked*

Explain why this is not done for *frolicsome* or *panic-stricken* or *traffic cop*.

Exercise 4

Try your hand at spelling these words containing the final -E and a suffix.

1.	agree	+ MENT	=	_____
2.	amuse	+ MENT	=	_____
3.	care	+ FUL	=	_____
4.	canoe	+ ING	=	_____
5.	come	+ ING	=	_____
6.	disagree	+ ABLE	=	_____
7.	engage	+ MENT	=	_____
8.	excite	+ MENT	=	_____
9.	immense	+ ITY	=	_____
10.	like	+ LY	=	_____
11.	safe	+ TY	=	_____
12.	sense	+ LESS	=	_____
13.	shine	+ ING	=	_____
14.	enlarge	+ MENT	=	_____
15.	entice	+ ING	=	_____
16.	perceive	+ ED	=	_____
17.	escape	+ ING	=	_____
18.	discharge	+ ED	=	_____
19.	relieve	+ ING	=	_____
20.	contrive	+ ANCE	=	_____

Exercise 5

Have someone read the following sentences from dictation as you spell the words correctly. There will be many examples of dropping or retaining the final -E.

1. While they were *staring* at the stars, they saw something *stirring* in the bushes.
2. It takes much *planning* to build a house *preferred* by others.
3. The *cannery* used plenty of *cane* sugar with such fruits as *pineapples* and peaches.
4. By using *scraps* of food, the cook managed to *scrape* together a fair meal after the *scrapping* of the parents was over.
5. The little *moppet* sat *moping* in her little chair while the mother *mopped* up the food that was lying *sloppily* on the floor.

6. After Maria's parents *refused* to buy her the new computer game, she *fumed* and *fussed effusively* and finally stamped out of the room.

7. By *dotting* your *i*'s and *crossing* your *t*'s you can take a small step toward *better spelling*.

8. While a troop of cavalry was *ridding* the woods of the stragglers, a second troop was *riding* into the village.

Exercise 6

Each of the following words has an error in the dropping or retention of final -E. Make the correction in the space to the left.

_____ 1. scarcly

_____ 2. vengance

_____ 3. truely

_____ 4. tastey

_____ 5. noticable

_____ 6. changable

_____ 7. perspireing

_____ 8. retireing

_____ 9. aweful

_____ 10. wisedom

_____ 11. assureance

_____ 12. insureance

_____ 13. outragous

_____ 14. servicable

_____ 15. couragous

_____ 16. gorgous

_____ 17. pronouncable

Chapter 13

DOUBLING FINAL CONSONANTS

Do you know the difference between *riding* a horse and *ridding* the house of undesirable visitors? Do you know when people are *hoping* and when they are *hopping*? These are some examples of words with doubled consonants. There is no reason why anyone should suffer while trying to remember whether to spell a word with one or with two final consonants, for there are rules that will take care of all cases.

How many times have you been puzzled about doubling a consonant?

Does *beginning* have two *n*'s in the middle?

Does *omitted* have two *t*'s?

Why has *benefiting* one *t*, while *admitting* has two?

These and all other questions are easily answered if you will remember these two rules. There are very few rules in English as sure to help you as these.

One-Syllable Words

First you must recall the meaning of the word *syllable*. A syllable is a unit of spoken language forming either a whole word (as *men*) or a division of a word (as *priv* in *priv·i·lege*). Look at these words.

run   *swim*   *hop*

Each of these has a vowel in the middle and a consonant at the end. These make up one syllable and such a word is called a one-syllable word. But look at these:

con·fer   *pre·fer*   *trans·fer*

You notice that we have at least *two* syllables in each word. Now we can proceed to the rules. Notice what happens to our three friends when we add *-ing*.

ru*nn*ing   swi*mm*ing   ho*pp*ing

The final consonant (*n*, *m*, *p*) has been doubled before a suffix beginning with a vowel. We could have added the suffix *-er*.

ru*nn*er   swi*mm*er   ho*pp*er

Rule 1

When a one-syllable word ends in one vowel and one consonant, that consonant is _doubled_ before a suffix beginning with a vowel.

Now discover for yourself what would happen to the final consonants of these words.

One-Syllable Words Doubling Consonant Before Suffix Beginning with Vowel

Word		+ _ER_		+ _ING_
hit	→	hi*tt*er	→	hi*tt*ing
spin	→	spi*nn*er	→	spi*nn*ing
wrap	→	wra*pp*er	→	wra*pp*ing
trim	→	tri*mm*er	→	tri*mm*ing

These words are easy.

The following words have more than one syllable but they follow the same rule as the words just described. They _double_ their final consonant before a suffix beginning with a vowel.

Word		+ _ER_		+ _ING_		+ Other Suffix
admit			→	admi*tt*ing	→	admi*tt*edly
begin	→	begi*nn*er	→	begi*nn*ing		
compel			→	compe*ll*ing		
confer			→	confe*rr*ing		
control			→	contro*ll*ing	→	contro*ll*able
commit			→	commi*tt*ing		
equip			→	equi*pp*ing		
omit			→	omi*tt*ing		

Words of More Than One Syllable

Rule 2

A word of more than one syllable ending in a single vowel and a single consonant, which has the accent on the final syllable, _doubles_ that consonant before a suffix beginning with a vowel. _Remember, the accent must be on the last syllable._

occ·ur´	ad·mit´	per·mit´

If the final syllable has no accent, there will be no doubling of the consonant. Thus, *benefit* will not double the *t*, because the accent is on the first syllable.

be´·ne·fit·ing   tra´·vel·ed

Note!

Study the suffixes to the following words. Each word satisfies three conditions.

1. **It is more than one syllable.**
2. **The last syllable has the accent.**
3. **The last syllable ends in *one* vowel and a *single* consonant.**

Two-Syllable Words Doubling Consonant Before Suffix Beginning with Vowel

Word	+ *ING*	+ *ED*	+ Other Suffix
abet →	abetting →	abetted →	abettor
abhor →	abhorring →	abhorred →	abhorrence
admit →	admitting →	admitted →	admittance
allot →	allotting →	allotted →	allottance
annul →	annulling →	annulled →	annulment (one *l* because the suffix begins with a consonant)
confer →	conferring →	conferred →	conference (one *r* because the accent is not on *fer* but *con*)
concur →	concurring →	concurred →	concurrence
defer →	deferring →	deferred →	deference (only one *r* because accent is *not* on last syllable)
dispel →	dispelling →	dispelled	
excel →	excelling →	excelled	
infer →	inferring →	inferred →	inference (one *r*. Why?)
occur →	occurring →	occurred →	occurrence
omit →	omitting →	omitted	
permit →	permitting →	permitted	
rebel →	rebelling →	rebelled →	rebellion
recur →	recurring →	recurred →	recurrence
refer →	referring →	referred →	reference (one *r*. Why?)
regret →	regretting →	regretted	
transfer →	transferring →	transferred	

Special Situations

Rule 3

When adding -*NESS* to a word, use *nn* if the original word ends in *n*.

EXAMPLES:
mean + *ness* = mean*ness*
plain + *ness* = plain*ness*
thin + *ness* = thin*ness*

Rule 4

Words ending in -*FUL* have a single *l* unless -*ly* is added.

EXAMPLES:
careful + *ly* = carefu*lly*
beautiful + *ly* = beautifu*lly*
dutiful + *ly* = dutifu*lly*
wonderful + *ly* = wonderfu*lly*

hopeful + *ly* = hopefu*lly*
useful + *ly* = usefu*lly*
youthful + *ly* = youthfu*lly*

Exercise 1

Below is a list of verbs of one syllable. Add -ing to each of them. Some will double their final consonant. Some will not. Why? Remember Rule 1. There must be only one *vowel and* one *consonant.*

_____ 1. cramp

_____ 2. drum

_____ 3. grin

_____ 4. hit

_____ 5. look

_____ 6. nod

_____ 7. pain

_____ 8. rest

_____ 9. rig

_____ 10. scrub

Six out of the ten doubled their consonants. The remaining four did not because they had a vowel and two consonants (cr-a-mp) *or two vowels and consonant* (l-oo-k).

How Consonants Determine Meaning

Now for a few pairs of words with different meanings, depending upon the doubling of the consonants.

bar	→	He *barred* the door.
bare	→	He *bared* his arm.
pin	→	Mary *pinned* her dress.
pine	→	Mary *pined* away.
plan	→	They *planned* a happy life.
plane	→	The carpenter *planed* the wood.
scrap	→	The two dogs *scrapped*.
scrape	→	Walter *scraped* his new knife on the cement floor.
wag	→	He *wagged* his head solemnly.
wage	→	He *waged* a bitter war.

Notice how the meaning is determined by the single or double consonant and why correct spelling is so important to convey your meaning.

Notice these few exceptions to the rule: *chagrined, gaseous, transferable, transference, transferee, facility.*

Exercise 2

Write correctly the words formed as the exercise indicates:

_____   1. defer + ed

_____   2. refer + ence

_____   3. shop + ing

_____   4. disapprove + al

_____   5. nine + teen

_____   6. hit + ing

_____   7. singe + ing

_____   8. fame + ous

_____   9. control + ing

_____   10. repel + ent

_____   11. desire + ing

_____   12. tire + less

_____ 13. true + ly

_____ 14. swim + er

_____ 15. trim + er

_____ 16. occur + ence

_____ 17. move + able

_____ 18. commit + ed

_____ 19. equip + age

_____ 20. excel + ing

Exercise 3

Write the present participle (+ ing) _and_ past participle (+ ed) _of the following verbs. Some will double the final consonant; others will not. When in doubt, refer to the rules on doubling final consonants._

Word	Present Participle	Past Participle
1. adapt	_____	_____
2. cramp	_____	_____
3. design	_____	_____
4. conceal	_____	_____
5. congeal	_____	_____
6. blot	_____	_____
7. stop	_____	_____
8. crush	_____	_____
9. excel	_____	_____
10. defer	_____	_____
11. envelop	_____	_____
12. extol	_____	_____
13. flutter	_____	_____
14. happen	_____	_____
15. hum	_____	_____
16. level	_____	_____
17. quarrel	_____	_____
18. rub	_____	_____
19. signal	_____	_____
20. retreat	_____	_____

Exercise 4

By adding the various endings, make new words. In some instances, the final consonant of the original word will be doubled. When in doubt, refer to the rules about doubling final consonants.

EXAMPLE:

Form an adjective of the word *style* by adding *-ish*.

Word	Suffix	New Word
style	-ish	stylish

_____   1. Form an adjective of *wit* by adding *-y*.

_____   2. Form a noun from the verb *spin* by adding *-er*.

_____   3. Form a noun from the noun *blot* by adding *-er*.

_____   4. Form a noun by adding *-er* to *design*.

_____   5. Form an adjective by adding *-ical* to *quiz*.

_____   6. Form a noun by adding *-er* to *shut*.

_____   7. Form a noun by adding *-er* to *slip*.

_____   8. Form a noun by adding *-eer* to *profit*.

_____   9. Form a noun by adding *-ing* to *meet*.

_____   10. Form a noun by adding *-er* to *dry*.

_____   11. Add *-able* to *inhabit* to form an adjective.

_____   12. Add *-er* to *toil* to form a noun.

_____   13. Add *-er* to *put* to form a noun.

_____   14. Add *-ment* to *develop* to form a noun.

_____   15. Add *-ment* to *defer* to form a noun.

_____   16. Add *-er* to *rub* to form a noun.

_____   17. Add *-er* to *develop* to form a noun.

_____   18. Make the feminine of *god*.

_____   19. Name the man who sells you drugs.

_____   20. Add *-er* to *trap* to form a noun.

DOUBLING FINAL CONSONANTS

Exercise 5

Add the indicated ending to each of the following words.

_____ 1. tearful + ly

_____ 2. careful + ly

_____ 3. open + ness

_____ 4. dutiful + ly

_____ 5. bountiful + ly

_____ 6. common + ness

_____ 7. mimic + ed

_____ 8. picnic + ing

_____ 9. mimic + ing

_____ 10. panic + y

Chapter 14

ENGLISH AS A SECOND LANGUAGE

Minimal Differences in Spelling

Spelling in English is difficult because one sound may be written many different ways. You cannot rely on phonetics to help you. In addition, it is easy to confuse words that have only slight differences in the way they are spelled. For many ESL students, vowels are the most difficult part of spelling English. In this section, you will see the way various English vowel sounds are commonly spelled. For each vowel sound, we give both the most common spelling or spellings and also additional spellings that are used less frequently.

The sound symbols used here are based on the pronunciation keys used in most dictionaries. You do not need to memorize these symbols. They are just here to help you recognize the sound that goes with the spelling. Sample words are included for the spellings of each sound.

After each set of sounds you will find an exercise to help you review.

ĭ as in *fit* and ē as in *feet*

The short vowel ĭ is most often spelled simply *i* or *y*. However, there are a number of other possible, though less common, spellings.

ĭ as in *fit*

Most Common Spellings

i   as in ch*i*p, f*i*nish, f*i*x, *i*nclude, k*i*ck, l*i*p, m*i*nt, p*i*g, p*i*ll, p*i*t, r*i*ng, sp*i*nach, spl*i*t, wh*i*ch, w*i*ll, w*i*n

y   as in anton*y*m, h*y*mn, lar*y*nx, m*y*th, ph*y*sical, s*y*ntax

Additional Spellings

e   as in *e*clipse, *e*cology, *e*conomy, *e*merge, *e*mit, *E*ngland, *E*nglish

ee   as in b*ee*n

o   as in w*o*men

ui   as in b*ui*lt, g*ui*ld, g*ui*nea pig

The $\bar{e}$ sound, similar to the Spanish *i,* has several common spellings in English, and a few less common ones. Like other long vowels in English, it is usually represented by a double vowel or by a pair of vowels.

$\bar{e}$ as in *feet*

Most Common Spellings

ee   as in *eerie, deep, keen, meet, see*

ea   as in *bean, each, tea, teach, wheat*

ie   as in *chief, priest, relieve, series*

Additional Spellings

ay   as in qu*ay*

e   as in conc*e*de, *e*ternal, sc*e*nic

ei   as in n*ei*ther, rec*ei*ve

eo   as in p*eo*ple

ey   as in k*ey*

i   as in fat*i*gue, mach*i*ne, rav*i*ne

Exercise 1

Complete each word with the correct letter or letters.

1. A sh _____ p is a furry white animal that says "ba-a-a."

2. A sh _____ p is a large boat.

3. Something that doesn't cost much money is ch _____ p.

4. Do you like to eat potato ch _____ ps while you watch television?

5. Don't l _____ ve yet. Stay a little longer.

6. Where do you l _____ ve?

7. It's cold in here. Let's turn on the h _____ t.

8. The batter h _____ t the ball.

9. When do you go to sl _____ p at night?

10. Be careful not to sl _____ p and fall on the ice.

ĕ as in *set* and ĭ as in *sit*

This is the same short ĭ sound you reviewed in the previous section. The short ĕ sound is spelled most often with the letter *e*. However, sometimes it is spelled with the combination *ea*, and there are a few other variations that are occasionally used.

ĕ as in *set*

Most Common Spellings

e   as in belt, bet, elementary, elephant, fellow, hello, lend, penny, rest, seldom, self, seven, whether, yes

Additional Spellings

ea   as in bread, breakfast, head, instead, pleasure, spread

a   as in many, anything

ai   as in said

ay   as in says

ie   as in friend

ue   as in guess, guest

Exercise 2

Complete each word with the correct letter or letters.

1. Jenny and I made a b _____ t on who was going to win the World Cup.

2. Linda b _____ t her tongue while she was eating her dinner.

3. Fill out the form with a l _____ d pencil.

4. Albert forgot to put the l _____ d on the pot.

5. You don't have to stand. There is room for you to s _____ t down.

6. Can you help me s _____ t the table for dinner?

7. You speak English very w _____ ll.

8. W _____ ll you help me with my homework?

9. Kim has to f _____ ll out an application for a job.

10. The little boy f _____ ll down when he was ice skating.

$\bar{a}$ as in *late* and $\breve{e}$ as in *let*

The $\bar{a}$ sound is most often spelled *a*, *ai*, or *ay*. The *a* spelling is usually followed by a consonant and a silent *e*. The *ay* spelling commonly comes at the end of a word.

$\bar{a}$ as in *late*

Most Common Spellings

a as in *able*, *age*, *ape*, *ate*, *aviator*, *bake*, *brave*, *fable*, *flake*, *game*, *grape*, *labor*, *lazy*, *plate*, *rave*, *spade*, *stake*, *wake*, *waste*

ai as in *braille*, *brain*, *complain*, *explain*, *jail*, *mail*, *plain*, *stain*, *straight*, *waist*

ay as in *bay*, *gay*, *hay*, *layer*, *may*, *mayor*, *player*, *pray*, *spray*, *stay*, *way*

Additional Spellings

ea as in *great*, *break*

ei as in *eight*, *neighbor*, *reign*, *reindeer*

ey as in *they*, *prey*

Exercise 3

Complete each word with the correct letter or letters.

1. Many species m _____ te in the spring.

2. I m _____ t my friend at the mall yesterday.

3. The patient has a severe p _____ n in his abdomen.

4. Could you lend me a p _____ n to write down the phone number?

5. When I was a little girl, I used to wear my hair in br _____ ds.

6. Would you like some butter on your br _____ d?

7. If you drop the glass, you will br _____ k it.

8. She always has orange juice for br _____ kfast.

9. If you leave the g _____ te open, the dog will run into the street.

10. Please g _____ t some bottled water at the supermarket on your way home.

$\bar{\imath}$ as in *my* and $\bar{a}$ as in *may*

The most common spelling for $\bar{\imath}$ is the letter i. Like the $\bar{a}$ sound, it is often followed by a consonant and a silent *e*, and it can also be followed by a silent *g* or *gh*. The $\bar{\imath}$ sound is sometimes spelled *y*, especially when it comes at the end of a word. Both the *i* and the *y* can be followed by a silent *e* at the end of a word.

$\bar{\imath}$ as in *my*

Most Common Spellings

i   as in bite, blind, bribe, diner, drive, fight, flight, grind, hive, lion, might, mine, mild, nine, quite, ride, sight, sigh, sign, tight, tire, while, white, wild

y   as in by, dry, fry, psychology, spy, style, type, try, why

ie   as in die, lie, tie

ye   as in dye, rye

Additional Spellings

ai   as in aisle

ei   as in height

uy   as in buy

Exercise 4

Complete each word with the correct letter or letters.

1. How h _____ gh is that mountain?

2. Do cows eat h _____ ?

3. The ship is moored in the b _____ .

4. The post office is right b _____ the supermarket.

5. Go to the post office to b _____ the stamps.

6. Are you going to p _____ with cash or a credit card?

7. It's as American as apple p _____ .

8. She has beautiful red hair. I can't believe she's going to d _____ it black.

9. What d _____ will they arrive?

10. Every year, thousands of people d _____ of heart disease.

ă as in *man* and ā as in *main*

The ă sound is almost always spelled *a*. This makes it one of the easiest vowel sounds to put in writing. Notice that the ă sound is often followed by a consonant, but never by a single consonant followed by a silent *e*. The silent *e* is used only when the vowel sound is ā.

ă as in *man*

Most Common Spellings

a   as in *ant, bad, black, bran, can, cat, gram, graph, grass, happy, jam, kangaroo, lamp, mash, matter, splash, tap*

Additional Spellings

ai   as in pl*ai*d

au   as in l*au*gh, *au*nt

Exercise 5

Complete each word with the correct letter or letters.

1. Oat br _____ n cereal has become very popular.

2. You can figure it out. Use your br _____ n.

3. When you are ready, just t _____ p on the door.

4. The police tied yellow t _____ pe around the scene.

5. The turkey was brought in on a silver pl _____ tter.

6. He certainly put enough food on his pl _____ te.

7. Those black creatures flying around the belfry are b _____ ts.

8. He has to decide whether to fish or cut b _____ t.

9. We need more information. This study doesn't provide enough d _____ ta.

10. One d _____ te every schoolchild knows is Independence Day.

ă as in *cat*, ŏ as in *cot*, and ŭ as in *cut*

The short vowels ŏ and ŭ, like the short ă, are almost always spelled with the single letter representing the vowel. If you can recognize these vowel sounds, you will be able to spell them without too much trouble.

ŏ as in *cot*

Most Common Spellings

o   as in b*o*dy, fl*o*ck, g*o*t, h*o*p, kn*o*t, l*o*g, n*o*t, pl*o*t, sp*o*t, tr*o*t

Additional Spellings

a   as in wh*a*t, w*a*sp

ŭ as in *cut*

Most Common Spellings

u   as in b*u*tter, cr*u*mb, fl*u*b, g*u*n, m*u*tt, r*u*n, st*u*mble, s*u*pper, tr*u*nk

Additional Spellings

ou   as in c*ou*sin, d*ou*ble

o   as in *o*ven, w*o*nder

Exercise 6

Complete each word with the correct letter or letters.

1. After the B _____ ttle of Waterloo, Napoleon's reign was over.

2. We ordered a b _____ ttle of wine with dinner.

3. The tiny little gn _____ ts that fly around on a summer evening can drive you crazy.

4. I have to untangle the cord. It's all tied up in kn _____ ts.

5. Almonds are my favorite n _____ ts.

6. His first play received terrible reviews, and was a total fl _____ p.

7. The baby birds are trying to fl _____ p their wings.

8. A slang word for a policeman is c _____ p.

9. You can wear a c _____ p on your head.

10. You drink coffee from a c _____ p.

Review Exercise A—ĭ, ī, ĕ, ē, ă, ā, ŏ, ŭ

Complete each word with the correct letter or letters.

1. My team can b _____ t your team.

2. Would you be willing to b _____ t on that?

3. I would, b _____ t I don't have any money.

4. You just know your team can't possibly w _____ n.

5. Don't wh _____ ne just because you lost.

6. He missed the m _____ n point of the argument.

7. All U.S. presidents, so far, have been m _____ n.

8. Jose is a good m _____ n.

9. I'll take either one. They s _____ m to be exactly the s _____ me.

10. Where have you b _____ n all this time?

ŏo as in *look* and ŏ as in *lock*

The short double ŏo sound is almost always spelled with a double *oo*, usually followed by a single consonant. The only problem for spelling is that you must remember to use the double letter and not confuse this sound with the short ŏ, usually spelled with a single *o*.

ŏo as in *look*

Most Common Spellings

oo   as in f*oo*t, p*oo*r

Additional Spellings

u   as in b*u*ll, p*u*t, c*u*re

ou   as in c*ou*ld, sh*ou*ld

Exercise 7

Complete each word with the correct letter or letters.

1. I love to read a good b _____ k.

2. My neighbors have a swing on their b _____ ck porch.

3. I'd enjoy fishing better if I didn't have to put the worm on the h _____ k.

4. He needed money, so he h _____ cked his trumpet at the pawn shop.

5. It was hot, so we went wading in the br _____ k.

6. The little girl was building a tower with her bl _____ cks.

â as in *care*, *ô* as in *core*, *û* as in *cur*

The *â* is usually spelled *a* or *ai*; the *û* sound is usually spelled with a *u*. Both are usually followed by an *r*. The *ô* sound, usually spelled *o*, has more variations in the consonants that can follow it.

â as in *care*

Most Common Spellings

a   as in *a*rea, b*a*re, d*a*ring, gl*a*re, sh*a*re, squ*a*re, w*a*res

Additional Spellings

ai   as in c*ai*rn, fl*ai*r, p*ai*r

ea   as in p*ea*r, t*ea*r (meaning "rip"), w*ea*r

e   as in wh*e*re

ô as in *core*

Most Common Spellings

o   as in b*o*rn, c*o*rd, l*o*ng, m*o*rning, *o*r, *o*re, sw*o*re, t*o*rch

Additional Spellings

a   as in h*a*lter, t*a*ll, w*a*lk, w*a*rm

au   as in *au*dition, c*au*ght, c*au*ldron, c*au*se, h*au*nt

aw   as in h*aw*k, s*aw*, y*aw*n

ou   as in b*ou*ght, f*ou*r

û as in *cur*

Most Common Spellings

u   as in b*u*rger, c*u*rl, f*u*r, st*u*rdy, s*u*rface, t*u*rkey, t*u*rn

Additional Spellings

e   as in p*e*rmanent, sw*e*rve

ea   as in *ea*rn

i   as in sh*i*rt, st*i*r, wh*i*rl

o   as in w*o*rld, w*o*rm

Exercise 8

Complete each word with the correct letter or letters.

1. They are forecasting f _____ r weather for the weekend—warm and sunny.
2. This is a present f _____ r you.
3. Animal rights activists object when people wear f _____ r coats.
4. I have to go to the hardware st _____ re.
5. It's considered rude to st _____ re at people.
6. That shirt is t _____ rn.
7. T _____ rn right at the next corner.
8. Where w _____ re you? I couldn't find you anywhere.
9. Miners dig for _____ re.
10. Would you like this one _____ r that one?

ä as in *card* and *ô* as in *cord*

The *ä* sound is also frequently followed by an *r*, but not always. It is usually spelled *a*.

ä as in *card*

Most Common Spellings

a   as in *a*re, *a*rch, *a*rm, c*a*lm, f*a*r, h*a*rsh, sc*a*rf, t*a*rnish, y*a*rn

Additional Spellings

ea   as in h*ea*rt

Exercise 9

Complete each word with the correct letter or letters.

1. You can walk from here. It isn't f _____ r.
2. Did you want three apples or f _____ r?
3. The farmer put the animals in the b _____ rn at night.
4. He has always lived in the house where he was b _____ rn.
5. It was a bad accident, and it left him with a sc _____ r on his cheek.
6. Is the ball game over already? What was the sc _____ re?
7. People used to dry, or p _____ rch, the corn to store it for the winter.

8. In the summer we like to sit on the front p _____ rch and watch the world go by.

9. He pursued his goal with great _____ rdor and enthusiasm.

10. Will the meeting please come to _____ rder?

ō as in *rote* and ōō as in *root*

The long single ō is most commonly spelled *o* or *oa*. When it is spelled *o*, it is often followed by a single consonant and a silent *e*. This is the same pattern you saw for the long ā sound. The long double ōō, which sounds like the Spanish *u*, is most commonly spelled *oo*, *ou*, or *u*. However, for both of these sounds a number of additional spellings are possible.

ō as in *rote*

Most Common Spellings

o   as in b*o*ne, c*o*zy, h*o*le, j*o*ke, n*o*te, *o*pen, *o*ver, p*o*ny, r*o*se, s*o*lo, wh*o*le

oa   as in b*oa*t, c*oa*l, l*oa*n, m*oa*n, r*oa*st, t*oa*st

oe   as in d*oe*, f*oe*, t*oe*

Additional Spellings

ou   as in b*ou*lder

ough   as in th*ough*

ow   as in b*ow*, fl*ow*, sh*ow*

ew   as in s*ew*

ōō as in *root*

Most Common Spellings

oo   as in bl*oo*m, b*oo*n, ch*oo*se, c*oo*l, h*oo*t, l*oo*ny, n*oo*se, r*oo*ster, t*oo*, z*oo*m

Additional Spellings

o   as in d*o*, t*o*, tw*o*

ou   as in gh*ou*l, r*ou*te, y*ou*

ough   as in thr*ough*

oe   as in sh*oe*

u   as in r*u*de

ue   as in bl*ue*, tr*ue*

ui   as in cr*ui*se

ew   as in cr*ew*, kn*ew*

Exercise 10

Complete each word with the correct letter or letters.

1. C _____ l mines are usually found in mountainous areas.

2. It gets c _____ l in the evening. You should bring a sweater.

3. I wouldn't touch that with a ten-foot p _____ le.

4. He does ten laps in the swimming p _____ l every day.

5. Of course you can stay with us. We have plenty of r _____ m.

6. When I'm in a new city, I like to just r _____ m around the streets.

7. As a general r _____ le, it's a good idea to take a taxi home late at night.

8. The actor considered that r _____ le the high point of his career.

9. It's always easier to do a job when you have the right t _____ ls.

10. You have to pay a t _____ ll on all the highways into the city.

oi as in *foil* and *ou* as in *foul*

The *oi* sound, spelled either *oi* or *oy*, always uses the *oy* spelling at the end of a word. The *ou* sound, spelled either *ou* or *ow*, always uses the *ow* spelling at the end of a word.

oi as in *foil*
Most Common Spellings

oi	as in b*oi*l, ch*oi*ce, cl*oi*ster, j*oi*nt, l*oi*n
oy	as in ann*oy*, b*oy*, cl*oy*

ou as in *foul*
Most Common Spellings

ou	as in b*ou*ndary, c*ou*nt, l*ou*d, *ou*t, s*ou*nd
ow	as in b*ow*, br*ow*n, c*ow*, cr*ow*d, h*ow*

Additional Spellings

ough	as in b*ough*

Exercise 11

Complete each word with the correct letter or letters.

1. Smoking is not all _____ ed anywhere in the building.

2. He called her name al _____ d, and everyone turned to look.

3. Pewter is an all _____ of tin and lead.

4. If you strike _____ l in your backyard, you'll be rich.

5. In the evening, you can hear an _____ l hoot.

6. Don't make so much n _____ se. You'll wake everyone up.

7. N _____ is the time for us to take action!

8. This ticket will be v _____ d if you don't use it by the date stamped on the back.

9. He v _____ ed to be true, but, alas, he was unfaithful.

10. Use n _____ ns and verbs when you write. Av _____ d too many adjectives.

Review Exercise B—*ŏŏ, ŏ, â, ô, û, ä, ō, ōō, oi, ou*

Complete each word with the correct letter or letters.

1. My father always c _____ rves the turkey on Thanksgiving.

2. Drive slowly. There are lots of c _____ rves on this road.

3. Put on your c _____ t before you go out in the cold.

4. We put an extra c _____ t in the room for the baby to sleep on.

5. We c _____ t quite a few fish in the lake last year.

6. He killed the g _____ se that laid the golden egg.

7. She g _____ s to school with me.

8. Smoking is n _____ t allowed here.

9. She always writes a thank-you n _____ te when someone gives her a present.

10. By aftern _____ n, n _____ ne of the snow was left. The sun had melted it.

Unaccented Syllables

Unaccented, or barely accented, vowels present a special problem for spelling. The sound is something like **uh**, but this sound can be represented by any of the vowels or even by a combination of vowels. This is a problem even for native English speakers, who often have trouble deciding, for example, if a word should end *-ence* or *-ance*. Pronunciation will not offer any help here.

Unaccented Syllables

a	as in *a*lone
ai	as in cert*ai*n
e	as in both*e*r
i	as in happ*i*ly
io	as in intent*io*n
o	as in cal*o*rie
u	as in min*u*s

Exercise 12

Complete each word with the correct letter or letters.

1. N _____ cessity is the mother of invention.

2. The parents and children had a very emot _____ ion _____ l reunion.

3. The province declared its independ _____ nce, and a civil war began.

4. In hot weather, everyone p _____ rspires.

5. He went to college for a lib _____ r _____ l arts degree.

Silent Letters

In English, there are a number of letters that are sometimes written but not pronounced. We have already mentioned the silent *e*, which comes after a single consonant and changes the pronunciation of the preceding vowel. For example, the addition of a silent *e* changes the short *ă* in hat to the long *ā* in hate.

In addition, there are a number of consonants that are often not pronounced, such as *g* and *k* when they come before an *n*. Following is a list of the most common silent letters.

Silent Letters	
c	as in science, scissors
d	as in Wednesday
g	as in gnaw, gnat, sign, reign
h	as in heir, honor, hour, shepherd
k	as in knee, knight, knife, knock, know
l	as in almond, calf, calm, folk, half, solder, talk, walk, yolk
n	as in condemn, damn, hymn, solemn
p	as in corps, cupboard, pneumonia, psychology, raspberry
t	as in fasten, glisten, hasten, hustle, listen, often, nestle, thistle

Exercise 13

Complete each word with the correct letter or letters.

1. You can cut the string with a _____ nife or with a pair of s _____ issors.

2. Ca _____ m down and try to ta _____ k slowly.

3. He's seeing a _____ sychiatrist who is willing to lis _____ en to his problems.

4. The _____ eir to the throne will rei _____ n over the country.

5. The condem _____ ed man ate a hearty dinner.

SPECIAL DEVICES

Chapter 15

THE HYPHEN

English is a language rich in compound words. Sometimes two nouns are combined as in *secretary-treasurer* because the new term combines the functions of both. The hyphen here shows that you are talking about one man or woman. Many compound words are adjectives formed from various parts of speech. For example, to say that a *car is of low price* sounds archaic. Instead, we write *low-priced* car.

In describing a suit that you could wear at once after you had bought it, you could write: *a garment that was already made*, or the much shorter, *ready-made* suit.

Many hyphenated words eventually become so familiar that they are written as one word. Certain magazines, like *Time* and *Newsweek*, frequently write as single words those words that texts and dictionaries still hyphenate. However, the trend today is away from the use of hyphens, often combining compound words that were previously hyphenated, such as *citywide*, *countdown*, and *stickup*.

Compound Adjectives

When to Hyphenate

There are eight types of such hyphenated adjectives.

1. Noun or adjective + participle.

   EXAMPLES:
      fire-fighting apparatus (noun + participle)
      bad-looking apples (adjective + participle)

2. Noun + adjective.

   EXAMPLES:
      good-natured man
      lily-white hands

3. Compound numbers between 21 and 99.

    EXAMPLES:
    > *twenty-fifth* person
    > the three hundred and *seventy-fifth* bill

4. Number + nouns.

    EXAMPLES:
    > the *five-year* plan
    > *thirty-cent* candies
    > twelve *two-year-olds*

5. Short adverbs (*best, far, ill, long, much, well*) + participle.

    EXAMPLES:
    > *best-known* author
    > *far-fetched* theory
    > *ill-gotten* gains
    > *long-needed* vacation
    > *well-founded* argument

6. Adjectives of nationality.

    EXAMPLES:
    > *Franco-Prussian* War
    > *Anglo-Saxon*
    > *Asian-American*

7. Two nouns forming an adjective.

    EXAMPLES:
    > a *father-son* event
    > a *brother-sister* act

8. Verb plus other elements forming an adjective.

    EXAMPLES:
    > The *would-be* actor
    > The *wait-and-see* plan for peace
    > A *hit-and-run* driver

When *Not* to Hyphenate

1. When the adjective follows the noun.

    EXAMPLES:

    She was an executive well known for her honesty.
    He was a man ill fitted for the job.

2. When two independent adjectives precede the noun and are not combined.

    EXAMPLES:

    Jack wore his old blue sweater.
    But: *Jack wore his sky-blue sweater* (only one adjective).
    She carried the tired, old dog.

3. When an adverb modifies an adjective.

    EXAMPLES:

    He was a highly paid executive.
    This was a nicely kept room.
    It was a newly born calf.

4. When a comparative or superlative form is one of the two modifiers.

    EXAMPLES:

    There was no kinder hearted person in the room.
    The lowest priced car was the compact.
    But: *A low-priced car was desired.*

5. When the compound modifier is a proper noun of two words.

    EXAMPLES:

    Thomas Mann was a Nobel Prize winner.
    He was the South American representative in the Security Council.

6. When one word in the compound modifier has an apostrophe.

    EXAMPLES:

    The first year's harvest was small.
    The third century's literature was most religious.
    The seventh day's fast was broken.

Exercise 1

Indicate at the left whether the following words are properly hyphenated. Place a C if correct and an X if wrong.

_____	1. well-fed cattle
_____	2. redcheeked youngster
_____	3. tenday reducing diet
_____	4. a three-month delay
_____	5. the twenty-second victim
_____	6. poorly lit interior of the hut
_____	7. state-wide elections
_____	8. eighty-dollar seats
_____	9. a seven-day wonder
_____	10. the kind-hearted teacher
_____	11. hornrimmed spectacles
_____	12. the legend of the saber toothed tiger
_____	13. This was indeed a well kept garden
_____	14. His ill-fated story was common knowledge
_____	15. My sister was a red-head
_____	16. a first class performance
_____	17. the silver plated fork
_____	18. the sky-blue water
_____	19. England's far-flung empire
_____	20. the far-off hills of Dune

Compound Nouns

By using the hyphen with two or more familiar words, new words have been added to our vocabulary.

1. Use the hyphen when two normally distinct functions are united in one person or thing.

    EXAMPLES:
    secretary-treasurer } *united*
    fighter-bomber   functions

    However, *do not* hyphenate double terms that represent a single office:

    EXAMPLES:
    Major General
    Secretary of Defense
    Lieutenant Commander } *single*
    General Manager   office
    Executive Assistant
    Manager Trainee

2. Use the hyphen when two nouns form a new noun. Usually the first acts with the force of an adjective.

    EXAMPLES:
    light-year
    foot-pound
    nation-state

3. Sometimes a noun will be combined with another part of speech to form an entirely new noun.

    EXAMPLES:
    son-in-law
    jack-in-the-box
    know-it-all

4. A verb may be combined with some other part of speech to make a noun.

    EXAMPLES:
    know-how
    A *do-nothing*   } verb plus object helps make new nouns
    A *cure-all*
    A *know-nothing*

    A *flare-up,*   *play-off*
    A *lean-to,*   *drive-in*   } verb plus preposition helps make new nouns
    A *go-between*   *shake-up*

Compound Numbers and Fractions

1. Use the hyphen in numbers from twenty-one to ninety-nine.
2. In fractions use the hyphen when the fraction is used as an adjective.

EXAMPLES:
> *The three and one-half pounds of butter.*
> *Two and one-eighth quarts of soymilk.*

Caution! _____

Do not use the hyphen when the fraction is not a single adjective.

EXAMPLES:
> The chairperson asked *one third* of the group to stay.
> He drank *one half* of the cup quickly.

Compounds with Certain Particles

1. All compounds with **self-** use the hyphen.

   EXAMPLES:
   > *self-sacrifice*
   > *self-interest*
   > *self-made* man

2. Compounds with **all-** use the hyphen.

   EXAMPLES:
   > *all-important*
   > *all-purpose*

3. Most compounds with **half-** use the hyphen.

   EXAMPLES:
   > *half-moon*
   > *half-truth*

   There are some exceptions to this rule.

   EXAMPLES:
   > *halfway*
   > *halfhearted*

4. Most compounds with **cross-** use the hyphen.

EXAMPLES:
cross-examine
cross-reference

There are exceptions to this rule.

EXAMPLES:
crosscut
crossbreed

5. With some exceptions, words with high, low, and full use the hyphen.

EXAMPLES:
high-class
low-grade
full-fledged

Caution!

Do *not* hyphenate the reflexives such as *yourself*, *himself*, *herself*, or *self* in such adjectives as *selfless, selfsame*.

6. The prefix **re-** takes the hyphen when it means *again*, especially if necessary to prevent confusion.

EXAMPLES:
re-form the squad
re-cover the pot
re-create the scene of the crime

Note!

- Note the difference between *reform* the prisoner and *re-form* the broken line of infantry.
- To eliminate the hyphen in *re-cover* and *re-create* might lead to nuspronunciation or misunderstanding.

7. Occasionally a hyphen is used with prefixes ending in the same vowel that begins the next word.

EXAMPLES:
co-owner
pre-engineered

In general, however, those words are written as one word, without a hyphen.

EXAMPLES:
cooperate
preeminent

8. Use a hyphen with some words beginning with **anti**.

EXAMPLES:
anti-Semitism
anti-imperialism

However, the trend today is to combine words that begin with **anti**.

EXAMPLES:
antioxidant
antiperspirant

9. Use a hyphen when a prefix is added to a word beginning with a capital letter.

EXAMPLES:
mid-Atlantic
pro-British

10. Use a hyphen with titles that are preceded by **vice-** or **ex-**, or are followed by **-elect**.

EXAMPLES:
Vice-President
President-elect
ex-Governor

Remember! _____

Consult the dictionary if you are in doubt about when to hyphenate.

Used for Clarity

Use a hyphen to avoid confusion of meaning. Look at the following sentence.

She is an old-furniture buyer for an antique store.

Without the hyphen, we would appear to be describing her as *an old buyer*. With the hyphen, it is clear that she buys old furniture.

Words That Are NEVER Hyphenated	
background	outline
downstairs	pastime
farewell	railroad
headline	semicolon
inasmuch	together
keyboard	warehouse
midday	yourself
nevertheless	

Words That Are ALWAYS Hyphenated	
brother-in-law	son-in-law
daughter-in-law	aide-de-camp
father-in-law	man-of-war
mother-in-law	runner-up
sister-in-law	jack-o'-lantern

Used to Divide Words

The hyphen is also used to divide a word at he end of a line of text. The word must be divided according to syllables. If you are unsure of where to break a word, consult the dictionary or the "10,000 Word Ready Reference Spelling List" at the back of this book. Most computer software programs have auto-hyphenate settings.

Words ALWAYS Written Separately			
some way	any day	each other	in fact
some day	any place	*en route*	in order
some place	by and by	every way	in spite
	by the bye	every time	no one
	by the way		

Caution!

Do not confuse *already*, an adverb expressing time, with *all ready*, an adjective meaning fully prepared.

EXAMPLES:
    The members of the team were *all ready* to go.
    He had *already* left.

Exercise 2

Spell the following words correctly by inserting the hyphen where it belongs. If the word is correctly spelled, write C *in the space to the left.*

_____   1. sisterinlaw

_____   2. man of war

_____   3. aidedecamp

_____   4. runon sentence

_____   5. down-stairs

_____   6. anti war rally

_____   7. ex-husband

_____   8. re-emerge

_____   9. self-centered child

_____   10. one quarter of the population

_____   11. runnerup

_____   12. drivein theater

_____   13. secretary-treasurer

_____   14. Lieutenant General

_____   15. tradein

_____   16. fire-fighting engine

_____   17. pro-European policy

_____   18. builtin arch

_____   19. The final play-off

_____   20. broken-down houses

Chapter 16

THE APOSTROPHE

To Show Contraction

1. Use the apostrophe to indicate a lost vowel.

   EXAMPLES:
   do n*o*t = don't
   can n*o*t = can't
   could n*o*t = couldn't
   we *a*re = we're
   you *a*re = you're
   they *a*re = they're
   he *i*s = he's
   she *i*s = she's
   it *i*s = it's

To Show Possession

To Show Possession: Common Nouns

1. Most frequently the apostrophe is used to show possession. A *singular noun* not ending in -*s* adds '*s*.

   EXAMPLES:
   The hat of the girl = the girl's hat
   The rights of the man = the man's rights

2. Add '*s* to a *singular noun* that ends in -*s* or an s-sound if a new syllable is formed by pronouncing the possessive.

   EXAMPLES:
   The hair of the actress = the actress's hair
   The daughter of the boss = the boss's daughter

3. To show possession with a *plural noun*, add *'s* if the noun does not end in *s*.

EXAMPLES:
    men's clothing
    women's hats
    children's shoes

4. If the *plural noun* ends in *-s* (as most nouns do), add only the apostrophe.

EXAMPLES:
    the doctors' fees
    the dentists' conference
    the teachers' demands

To Show Possession: Proper Nouns

1. To show possession of a *singular proper noun* not ending in *-s*, add *'s*.

EXAMPLES:
    Mr. Mann's library
    Miss Smith's dog
    Dr. Levitt's office

2. When the *proper noun* ends in *-s* and has only one syllable, add *'s*.

EXAMPLES:
    Alger Hiss's case
    Rudolf Hess's escape

3. When the *proper noun* ending in *-s* has two or more syllables, add only the apostrophe.

EXAMPLES:
    Mr. Dickens' readings
    Roger Williams' expulsion

To Show Possession: Compound Nouns

1. The apostrophe is used only after the last noun in the compound.

EXAMPLES:
    my mother-in-law's house
    the man-of-war's deck

To Show Possession: Indefinite Pronouns

1. Use the same rules for indefinite pronouns as those above for common nouns.

   EXAMPLES:
   One's honor is at stake. (*singular*)
   The others' hats were soiled while ours were clean. (*plural*)

To Show Possession: Personal Pronouns

1. Personal pronouns *never* use the apostrophe for their possessive case.

   EXAMPLE:
   his, hers, its, ours, theirs

2. Be especially careful with *whose*. What is the difference between:

   Whose house is this?
   and
   Who's there?

To Avoid Repetition of *S* Sound

1. To avoid the repetition of the *s*-sound, just add the apostrophe.

   EXAMPLE:
   for mildness' sake

To Indicate Double Ownership

1. When you wish to indicate *ownership by two or more* persons, use the apostrophe *only* for the last.

   EXAMPLES:
   Lewis and Clark's expedition
   Jim and Joe's locker
   Smith, Kline and French's drugs

2. If you are talking about *separate ownership*, use the apostrophe after each noun.

   EXAMPLE:
   The president's and secretary of state's reports
   This means there were two reports, one by each officer.

Remember!

The apostrophe means "belonging to whatever immediately precedes it," *except* **when it is used to indicate a lost vowel.**

EXAMPLES:

children's—belonging to children

men's—belonging to men

boss's—belonging to a single boss

bosses'—belonging to more than one boss

Exercise

Rewrite the following phrases, using the apostrophe to show possession:

_____   1. The hat of the young girl

_____   2. The votes of the members

_____   3. The styles of the ladies

_____   4. The paws of the cats

_____   5. The decorations of the sailors

_____   6. The hat of the professor

_____   7. A shoe of a woman

_____   8. The voice of the soprano

_____   9. The tail of the dog

Add the apostrophe in the following sentences to show omission of a letter.

_____   10. They do not vote often.

_____   11. We have not any money.

_____   12. The allies could not agree on the campaign.

_____   13. You are always late.

_____   14. They can not always win.

_____   15. It is too late to go now.

_____   16. Let us wait a little longer.

_____   17. We would not take "no" for an answer.

Chapter 17

CAPTIAL LETTERS

Basic Principles

What to Begin with a Capital Letter

1. The first word of a sentence.
2. The first word of a quoted sentence.
3. The first word, and important words, in titles of books or themes.
4. Proper nouns.
5. The pronoun *I*.
6. The first word of a salutation and complimentary closing of a letter.

Proper Nouns

When to Capitalize

Proper Names
Sioux City
Eastern District High School
State Legislature
United Nations

Definite place names
Madison Avenue

Family relationships
Aunt Jane
Uncle Bill (but when preceded by a possessive: my uncle Bill)

Substitute for person's name (especially in direct address)
"Hurry up, Aunt!"
"Yes, Mom, I'm hurrying!"
Dear Sir
Dear Madam

Definite events
May Day
War of 1870

Races, Languages, Religions
German
Hindu
French
Caucasian
Mongolian
Judaism

Titles
Uncle Don
Dr. Jones

Organization Names
The Odd Fellows (club)
Bethlehem Steel Corporation
Methodist Episcopal Church
The Farmer-Labor Party

Deity (and words associated with Deity)
God
Christ
Buddha
Scriptures

Trade names
Hathaway shirt
Revlon's lotion

Note!

Capitalize only the part of the *trade name* that differentiates it from all other brands.

When NOT to Capitalize

Words that are not a speclflc name
our high school
the cold stream

Point of the compass
four degrees north

The names of the seasons
spring
summer
autumn
winter

Studies other than languages
chemistry
biology

A title after a modifier
my uncle
a doctor
I have two brothers
my cousins

Books, Plays, Music

Remember This Rule in Capitalizing a Title!_____

Don't cap the "CAPS." The last "CAP" stands for

> **C—conjunctions (and, but, or, for, nor)**
> **A—articles (the, a, an)**
> **P—prepositions (of, to, for, from)**

EXAMPLES:
Book: *Moby Dick*
Play: *Hamlet*
             My Fair Lady
Music: "Let it Be"
             "Moondance"

Exercise

Try your hand at capitalizing the words that need capitals.

1. We stopped at the hotel westover.
2. The buick cars are well advertised.
3. We celebrate decoration day.
4. the north side high school
5. We saw the lion king.
6. They sang irish folk songs.
7. In english courts, the bible is kissed.
8. Harriet Beecher Stowe's uncle Tom is known wherever the book is read.
9. They walked along fifth avenue.
10. Many people ask for washington coffee.
11. Our vacation to britain lasted three weeks.
12. Bard college is in new york.
13. the taming of the shrew is a play written by shakespeare.
14. My courses in college include mathematics, english, and french.
15. Last spring we visited aunt emily who lives out west.

Chapter 18

SPELLING ABBREVIATIONS

The Calendar

Day, Month, Time

Days of the Week	
Abbreviation	**Weekday**
Sun.	Sunday
Mon.	Monday
Tues.	Tuesday
Wed.	Wednesday
Thurs.	Thursday
Fri.	Friday
Sat.	Saturday

Months of the Year	
Abbreviation	**Month**
Jan.	January
Feb.	February
Mar.	March
Apr.	April
Aug.	August
Sept.	September
Oct.	October
Nov.	November
Dec.	December

Time	
Abbreviation	**Time**
A.D.	anno Domini (Latin for "In the year of the Lord")
B.C.	before Christ
A.M.	ante meridiem (Latin for "before noon")
P.M.	post meridiem (Latin for "after noon")
EST	Eastern Standard Time

Business and Postal Terms

Business Terms

Business Terms	
Abbreviation	**Term**
acct.	account
ans.	answer
assn.	association
Ave.	avenue
bldg.	building
Blvd.	boulevard
bros.	brothers
C.O.D.	collect on delivery
dept.	department
Esq.	esquire
etc.	and so forth
F.O.B.	freight on board
Inc.	incorporated
Jr.	junior
Ltd.	limited
mfg.	manufacturing
Mts.	mountains
no.	number
P.O.	post office
P.S.	postscript (written after the letter)
recd.	received
R.F.D.	rural free delivery

Abbreviation	Term
R.R.	railroad
R.S.V.P.	reply, if you please (French: répondez s'il vous plaît)
Sr.	senior
SS	steamship
St.	street

Postal Terms

Each state abbreviation consists of two capital letters.

State Abbreviations

Abbreviation	State	Abbreviation	State
AL	Alabama	MT	Montana
AK	Alaska	NE	Nebraska
AZ	Arizona	NV	Nevada
AR	Arkansas	NH	New Hampshire
CA	California	NJ	New Jersey
CO	Colorado	NM	New Mexico
CT	Connecticut	NY	New York
DE	Delaware	NC	North Carolina
DC	District of Columbia	ND	North Dakota
FL	Florida	OH	Ohio
GA	Georgia	OK	Oklahoma
HI	Hawaii	OR	Oregon
ID	Idaho	PA	Pennsylvania
IL	Illinois	PR	Puerto Rico
IN	Indiana	RI	Rhode Island
IA	Iowa	SC	South Carolina
KS	Kansas	SD	South Dakota
KY	Kentucky	TN	Tennessee
LA	Louisiana	TX	Texas
ME	Maine	UT	Utah
MD	Maryland	VT	Vermont
MA	Massachusetts	VA	Virginia
MI	Michigan	WA	Washington
MN	Minnesota	WV	West Virginia
MS	Mississippi	WI	Wisconsin
MO	Missouri	WY	Wyoming

Personal Titles

Titles	
Abbreviation	**Title**
Asst.	Assistant
Capt.	Captain
Com.	commander
	commissioner
	commission
	committee
D.D.S.	Doctor of Dental Surgery
Dr.	Doctor
Gov.	Governor
Hon.	Honorable
Lt.	Lieutenant
M.D.	Doctor of Medicine
Mr.	Mister
Mrs.	Mistress
Ms.	Miss, Mrs.
Ph.D.	Doctor of Philosophy
Pres.	President
Prof.	Professor
Rev.	Reverend
R.N.	Registered Nurse
Supt.	Superintendent
Sec. or Secy.	Secretary
Treas.	Treasurer

Measurement Terms

Standard Measurement	
Abbreviation	**Term**
in.	inch
ft.	foot
yd.	yard
oz.	ounce
lb.	pound
bu.	bushel
doz.	dozen
hr.	hour
yr.	year

Metric Measurement	
Abbreviation	**Term**
l.	liter
mg.	milligram
kg.	kilogram
cm.	centimeter
mm.	millimeter
km.	kilometer

Exercise 1

In the space to the left, put the correct spelling of the abbreviations of the following words:

_____	1. Secretary
_____	2. Treasurer
_____	3. Collect on Delivery
_____	4. Before noon
_____	5. Junior
_____	6. dozen
_____	7. August
_____	8. Doctor of Medicine
_____	9. Honorable
_____	10. year
_____	11. Saturday
_____	12. Rural Free Delivery
_____	13. Reply if you please
_____	14. Esquire
_____	15. Department
_____	16. pound
_____	17. Governor
_____	18. Dentist
_____	19. Reverend
_____	20. Boulevard

Exercise 2

Write the words for which the following abbreviations are given:

_____	1. Ph.D.
_____	2. Ave.
_____	3. in.
_____	4. etc.
_____	5. no.
_____	6. Bros.
_____	7. P.S.
_____	8. R.R.
_____	9. Sept.
_____	10. F.O.B.
_____	11. Prof.
_____	12. Asst.
_____	13. E.S.T.
_____	14. Gov.
_____	15. Wed.
_____	16. Asst.
_____	17. SS
_____	18. St.
_____	19. recd.
_____	20. dept.
_____	21. M.D.
_____	22. Treas.
_____	23. Sat.
_____	24. Hon.
_____	25. Rev.
_____	26. Sec.
_____	27. D.D.S.
_____	28. Capt.
_____	29. Mar.
_____	30. P.M.

TROUBLESOME WORDS

Chapter 19

HOMONYMS AND HOMOPHONES

arlier in this book we pointed out the necessity of listening carefully. Careless listening can give you a wrong mental picture of a word and thus you take the first step toward misspelling it.

There are many words that are pronounced and spelled alike but differ in meaning. They are called HOMONYMS. *Quail*, meaning a bird, and *quail*, meaning to recoil in dread, are homonyms. So are *pole*, meaning a stake, and *pole*, meaning the end of a magnet.

There are hundreds of other words that are pronounced alike but differ in spelling, derivation, and meaning. They are called HOMOPHONES. *Altar/alter, chord/cord,* and *minor/miner* are homophones. So are *awl/all, bear/bare.*

Homophones are more likely to cause spelling errors than homonyms.

In the following lists, many of the confusing pairs that cause spelling difficulties are defined and illustrated in sentences. Spelling exercises appear at intervals.

Homonyms and Homophones

Key

n. = noun
v. = verb
adj. = adjective
pp. = past participle
adv. = adverb
pro. = pronoun
prep. = preposition

aisle, n.   a narrow passage
   The bridal couple walked down the **aisle**.

isle, n.   an island
   Poets sometimes write about the Golden **Isles**.

already, adv.   by this time
   We had **already** eaten our lunch.

all ready, adj.   all are ready
　　We were **all ready** to leave.

altar, n.   a tablelike structure used for religious purposes in a church or out of doors
　　The bridal couple came toward the **altar**.

alter, v.   to make a change
　　Plastic surgeons can **alter** features.

altogether, adv.   entirely
　　I **altogether** disapprove of such behavior.

all together, adj.   all in one place
　　The prisoners were placed **all together** in one room.

berth, n.   a place to sleep
　　We ordered a **berth** on the train.

birth, n.   act of being born
　　The **birth** of the prince caused much joy.

bloc, n.   a combination of persons with a common purpose
　　The radicals voted as a **bloc** in the legislature.

block, n.   a solid piece of material
　　He put his fountain on a **block** of concrete.

boarder, n.   one who is provided with meals and lodging
　　The **boarder** paid his rent to his landlady.

border, n.   a boundary
　　The **border** between the U.S. and Canada is not fortified.

born, pp.   that which has been given birth
　　The baby was **born** at dawn.

borne, pp.   carried
　　The countess was **borne** in her sedan chair.

brake, n.   an instrument to stop something
　　Because the **brake** was broken, the car rushed downhill.

break, v.   to smash, cause to fall apart
　　Be careful not to **break** these rare glasses.

bridal, adj.   pertaining to a wedding
　　The **bridal** gown was made of taffeta.

bridle, n.   part of a harness
 The horse pulled at his **bridle**.

bridle, v.   to restrain
 Some gossips need to **bridle** their tongues.

canvas, n.   a kind of rough cloth
 The sailor's duffel bag was **canvas**.

canvass, v.   to solicit
 Election workers went out to **canvass** the neighborhood.

capital, n.   a major city of a state or nation; also, something of extreme importance;
   also, stock of wealth
 Albany is the **capital** of New York.
 Kidnapping in some states is a **capital** offense.
 Liberia welcomes foreign **capital**.

capitol, n.   a building
 In Washington the **capitol** is popular with visitors.

chord, n.   a pleasant combination of tones
 The pianist electrified his audience with his opening **chords**.

cord, n.   a rope
 Can you get me some **cord** to tie these books?

cord, n.   a unit to measure fuel wood
 He chopped three **cords** of wood today.

coarse, adj.   vulgar
 Such **coarse** language cannot be permitted.

course, n.   a way to be followed
 In this emergency, only one **course** was indicated.
 John took the academic **course** in high school.

complement, n. or v.   something that completes another
 The fresh **complement** of soldiers saved the day.

compliment, n. or v.   something said in praise
 The president **complimented** the soldier for his bravery.

correspondence, n.   letters exchanged
 The **correspondence** between the two adversaries was lively.

correspondents, n.   those communicating by letter
 He had numerous **correspondents** to whom he wrote often.

Exercise 1

Underline the correct word in parentheses.

1. This story cannot (alter, altar) the situation.
2. Some experts think that cargo will soon be (born, borne) in submarines.
3. If you put your foot on the (break, brake) you will stop the car.
4. Many sincere people oppose (capital, capitol) punishment.
5. The center (aisle, isle) of the theater was very wide.
6. When the search party arrived, the fire had (all ready, already) died out.
7. Many friends and relatives attended the (bridle, bridal) ceremony.
8. The old bridge was (altogether, all together) dangerous.
9. When the attack was sounded, the marines were (all ready, already).
10. Many families have not had to touch their (capitol, capital) for a long time.

council, n.   a deliberative body
> The city **council** was called into special session.

counsel, n.   advice; also an attorney
> My **counsel** in this case is to avoid temperature extremes.
> The defendant's **counsel** made a stirring plea.

councilor, n.   one who is a member of a council
> The newly elected **councilor** was given an ovation.

counselor, n.   an advisor, usually legal
> In America we use the expression **counselor**, whereas in Britain it is solicitor or barrister.

core, n.   a center of fruit
> The **core** of my apple was rotten.

corps, n.   a unit of people
> General Smith commanded the Second Army **Corps**.

descent, n.   a going down
> The flight's **descent** was smooth.

dissent, n.   a disagreement
> Justice Holmes' **dissents** were famous.

desert, v.   to leave behind
> It is a terrible crime to **desert** one's child.

dessert, n.   sweets after a meal
>   We had sliced peaches for **dessert**.

dual, adj.   double
>   Dr. Jekyll and Mr. Hyde were the **dual** personalities of one man.

duel, n.   combat of two men
>   Hamilton was killed in the **duel** with Burr.

feint, v.   to make a pretense of
>   The boxer **feinted** with his left, then struck with his right.

faint, v.   to lose consciousness
>   We nearly **fainted** from hunger.

flair, n.   instinctive attraction to
>   The model had a **flair** for style.

flare, v.   to shine with a sudden light
>   A match **flared** in the darkness.

fowl, n.   a bird of any kind
>   The butcher sold freshly killed **fowl**.

foul, adj.   offensive to the senses
>   The air in the dungeon was **foul**.

gate, n.   a means of entrance or exit
>   The rusty **gate** was ajar.

gait, n.   a manner of walking
>   The old man's **gait** was slow and uncertain.

heir, n.   one who inherits property
>   The eldest son was the **heir** to his father's estate.

air, n.   atmosphere
>   The mountain **air** was chilly.

horde, n.   a crowd or throng
>   A **horde** of barbarians once sacked Rome.

hoard, n. a hidden supply
>   The miser added the coin to his **hoard**.

hostel, n.   an inn
>   The young cyclists stayed overnight at a **hostel**.

hostile, adj.   unfriendly
  The lawyer cross-examined the **hostile** witness.

instance, n.   example
  The lawyer gave **instance** after **instance** of good behavior.

instants, n.   plural, meaning moments
  Pain was stopped for several **instants** before the operation was continued.

its, pro.   The possessive case of it
  The baby played with **its** finger.

it's, abbreviated form of **it is**
  It's too late to go to any restaurant now.

led, v.   the past tense of **lead**
  The colonel **led** his men to safety.

lead, n.   (lĕd) a metal
  Plumbers make use of **lead** frequently.

libel, n.   a defamatory statement
  The politician sued the newspaper for **libel**.

liable, adj.   likely
  The sidewalk is so icy that you're **liable** to fall.

Exercise 2

Underline the correct word in parentheses.

1. England called its Privy (Council, Counsel) into session.

2. It takes a 40° angle to (compliment, complement) an angle of 50° to make a right angle.

3. To get out of the swamp, there was only one (course, coarse) to follow.

4. The (desert, dessert) at the end of the banquet was delicious.

5. (It's, Its) amazing how much you can get in a library.

6. The legislature passed the bill without any (dissent, descent).

7. The teacher (lead, led) his class outside.

8. The witness refused to answer any question without advice from his (counsel, council).

9. Joseph ate his apple down to the (corps, core).

10. The judge said that he had a (dual, duel) responsibility.

miner, n.   one who extracts minerals from the earth
Mark Twain frequently wrote about **miners** in the Old West.

minor, adj., n.   unimportant; below legal age
This injury to the skin was a **minor** one.
Alcoholic beverages may not be sold to **minors**.

peace, n.   a state of quiet; freedom from war
The U.N. tries hard to keep the **peace**.

piece, n.   a portion
A **piece** of pie costs fifty cents here.

pedal, n.   a foot lever
The bicycle was so high that the child's foot could not reach the **pedal**.

peddle, v.   to travel about with wares for sale
He earned a small income by **peddling** vegetables.

plain, adj., n.   *as an adjective,* simple, unadorned
In this small town we live in **plain** houses.
as a noun, a flat area of land
Many pioneers perished while crossing this **plain**.

plane, n.   an airplane; a tool; a flat surface
The **plane** made a forced landing.
To smooth the surface, the carpenter used a **plane**.

principal, adj., n.   *as an adjective,* main, important
These were the **principal** points in the CEO's speech.
as a noun, the head official in a school
A **principal** in a modern high school must be a good administrator.

principle, n.   a statement of a rule in conduct or in science or mathematics
Archimedes discovered the **principle** of buoyancy in liquids.
A candidate for high office must be a man of **principle**.

raise, v.   to help to rise to a standing position
When the old man fell, several helped to **raise** him.

raze, v.   to destroy to the ground
The building was **razed** because it was old and unsafe.

review, n.   a reexamination
The teacher conducted a **review** before the test.

revue, n.   a theatrical production of songs, skits, and dances
The dramatic society wanted to present a **revue**.

shear, v.   to cut or clip
     With sharp scissors, the tailor was able to **shear** the cloth.

sheer, adj.   straight up and down without a break
     The **sheer** precipice was a hundred feet high.

sight, n.   something that is seen
     The skyline of New York is an impressive **sight**.

site, n.   location of a planned building
     The architect studied the **site** carefully.

soar, v.   to fly high
     The hawk **soared** high in the sky.

sore, adj.   painful
     Unaccustomed to exercise, his muscles were **sore**.

stationary, adj.   fixed, attached
     The old-fashioned schoolroom had **stationary** desks and chairs.

stationery, n.   paper used in correspondence
     Maya designs beautiful **stationery** on her computer.

straight, adj.   direct
     The path leading to the house was **straight**.

strait, n.   a waterway
     The captain steered the ship through the **strait**.

tail, n.   the end of a body of an animal
     The cat's **tail** was accidentally caught in the door.

tale, n.   a narrative
     The prisoner told a long and sorrowful **tale**.

taut, adj.   tightly drawn
     The lines that held the sails were **taut**.

taught, v.   instructed
     The pupils were **taught** the elements of algebra.

team, n.   group on one side
     Our hockey **team** was the best in the league.

teem, v.   to become filled to overflowing
     The mountain lake **teemed** with fish.

there, adv.   an adverb of place
He placed the package **there**.

their, pro.   a possessive pronoun
The students brought **their** books.

they're pro. + v.   contraction of they are
"**They're** here," the children shouted.

to, prep.   *preposition with a verb to make an infinitive*
To err is human; **to** forgive, divine.
preposition with noun or pronoun
Please take this book **to** him.
Deliver this package **to** mother.

too, adv.   also, more than enough
We arrived late for the ceremony **too**.
Such bad behavior in class was **too** much for the teacher.

two, numeral, the number 2
He had **two** letters of recommendation.

vain, adj.   conceited
The **vain** teacher thought her students liked her.

vane, n.   weathercock
The farmer glanced at the **vane** to see the wind's direction.

vein, n.   blood vessel
The chef dropped her knife and accidentally punctured a **vein**.

veracious, adj.   truthful
The jury believed that the witness's report was **veracious**.

voracious, adj.   having a huge appetite
Most large animals are **voracious**.

vial, n.   a small vessel for liquids
The druggist gave the customer a **vial** of medicine.

vile, adj.   morally despicable
The judge said the criminal's offense was **vile**.

waist, n.   middle section of the body; a garment
Tonya has a narrow **waist**.
The bridal gown's **waist** was made of lace.

waste, v., n.   to squander; material that is squandered
  To **waste** food is almost a crime when so many starve.
  Many manufacturers dispose of industrial **wastes** through incineration.

week, n.   a period of seven days
  There are four **weeks** in a month.

weak, adj.   lacking strength
  The beggar was **weak** and frail from lack of food.

weight, n.   the amount that an object registers on a scale
  The child's **weight** was below normal.

wait, n.   a period of waiting
  The commuters had a long **wait** for the train.

who's, personal pro.   a contraction of who is
  "**Who's** there?" she asked.

whose, possessive of who
  Whose coat is this?

your, possessive of you
  This is **your** hat.

you're, a contraction of you are
  "**You're** elected," the chairman shouted.

Exercise 3

Underline the correct word in parentheses.

1. An appendectomy can hardly be considered (minor, miner) surgery.

2. He was a great admirer of (peace, piece) by friendly negotiation.

3. Because of motor difficulties the (plane, plain) had to make a forced landing on the (plane, plain).

4. The (principle, principal) causes of World War II are not easy to state.

5. The young girl placed the belt around her (waste, waist).

6. The sailors threw (their, there) caps into the air.

7. This insolence was (to, too, two) much to bear.

8. It is not necessary to use expensive (stationery, stationary) on minor occasions.

9. We could never discover (whose, who's) book it was.

10. "(They're, their) here," exclaimed the teacher.

Other Confusing Pairs of Words

There are many other word pairs that are often confused because they sound almost alike, as *illusion* and *allusion*. Strictly speaking, such pairs are not homonyms or homophones. However, they cause spelling difficulties and for that reason are listed and defined below. So, too, are words that resemble one another so closely in spelling that they are a frequent source of trouble, as *moral* and *morale*, and *dairy* and *diary*.

advice, n.   counsel
>We asked the teacher for **advice**.

advise, v.   to give counsel
>Our parents are ready to **advise** us.

affect, v.   to influence
>The heartwarming story **affected** readers.

effect, v.   to bring about a result
>By his skill and knowledge, the doctor **effected** a cure.

ally, v.   to join with
>England can usually be expected to **ally** herself with the United States.

ally, n.   one who joins with another
>France was our **ally** in World War II.

alley, n.   a narrow thoroughfare
>The cat disappeared down the **alley**.

allusion, n.   a reference to
>The judge made an **allusion** to an old ruling.

illusion, n.   a deception
>Magicians create **illusions**.

angel, n.   a supernatural being
>Disputes about **angels** are found in medieval thought.

angle, n.   corner; point of view
>Advertisers are always looking for a new **angle**.

ascent, n.   act of mounting upward
>The **ascent** of Mount Everest is hazardous.

assent, n.   agreement
>The father gave his **assent** to his daughter's marriage.

beside, prep.   by the side of
The bride stood **beside** her husband.

besides, adv.   in addition to
Besides a bonus, he received a raise.

breath, n.   an exhalation
The **breath** froze in the cold air.

breathe, v.   to take in or let out breath
The doctor asked the patient to **breathe** in deeply.

cloths, n.   bits of cloth
Try using new **cloths** for your sewing project.

clothes, n.   covering for the human body
Beau Brummel's **clothes** were the talk of London.

complacent, adj.   self-satisfied
When he received the prize he had a **complacent** smile.

complaisant, adj.   inclined to please or oblige
He was so **complaisant** that people liked to deal with him.

consul, n.   an official in one country representing another
The Russian **consul** in the United States represents his country's interests.

counsel, n.   an attorney
The **counsel** for the defense entered a plea of guilty.

corporal, adj.   relating to the body
Teachers no longer use **corporal** punishment.

corporeal, adj.   relating to physical rather than immaterial
Ghosts do not have a **corporeal** existence.

credible, adj.   believable
The witness made her story **credible**.

creditable, adj.   praiseworthy
The soldier's action was **creditable**.

device, n.   a contrivance
The inventor showed his new **device** for producing electricity.

devise, v.   to make a contrivance
The inventor **devised** a new means of producing electricity.

elicit, v.   to bring out
> By patiently questioning, the investigator **elicited** the truth.

illicit, adj.   unlawful
> The moonshiners operated an **illicit** distillery.

emigrant, n.   one who leaves a country for another
> America welcomes **emigrants** of good character from many lands.

immigrant, n.   one who comes to another country after leaving his own
> Forty million **immigrants** brought many resources to America.

formally, adv.   done in a formal or regular manner
> The bridegroom was dressed **formally**.

formerly, adv.   earlier
> **Formerly**, young employees had to wait a long time for promotion.

ingenious, adj.   clever, tricky
> The device for operating the ship was **ingenious**.

ingenuous, adj.   open, frank, innocent
> The **ingenuous** countenance of the witness won over the jury.

later, adv.   comparative degree of late
> It's **later** than you think.

latter, adv.   of two things, the one mentioned second
> Of the two desserts, ice cream or sherbet, I chose the **latter**.

Exercise 4

Underline the correct word in parentheses.

1. He likes to wear brightly colored (clothes, cloths).

2. This development in art comes in a (later, latter) period in history.

3. Refugees in Hong Kong rushed to the American (consul, counsel) for safety.

4. Before signing this contract, you should get legal (advice, advise).

5. He placed the boxes (beside, besides) the wall.

6. During the early part of this century, many (immigrants, emigrants) from England went to Australia.

7. All those who attended the banquet were (formerly, formally) attired.

8. The young child had an (ingenious, ingenuous) countenance.

9. The United States has been an (ally, alley) of England.

10. The orator's speech was full of literary (illusions, allusions).

loose, adj.   free, unattached
The screw was **loose**.

lose, v.   to miss from one's possession
I would not like to **lose** any more money at the races.

moral, adj., n.   pertaining to the good and proper
We live by **moral** law as well as the court's law.

morale, n.   state of well-being of a person or group
The **morale** of our team was high.

personal, adj.   pertaining to a person or individual
Our quarrel in the office was not due to a business but to a **personal** argument.

personnel, n.   the body of persons employed in some service
Because he had a deep understanding of people, he was appointed **personnel** manager.

quiet, adj.   free from noise
In hospital areas, **quiet** must be preserved.

quite, adj.   entirely, completely
The patient was **quite** conscious throughout the operation.

respectfully, adv.   showing deference
The servant spoke **respectfully** to his employer.

respectively, adv.   in the order given
The manager spoke to the bookkeeper, salesperson, and typist **respectively**.

than, a conjunction
Gold is heavier **than** silver.

then, adv.   an adverb of time
We shall await you **then**.

Exercise 5

Underline the correct word in parentheses.

1. The new bonus structure raised the (moral, morale) of our sales team.

2. Such demands are (quiet, quite) impossible to meet.

3. Problems of (personal, personnel) always arise where there are many employees.

4. The (loose, lose) stone caused the scout to slip.

5. Love is more powerful (then, than) hate.

6. I was (formally, formerly) dressed for the occasion.

7. Where did you (lose, loose) the money?

8. Every fable has a (moral, morale).

9. The tree-shaded street was (quite, quiet) deserted.

10. Rather (than, then) take a risk, he put his money in a bank.

Chapter 20

WORD BUILDING

When learning an instrument, the monotony of scale exercises can be tiresome. Without these scales, however, no virtuoso would ever develop. Spelling, too, has its scales and exercises. They may seem just as boring as the musical exercises, but they are similarly valuable.

Study the following word families. Sometimes you will forget the spelling of one of these words. If you can remember its brother or sister, you will not have to consult the dictionary. A little time spent with these now will mean much time saved later.

Word Families

Words and Variations

Word		Related Words	
abolish	abolish*ed*	abolish*ing*	aboli*tion*
accomplish	accomplish*ed*	accomplish*ing*	accomplish*ment*
account	account*ed*	account*ing*	account*ant*
acknowledge	acknowledg*ed*	acknowledg*ing*	acknowledg*ment*
advise	advis*ed*	advis*ing*	advis*er* (or advis*or*)
allude	allud*ed*	allud*ing*	allu*sion*
almost	al*ways*	al*ready*	al*together*
appear	appear*ed*	appear*ing*	appear*ance*
arrange	arrang*ed*	arrang*ing*	arrange*ment*
arrive	arriv*ed*	arriv*ing*	arriv*al*
assist	assist*ed*	assist*ing*	assist*ance*
begin	beg*an*	begin*ning*	begin*ner*
believe	believ*ed*	believ*ing*	believ*er*
busy	bus*ied*	busy*ing*	bus*iness*
change	chang*ed*	chang*ing*	change*able*
choose	chos*e*	choos*ing*	chos*en*
complete	complet*ed*	complete*ly*	comple*tion*
confide	confid*ent*	confid*ence*	confid*entially*
conscience	conscien*tious*	*sub*conscious	*un*conscious

156

Word		**Related Words**	
consider	considered	considerable	consideration
continue	continued	continuation	continually
control	controlling	controller	controllable
critic	critical	criticize	criticism
deceive	deceit	deception	deceiver
decide	decided	decision	deciding
define	definite	definition	definitely
describe	descriptive	describing	description
desire	desirous	desiring	desirable
embarrass	embarrassed	embarrassing	embarrassment
endure	endured	endurable	endurance
equip	equipped	equipping	equipment
every	everybody	everywhere	everyone
exceed	exceeded	exceeding	exceedingly
excel	excelled	excellent	excellence
excite	exciting	excitement	excitable
exist	existed	existing	existence
experience	experienced	experiencing	experiment
extend	extended	extensive	extension
impress	impressed	impressive	impression
intend	intended	intensive	intension
interfere	interfered	interfering	interference
interrupt	interrupted	interrupting	interruption
obey	obedient	obedience	obeisance
occasion	occasioned	occasional	occasionally
peace	peaceful	peaceable	peaceably
permit	permitted	permissible	permission
persist	persisted	persistent	persistence
pity	pitied	pitying	pitiable
possess	possessed	possessive	possession
practice	practical	practiced	practicable
prefer	preferred	preferring	preference
recognize	recognized	recognition	recognizable
separate	separation	inseparable	separately
sincere	sincerity	insincere	sincerely
surprise	surprised	surprisingly	surprising

Exercise

Indicate by the letter C *if the following words are correctly spelled. Correct all errors in the space to the left.*

_____	1. arranger	_____	21. necessarly
_____	2. choosers	_____	22. transferred
_____	3. difinative	_____	23. cancel
_____	4. preferential	_____	24. changable
_____	5. inseparable	_____	25. judgement
_____	6. hypocritical	_____	26. accomadate
_____	7. undefineable	_____	27. gaurantee
_____	8. undesireable	_____	28. reciepts
_____	9. pityless	_____	29. secretary
_____	10. unaccountable	_____	30. business
_____	11. unchangeable	_____	31. choosen
_____	12. incompletely	_____	32. posessed
_____	13. disarrange	_____	33. reconized
_____	14. confiding	_____	34. sincereity
_____	15. confidential	_____	35. existance
_____	16. indecisive	_____	36. embarassed
_____	17. non-existant	_____	37. excellent
_____	18. preferrable	_____	38. exciteable
_____	19. experiential	_____	39. prefered
_____	20. unendureable	_____	40. ocassion

Chapter 21

MOST FREQUENTLY MISSPELLED WORDS

The One Hundred Pests

One Hundred Commonly Misspelled Words

ache	dear	instead	raise	too
again	doctor		read	trouble
always	does	just	ready	truly
among	done			Tuesday
answer	don't	knew	said	two
any		know	says	
	early		seems	used
been	easy	laid	separate	
beginning	enough	loose	shoes	very
believe	every	lose	since	
blue			some	wear
break	February	making	straight	Wednesday
built	forty	many	sugar	week
business	friend	meant	sure	where
busy		minute		whether
buy	grammar	much	tear	which
	guess		their	whole
can't		none	there	women
choose	half		they	won't
color	having	often	though	would
coming	hear	once	through	write
cough	heard		tired	writing
could	here	piece	tonight	wrote
country	hoarse			
	hour			

Business Terms

The 500 words that follow are those that are most commonly misspelled in business correspondence. If you want to improve your business effectiveness, study these words closely until you can spell every one correctly.

The list was compiled by the National Office Management Association after a comprehensive study of 10,652 letters collected from business concerns and government agencies located throughout the country.

The words are not strange or unusual. They appear frequently in business letters. Many of them appear on other pages of this book. Mastery of this list will protect you against the spelling mistakes committed by many business men and women.

Commonly Misspelled Business Terms

A

accept
accommodate
accountant
accumulate
acknowledgment
acquainted
acquire
acquisition
acquitted
actually
additionally
address
adjustable
administration
advances
advertisement
advisability
advise
affects
affidavit
affirmative
agency
aggravate
allotment
allowance
all right
alphabetic
aluminum
analysis
analyze
anniversary
announcement

anthracite
anticipating
anxiety
apology
apparatus
appearance
applicant
appraisal
appropriation
approval
argument
arrears
arrival
articles
assessable
assignment
assistance
associate
assured
attached
attorney
attempt
attendance
attractive
auditor
available
aviation

B

baggage
balance
bankruptcy
banquet

barrel
barter
becoming
beneficiary
benefited
biased
bituminous
bookkeeping
borrower
brief
broadcast
brokerage
budget
bulletin
bureau
business

C

calculator
calendar
campaign
canceled
candidate
capacity
capitalization
carbon
carrier
cartage
carton
certificate
chattel
circular
clearance

coincidence
collapsible
collateral
collision
column
combination
combustible
commerce
commission
committee
commodity
community
companies
comparative
compel
compensation
competent
complaint
complimentary
concession
condemn
conference
confirmation
congestion
conscientious
consequence
considerable
consignee
consolidated
construction
consumer
container
contemplating
contemporary
contingent
convenience
conveyance
cooperate
corporation
corroborate
corrugated
counterfeit
coupon
courteous
credentials
creditor
curiosity
currency
customer
cylinder

D
decision
defendant
deferred
deficit
definite
defray
demonstration
depreciation
description
desperate
destination
deteriorate
determination
develop
dictionary
director
disappear
disappoint
disastrous
disbursements
discernible
discontinued
discrepancy
discuss
dispatch
dissatisfaction
dissolution
distinction
distinguish
distributor
dividend
document
doubt
duplicate
durable

E
earliest
earnest
easier
economic
eighth
elevator
eligible
embarrass
emergency
enormous
enterprise
envelope

equally
equipped
especially
estimate
essentially
eventually
evidence
exaggerate
examination
exasperate
excellent
except
exchange
executive
exhibition
existence
expedite
explanation
extension

F
facilitate
February
financier
foreclosure
forehead
forfeit
formally
formerly
forty
franchise
fundamental
furniture
futile

G
generally
genuine
government
grammar

H
handkerchief
hastily
hazard
height
hoping
hosiery
humorous

I
illegible
immediately
impracticable
inasmuch
inconsistent
inconvenience
incorporated
incredible
increment
indelible
indemnity
indispensable
inducement
industrial
inevitable
inferred
inflation
infringement
initiate
inquiry
insolvency
inspection
instance
institution
instructor
insurance
integrity
intelligence
interpretation
inventory
investigate
invoice
involved
itemized
itinerary
its

J
jobber
journal

K
keenness
knowledge

L
laboratory
ladies
latter

leased
ledger
legitimate
leisure
liabilities
library
license
likable (*or* likeable)
liquidation
literature
lucrative
luscious
luxury

M
machinery
maintenance
management
manila
manufacturer
margin
material
maturity
mechanical
medicine
memorandum
mercantile
merchandise
merge
middleman
mimeograph
miniature
miscellaneous
misrepresent
misspelled
moistener
monopoly
mortgage
movie
mucilage
municipal

N
necessary
ninth
notary
noticeable
notwithstanding
nowadays

O
obliging
observation
obsolete
obstacle
occasionally
occurred
omission
oneself
opportunity
optimism
option
ordinance
organization
outrageous
overdraw
overhead
oxygen

P
pamphlet
parallel
parenthesis
parliament
particularly
pavilion
peaceable
peculiarities
pecuniary
percent
perforation
performance
permanent
permissible
perpendicular
perseverance
personal
personnel
persuade
perusal
petition
petroleum
photostat
physical
physician
plaintiff
plausible
policy
practically
precedence

precise
preface
preference
prescription
presence
presidency
prestige
primitive
principal
principle
privilege
procedure
process
professional
prominence
promissory
pronunciation
prospectus
psychology

Q

qualification
quantity
questionnaire
quotation

R

readjustment
really
reasonable
rebate
receipt
recognize
recommend
reconstruction
reference
regardless
register
reimburse
reinforcement
relations
remedied
remittance
representative
requisition
resign
respectfully
respectively
responsible

restaurant
ridiculous
rural

S

sacrifice
salary
salutation
sanitary
satisfactory
schedule
scissors
secretarial
security
seize
separate
several
significance
similar
simultaneous
sincerely
sociable
society
solemn
solvent
sometimes
source
southern
souvenir
specialize
specify
spectacular
speculate
statement
stationary
stationery
statistics
straightened
strenuous
strictly
sublet
subsidize
substantial
substitute
subtle
successful
suggestion
summary
superfluous

superintendent
surplus
surprise
susceptible
syllable
syndicate
systematize

T

tangible
tariff
tendency
testimonials
tickler
together
transferred
transparent
treasurer
triplicate
Tuesday
turnover
typewriter
typical
typographical

U

unanimous
university
unmistakable
utilities
utilize

V

verification
vicinity
visible
volume
voucher

W

waive
warrant
Wednesday
whatever
wholesale
wholly
women

Chapter 22

COMPUTER TERMS

Computers have their own "languages," and new technology is emerging at rapid speeds. Developers, as well as end-users, continue to expand our computer-related vocabulary, and an increasing number of technical terms have entered our common usage. As vocabulary evolves with technology, new words enter; others become obsolete. Daisy wheel typewriters and records stored on microfiche have given way to modern computer input and disc storage.

Computer Acronyms

We have already addressed acronyms, which are common in computer terms. We may be familiar with many of these acronyms, or even use them daily, without knowing the words they stand for. This is exactly why acronyms are especially useful with computer and technological terms. We do not need to know that DSL is a "digital subscriber line" to get connected to the Internet. Other terms, such as instant messenger (IM), are simply shortened for convenience. Some examples follow:

FTP   File Transfer Protocol
DVD   Digital Versatile Disc (formerly Digital Video Disc)
DSL   Digital Subscriber Line
ASCII   American Standard Code for Information Interchange
MAC   Macintosh Computer
HTML   Hypertext Markup Language
URL   Uniform Resource Locator
PDA   Personal Digital Assistant
CD   Compact Disc
IM   Instant Messaging
WYSIWYG (pronounced wisiwig): What You See Is What You Get

Online Shorthand

Language shortcuts are being created and refined all the time through e-mail and instant messaging. While these are commonly used online, too often people assume everyone knows them. These language shortcuts are evolving slang and are not necessary to learn, but they are nevertheless a growing subset of slang language. If you do sometimes use them, you should be careful to avoid their use in business and with those who may not know the newest online slang.

A few examples follow:

LOL   laughing out loud
BRB   be right back
CU Later   See you later.

One Word or Two?

Web site, website
Web page, webpage
e-mail
Webcam
Webcast
Webmaster

Web site and web page are most often defined as being either one or two words. These are examples of words that have changed over time. *Webmaster* is one word. The words webcam and webcast are also each one word. While some people write *email* as one word, e-mail is still the more commonly listed choice.

Computer-Age Generated Words

Many words are developed by those in the technical field long before they come to common usage. The term "bit" was coined by the statistician John Tukey in 1949. He was looking for a shortened form of "Binary Digit." According to Tukey, he had considered "bigit" or "binit," but abbreviation evolved over lunch to become the bite-sized word "bit."

If you recall homonyms and homophones, *bit* (small bit of computer information) would be a homonym for *bit* as in small bite). From the word *bit*, new words have been created to refer to the technology. (*Byte* and *nybble* are homophones for *bite* and *nibble*.) Of course, mega is a standard prefix for something large (and one million *bytes* would be a *megabyte*).

Bit: a shortened term for Binary Digit
Byte: a sequence of bits
Nybble : a small byte
Megabyte: one million bytes

Common Computer Words

Most of the following phrases are in common use. Study only the words that concern you. Because the goal here is spelling and not in-depth computer knowledge, we provide the most basic terms and ask that you focus on words that might be part of your vocabulary.

Bandwidth
Baud Rate
Bluetooth
Blog
Blogger
Broadband
Compatibility
Computerized
Connection
Cursor
Database
Debug
Decode
Digital
Disk (also Disc)
Download
Downloadable
Electronic
Ethernet
Expandable
Glitch
Graphics
Hard drive
Hardware
Hyperlink
Hypertext
Inkjet
Interactive
Interface
Internet

Laptop
Laser
Macintosh
Matrix
Megabyte
Megapixel
Microprocessor
Modem
Monitor
Multimedia
Multitasking
Network
Newsgroup
Output
Peripheral
Pixel
Pixilated
Processor
Programmer
Retrieval
Server
Spam (unsolicited bulk e-mails)
Spell-check, Spell-checker
Software
Suite
Surfer
Telecommuting
Template
Terminal
Upload

Exercise

From each group select the correctly spelled word and place the letter before it in the space at the left.

_____ 1. *a.* didgital   *b.* digitle   *c.* digital   *d.* digatal

_____ 2. *a.* retrieval   *b.* retreival   *c.* retrievle   *d.* retreeval

_____ 3. *a.* acronim   *b.* acranym   *c.* acarnym   *d.* acronym

_____ 4. *a.* retrieval   *b.* retreival   *c.* retreivle   *d.* retrievel

_____ 5. *a.* access   *b.* acess   *c.* acces   *d.* acesse

_____ 6. *a.* compatability   *b.* compatibility   *c.* commpatability   *d.* compattability

_____ 7. *a.* periferal   *b.* peripheral   *c.* peripherle   *d.* peripharal

_____ 8. *a.* inter-face   *b.* inter face   *c.* interface   *d.* intraface

_____ 9. *a.* interractive   *b.* inneractive   *c.* interactive   *d.* enteractive

_____ 10. *a.* nybble   *b.* nibbel   *c.* nible   *d.* nibel

_____ 11. *a.* exapndable   *b.* expandible   *c.* expandabel   *d.* expandibel

_____ 12. *a.* softwere   *b.* software   *c.* softwear   *d.* software

_____ 13. *a.* programer   *b.* programmar   *c.* programmer   *d.* programar

_____ 14. *a.* processer   *b.* proceser   *c.* processor   *d.* procesor

_____ 15. *a.* tele-comuting   *b.* telecomuting   *c.* telecommuting   *d.* tele-commuting

_____ 16. *a.* Mackintosh   *b.* Macintosh   *c.* McIntosh   *d.* Macentosh

_____ 17. *a.* mailmerge   *b.* mail-merge   *c.* male merge   *d.* mail merge

Chapter 23

MEDICAL TERMS

T he expansion of medical research and services and growing interest in nutrition and alternative treatments has made many medical and health terms commonplace. In this chapter, some of the most common abbreviations and terms related to disease, treatment, and health are briefly defined. In some cases, areas of common spelling difficulties are italicized.

Medical Terms

Medical Abbreviations	
Abbreviation	**Term/Definition**
AIDS	Acquired Immunodeficiency Syndrome
CATSCAN (CT Scan)	Computerized Axial Tomography Scan
	A radiological diagnostic technique in which a series of x-rays are computerized to show a scan (picture) of the body
Chol.	Cholesterol
DOA	Dead on arrival
ECG or EKG	Electrocardiogram
EEG	Electroencephalogram
HIV	Human Immunodeficiency Virus
HMO	Health Maintenance Organization
IUD	Intrauterine device
IV	Intravenously
LPN	Licensed Practical Nurse
MRI	Magnetic Resonance Imaging
PCP	Pencyclidine
PCP	Primary Care Physician
PT	Physical Therapist
RN	Registered Nurse
RPH	Registered Pharmacist

Medical Terms

Term	Definition
A	
abrasion	Superficial tearing of the skin
abscess	Localized buildup of pus
acne	Inflammation of oil glands
acupressure	Treating acupuncture points without needles
acupuncture	Puncture of skin by needle to relieve pain
allergy	Hypersensitive reaction to certain substances
allopathic	Traditional Western medicine
alternative	Different from the traditional course of action
alternative health practitioners	There is a vast array of alternative professionals, including: acupuncturist, herbalist, holistic practitioner, homeopath, hypnotherapist, naturopath
ambulance	Vehicle equipped for transportation of ill or wounded to hospital
ambulatory	Able to walk about
amnesia	Loss of memory
analgesic	Substance providing relief from pain
anesthesia	Loss of sensation or feeling
aneurysm	Abnormal widening of vein or artery
antibiotic	Antibacterial substance
antioxidant	Substance that protects body cells from the damaging effects of oxidation
aorta	Artery carrying blood from the heart
arteriosclerosis	Hardening of the arteries
ayurvedic	Ancient Hindu science of health and medicine
B	
benign	Harmless
biofeedback	Monitoring function, such as heart rate or blood pressure; using that feedback for health
biopsy	Examination of small sample of tissue
bony	Relating to bone
C	
calcify	To make stony by deposit of calcium salts
calorie	Measure of energy (heat) in nutrition
capillary	Thin-walled blood vessel
carcinogenic	Cancer-causing substance
carcinoma	Type of cancer
caries	Tooth or bone decay
cartilage	Type of connective tissue
cholesterol	Fatty substance found in blood
coagulant	That which produces clotting

Term	Definition
coli*c*ky	Pertaining to paroxysmal pain
comp*lem*entary	One treatment that works alongside another
convale*s*cent	Recovering from illness
cuti*cle*	Dead skin at base of fingernail or toenail
cyst	Abnormal fluid or gas-fllled cavity

D

diaphra*g*m	Large muscle between chest and abdomen
dia*rrh*ea	Loose or watery stools
diet*ary*	Related to diet

E

ec*z*ema	Skin rash characterized by itching
emb*ryo*	Fetus in first 8 weeks after conception
en*e*ma	Fluid injected through rectum to lower bowel
epi*lepsy*	Disease of nervous system characterized by convulsive seizures

G

gla*u*coma	Disease of the eye caused by increased pressure within the eye
gyn*e*cologist	Specialist in women's diseases

H

hemo*rrh*age	Abnormal bleeding caused by rupture or tear of a blood vessel
he*p*atitis	Inflammation of the liver
herbal	Made from herbs
holistic	Taking into account the whole body and mind
home*o*pathy	An alternative, natural therapy
home*o*sta*s*is	Internal balance
hygi*e*ne	Science of health preservation
hy*p*nosis	Trancelike state
hypo*ch*ondriac	One who is excessively anxious about supposed ill health
hysterectomy	Surgical removal of uterus

I

*iatro*genic	Illness caused by medical intervention
indigest*i*ble	Not easily digested
infe*ctious*	Capable of being easily diffused or spread
in*o*culate	To inject a substance into the skin or tissues
intra*venous*	Into or within a vein

J

jug*u*lar	Relating to a large vein in the neck

Term	Definition
K	
ki*n*etic	Pertaining to motion
L	
larynx	Voicebox
leu*k*emia	Malignant disease of the white blood cells
ly*mph*	Transparent yellowish fluid containing cellular elements
M	
mas*tect*omy	Surgical removal of breast
mens*trua*tion	Monthly discharge of blood and tissue from the uterus
metabolism	Processing of a substance within the body
mi*graine*	Periodic severe headaches
mu*cus*	Viscous fluid produced by certain glands in the body
N	
nau*sea*	Desire to vomit
neural*gia*	Sharp pain produced by nerve stimulation
neu*ritis*	Inflammation of nerve
nutrient	Source of nourishment in food
nutrition	Nourishment in food
O	
o*phthal*mologist	Specialist in diseases of the eye
op*i*ate	Opium-like narcotic
osteo*porosis*	Disease in which bones become abnormally thin and brittle
P	
paraplegic	One who is paralyzed from the waist down
pharmaceutical	Drug treatment
*phle*bitis	Inflammation of a vein
ph*legm*	Mucus produced by the lungs
*ph*obia	Abnormal fear
*pn*eumonia	Inflammation of lung tissue
preventive, preventative	Measures or substances taken to prevent disease
pro*phyl*axis	Prevention of disease
psy*chia*try	Branch of medical science dealing with mental health
R	
rab*ies*	Hydrophobia
re*gimen*	A systematic course of treatment
remedy	Treatment to remove pain or treat disease

Term	Definition
S	
sac*ch*arin	Sugar substitute
sa*li*va	Secretion of salivary glands
sick*le* cell anemia	Hereditary form of malformation of red blood cells
s*yr*inge	Device for injecting liquids
T	
therapeutic	Method or substance used or practiced to cure or relieve symptoms of disease
tho*rac*ic	Pertaining to the chest
tonsi*ll*ectomy	Surgical removal of tonsils
tourni*quet*	Device for stopping bleeding
tox*ic*ity	State of being poisonous
U	
ulcerous	Pertaining to loss of tissue
ure*mia*	Accumulation of toxic substances caused by certain kidney diseases
urin*ary*	Pertaining to urine
V	
va*cc*ination	Inoculation to stimulate immunity to disease
va*cc*ine	Altered microorganisms that stimulate immunity
ver*tebr*a	Roundish bone in spinal column
vi*a*ble	Capable of survival
vir*al*	Pertaining to a virus
W	
*wh*ooping cough	Children's disease characterized by violent, paroxysmal cough

Exercise

From each group select the correctly spelled word and place the letter before it in the space at the left.

_____ 1. *a.* diarhea   *b.* diahea   *c.* dierrhea   *d.* diarrhea

_____ 2. *a.* innoculate   *b.* inocculate   *c.* inocullate   *d.* inoculate

_____ 3. *a.* anisthesia   *b.* anesthesia   *c.* anessthesia   *d.* annesthesia

_____ 4. *a.* calory   *b.* calorie   *c.* calore   *d.* callorie

_____ 5. *a.* hemorrhage   *b.* hemorhage   *c.* hemmorhage   *d.* hemorrage

_____ 6. *a.* rabes   *b.* rabies   *c.* rabeis   *d.* rabbies

_____ 7. *a.* tonsilectomy   *b.* tonsilecimy   *c.* tonsillectimy
   d. tonsillectomy

_____ 8. *a.* abscess   *b.* absess   *c.* abses   *d.* absces

_____ 9. *a.* capillary   *b.* capilary   *c.* cappilary   *d.* capillery

_____ 10. *a.* colicy   *b.* colicky   *c.* collicky   *d.* collichy

_____ 11. *a.* larnyx   *b.* larinx   *c.* larynx   *d.* larinks

_____ 12. *a.* arterosclerosis   *b.* artiriosclerosis   *c.* arteriosclerosis
   d. arterioslerosis

_____ 13. *a.* indigestable   *b.* indigestible   *c.* indegestible   *d.* indegistible

_____ 14. *a.* diafram   *b.* diaphram   *c.* diraphragm   *d.* diaphragm

_____ 15. *a.* sacharin   *b.* saccarin   *c.* saccharin   *d.* saccharrin

MEASURING YOUR PROGRESS

Chapter 24

ACHIEVEMENT TESTS

Achievement Test 1

Score ____

Chapters 1–4

Indicate by writing T or F to the left whether the following statements about English spelling are true or false. (Answers begin on page 206.)

____ 1. English spelling is difficult because it is not phonetic.

____ 2. At one time in the history of English the endings in *through, thorough, plough* were pronounced.

____ 3. The letter *p* in *ptomaine, pterodactyl,* and *ptarmigan* is pronounced in Modem English.

____ 4. New words are invented by scholars.

____ 5. Such words as *birth—berth, air—heir* are called antonyms.

____ 6. Many poor spellers do not hear words correctly.

____ 7. *Media* is the plural of *medium.*

____ 8. There are no rules in spelling that are worth learning.

____ 9. The most reliable source of information for spelling is in the dictionary.

____ 10. Acronyms are useless you know what they stand for.

____ 11. The sounds of English vowels have not changed through the centuries.

____ 12. When a word must be divided at the end of a line, the hyphen should always come after a vowel.

____ 13. Good examples of homonyms are *fright—freight; sleigh—sleight; tray—trait.*

____ 14. Syllables determine where to divide a word at the end of a line.

____ 15. Dictionaries vary their spelling in accordance with the areas of the country.

_____ 16. To become a better speller you must read everything very slowly.

_____ 17. Many good spellers can tell that a word is misspelled by its appearance (or configuration).

_____ 18. All good spellers inherit this ability.

_____ 19. Sometimes you can discover your own spelling devices to help you.

_____ 20. A good way to recall the spelling of *stationary* is to think of *station*.

_____ 21. Computer spell-checkers should be used, but not relied on.

_____ 22. The section on correct spelling in a good dictionary is entitled *Orthography*.

_____ 23. The words *center* and *centre* are examples of *homonyms*.

_____ 24. The words *theater* and *theatre* are examples of *antonyms*.

_____ 25. There is little value in compiling your own list of misspelled words.

_____ 26. In learning how to spell the word *superintendent* it is advisable to pronounce each syllable distinctly.

_____ 27. The letter *b* in *debt* and *doubt* is not pronounced in Modern English.

_____ 28. In learning how to spell a new word it is helpful to write it several times correctly.

_____ 29. The trouble with English spelling is that there are no rules.

_____ 30. Computer spellcheckers can recognize homonyms.

_____ 31. There is no difference in pronunciation between *trough* and *through*.

_____ 32. *Tough* and *rough* are homonyms.

_____ 33. *Through* and *true* have the same final sound.

_____ 34. The final sound in *knight* and *tight* is pronounced $\bar{\imath}t$.

_____ 35. Many English words derived from ancient Greek have silent letters as in *psyllium* and *pseudonym*.

_____ 36. *Moat* and *mote* are examples of homophones.

_____ 37. Words like *privilege* and *government* are frequently misspelled by omitting a letter.

_____ 38. Skimming will make you a better speller.

_____ 39. Careful observation will help you to become a better speller.

_____ 40. It is possible to train your eyes to recognize misspelled words by their appearance.

_____ 41. You can remember the correct spelling of the word *principle* by associating it with ru*le*.

_____ 42. To fix the correct spelling of *separate*, think of *sepa* plus *rate*.

_____ 43. By recalling the spelling of *where,* you can spell *there* correctly.

_____ 44. The words *hair* and *heir* are pronounced the same.

_____ 45. Though "practice makes perfect," many professional writers are sometimes plagued by misspellings.

_____ 46. The ultimate aim of learning to spell is to avoid constantly consulting the dictionary.

_____ 47. *Bark* (of a dog) and *bark* (of a tree) are homonyms.

_____ 48. Some people might learn to spell *their* correctly by associating it with *heir.*

_____ 49. The words *rough* and *ruff* are true homophones.

_____ 50. The words *bough* and *rough* are identical in sound.

_____ 51. Words in English derived from ancient Greek are pronounced exactly as they were in Greece.

_____ 52. English words are spelled exactly as they sound.

_____ 53. The best way to study spelling is to memorize all the words you need.

_____ 54. *Beet* and *beat* are true antonyms.

_____ 55. Because there are the letters *gh* in *night* and *sight,* they should be pronounced.

_____ 56. A person writing *litature* instead *of literature* has probably not heard the word correctly.

_____ 57. Because the *b* in *debt* is silent, the *b* in *debit* should also be silent.

Achievement Test 2

Score ____

Chapter 6

Underscore the word spelled correctly in the parentheses.

1. The agent signed the (receipt, reciept) for the rent.
2. It was a great (relief, releif) to go home at last.
3. Mary gave a loud (shriek, shreik) and ran.
4. The marines refused to (yeild, yield) their positions.
5. He was a perfect (fiend, feind) in his behavior.
6. His (acheivement, achievement) was remarkable.
7. Once we have lost our reputation, it is difficult to (retreive, retrieve) it.
8. It takes a good (freind, friend) to make one.
9. The slain leader was carried to the (beir, bier).
10. He was (chief, cheif) of the whole island.
11. We were (receiveing, receiving) visitors all day.
12. It is difficult to (deceive, decieve) people all the time.
13. Strenuous efforts are required to (achieve, acheive) a scholarship.
14. Astronomers can now (percieve, perceive) stars that are quite small.
15. Our (neighbors, nieghbors) to the south were angry at our behavior.
16. Careless training may lead to such (mischievious, mischievous) behavior in childhood.
17. The last (frontier, fronteir) is now in space.
18. Although the (ceiling, cieling) was low, he bought the house.

Achievement Test 3

Score _____

Chapters 7–8

In the following sentences the italic words are sometimes correctly spelled, sometimes misspelled. In the spaces to the left, place C if the spelling is correct. Write the correct spelling for all misspelled words.

_____ 1. Our lighter team was at a *dissadvantage.*

_____ 2. Park all *disabled* cars here.

_____ 3. Any *mistatement of* fact will be punished.

_____ 4. The old man could not *reccollect* anything that had happened.

_____ 5. The doctor *recommended* an aspirin.

_____ 6. This procedure was an *inovation.*

_____ 7. Let's *rennovate* your apartment.

_____ 8. Actions such as these are *unatural.*

_____ 9. This apartment had been *unoccupied* for a month.

_____ 10. Congress tried to *overide* the veto.

_____ 11. For misbehaving the sergeant was *dimoted.*

_____ 12. Sugar will easily *disolve* in water.

_____ 13. As a lawyer, Clarence Darrow was *preminent.*

_____ 14. One should always have some *anteseptic* handy for unexpected cuts.

_____ 15. His behavior under fire was *degrading.*

Select the correct choice of the two in parentheses:

_____ 16. By crossing the state border they ran into difficulty with the (intra-state, interstate) commission.

_____ 17. Do not (interrupt, interupt) an older person.

_____ 18. At the end of his letter he added a (poscript, postscript).

_____ 19. Many (suburban, subburban) communities are growing.

_____ 20. When the lights blew out we called the (superrintendent, superintendent).

_____ 21. Quite a few hotels here welcome (transient, transent) guests.

_____ 22. The judge ruled that this evidence was not (admissible, admissable).

_____ 23. Such arguments are (laughible, laughable).

_____ 24. It was (unthinkable, unthinkible) that he could lose the game.

_____ 25. For many years he was the most (eligible, eligable) bachelor in town.

_____ 26. England has always been (invincible, invincable) in a crisis.

_____ 27. (Legible, legable) handwriting is a delight for the reader.

_____ 28. Make yourself (comfortable, comfortible).

_____ 29. Many foods are (perishible, perishable) unless properly refrigerated.

_____ 30. Evidence of the disease was not yet (demonstrable, demonstrible).

In thefollowing sentences the italic words are sometimes correctly spelled, sometimes misspelled. In the spaces to the left, place C if the spelling is correct. Write the correct spelling for all misspelled words.

_____ 31. The debater made a _mistake_.

_____ 32. I don't _reccolect_ what happened.

_____ 33. _Professional_ ball players receive high salaries.

_____ 34. His sleight of hand was _unoticeable_.

_____ 35. That player is vastly _overated_.

_____ 36. Sometimes it is better if one doesn't know his _anticedents_.

_____ 37. Iodine is still a popular _antiseptic_.

_____ 38. "Don't _interrupt_ me," she exclaimed.

_____ 39. Lincoln was not very happy when several states _seseded_ from the Union.

_____ 40. The doctor diagnosed the disease as a _preforated_ ulcer.

_____ 41. We must look at things in their proper _prespective_.

_____ 42. Let us _proceed_ with the business.

_____ 43. A _percocious_ child can learn to play chess well.

_____ 44. This water is hardly _drinkible_.

_____ 45. Some mountains are _inaccessable_.

_____ 46. The _combustible_ materials were placed in fire-proof bins.

_____ 47. Sasha is _eligable_ for a promotion.

_____ 48. There are some schools for _incorrigible_ youngsters.

_____ 49. "Such language is _detestable_," said the teacher.

_____ 50. He was an old _acquaintence_.

_____ 51. The face of the *defendent* became pale as the verdict was read.

_____ 52. Sometimes little things turn out to have great *significence*.

_____ 53. The mechanics overhauled the airplane motor in a *hanger*.

_____ 54. The *collar* of his shirt was frayed.

_____ 55. The online business advertised in a local newspaper for an experienced *operator*.

_____ 56. Most department store customers prefer to use an *escalator* when they wish to ascend to another floor.

_____ 57. The *radiater* of the car started to boil over in the hot weather.

_____ 58. Readers who disagree with a newspaper's editorial position should write a letter to the *editor*.

_____ 59. One of the duties of a *superviser* is to train employees.

_____ 60. The *purchaser* is protected by a money-back guarantee.

Achievement Test 4

Score _____

Chapters 9–11

Underline the word spelled correctly in the parentheses.

1. All the (buffaloes, buffalos) were killed in this territory.

2. The president sent through his two (vetoes, vetos) to Congress.

3. All the (tomatoes, tomatos) had ripened.

4. We examined six (pianos, pianoes) before we selected one.

5. Cowboys learn how to do many stunts with their (lassoes, lassos).

6. Among the (calfs, calves) were some spotted ones.

7. All the (leafs, leaves) fell down.

8. Many old (beliefs, believes) must be disregarded.

9. Napoleon crushed many (armies, armys) in his time.

10. This farm still made use of (oxes, oxen).

11. Hailstones fell down several (chimneys, chimnies).

12. In this machine, there were many levers and (pulleys, pullies).

13. The players took several practice (volleys, vollies) before the game.

14. The (salaries, salarys) of his employees were frequently raised.

15. The Greeks composed the greatest dramatic (tragedeys, tragedies).

16. The judge pronounced his sentence (angrily, angryly).

17. It is advisable occasionally to be (mercyful, merciful).

18. The bandleader played several (medleys, medlies).

19. A public (conveyance, conveyence) was supplied to the general.

20. Good posture always (dignifies, dignifys) the person.

21. My father reminded us that we would be (dineing, dining) at six.

22. It was the loveliest sight (imagineable, imaginable).

23. (Judging, Judgeing) from the attendance, the play was a hit.

24. Her success in college was (surpriseing, surprising).

25. Thoreau was (writeing, writing) a great deal while staying at Walden Pond.

26. The wounded dog was (whining, whineing) all night long.

27. All those (desireous, desirous) of success must work hard.

28. The (density, denseity) of the atmosphere is being studied.

29. The lecturer spoke clearly and (sincerely, sincerly).

30. Certain traits sometimes run in (families, familys).

31. We both like (dining, dineing) out frequently.

32. This trail is not for the birds but for (donkeys, donkies).

33. Much (encouragment, encouragement) was required before the baby would walk.

34. Space travel is no longer (unimagineable, unimaginable).

35. This line had the fewest (casualties, casualtys).

36. We noticed that all the ants seemed (busily, busyly) engaged in building a new home.

37. Jascha Heifetz was (accompanied, accompanyed) by an accomplished pianist.

38. When Erin ran late, her mother was (worried, worryed).

39. Reynolds frequently (portrayed, portraied) the English nobility of the 18th century.

40. His insights frequently seemed touched with (sublimity, sublimeity).

41. Such actions at this time seemed (inadvisable, inadviseable).

42. By careless handling, she seemed to be (singing, singeing) her hair.

43. In expository writing (vagueness, vaguness) is not tolerated.

44. We learn more by listening than (argueing, arguing).

45. Considering everything, it was a (lovely, lovly) wedding.

46. Such (couragous, courageous) action was rarely seen.

47. Dinner at this late hour was (tastless, tasteless).

48. Working long on the (contriveance, contrivance) made him a bit fanatic about it.

49. (Anniversaries, anniversarys) should be celebrated properly.

50. A pair of (oxes, oxen) is a rarity on a farm today.

51. The printer corrected the (proofs, prooves) of the new book.

52. My friend liked all his (brothers-in-law, brother-in-laws).

53. The castle was (beseiged, besieged) for ten days.

54. Mary's (likeness, likness) was obvious in the portrait.

55. After many lessons he learned to dance (gracfully, gracefully).

56. This celebration was (truly, truely) magnificent..

57. The comic made his living by (mimicing, mimicking) others.

58. Some ranches have as many as 10,000 (sheeps, sheep).

59. All the (alumni, alumnuses) of Fairweather College returned on Founder's Day.

60. Before the American public high schools, there were many (academies, academys).

61. It is very difficult to discover a single (curricula, curriculum) that can satisfy all people.

62. Ehrlich stained many (bacilli, bacilluses) in his career.

Achievement Test 5

Score ____

Chapters 12–15

Underline the word spelled correctly in the parentheses.

1. He wanted to buy a (low-priced, low priced) car.
2. This author was (best known, best-known) for his characterization.
3. She was the (thirty-first, thirty first) queen to be chosen.
4. This hypothesis was a little (far-fetched, far fetched).
5. The ewe was (newly-born, newly born).
6. It was the (highest priced, highest-priced) dress in the store.
7. It was a successful (pre-election, preelection) bet.
8. To get this loan, you must have a (coowner, co-owner).
9. They cheered the (exGovernor, ex-Governor).
10. (Vice-Admiral, Vice Admiral) Rooney was promoted.
11. The doctors (conferred, confered) for two hours.
12. We had no (preference, preferrence) in this matter.
13. After many trials, he was (transferred, transfered) to another prison.
14. The girl quickly tore the (wrapings, wrappings) from the package.
15. Many new bills are thrown into the legislative (hoper, hopper).
16. Mulvaney was the best (hitter, hiter) in the league.
17. Turkey, plus all the (trimings, trimmings) was served yesterday.
18. The Dupont Company had a (controlling, controling) interest in the firm.
19. Our graduates (excelled, exceled) over all others at Yale.
20. The prisoner never (regretted, regreted) his misdeeds.
21. The house had a (low-ceiling, low ceiling).
22. (One half, one-half) of the audience left at the end of the first act.
23. All night the tune kept (dining, dinning) in her head.
24. The duchess wore a (low necked, low-necked) gown at the party.
25. The employer demanded several (references, referrences).
26. We are all (hoping, hopping) for permanent peace.
27. Such freak accidents seldom (occured, occurred).

28. The guilty culprit wore a (hangdog, hang-dog) look.

29. America, at that time, had (unparalleled, unparaleled) prosperity.

30. It was the (twenty ninth, twenty-ninth) celebration of the ending of the war.

31. The (pre-dawn, predawn) flight was a success.

32. My cousin was the (high scorer, high-scorer) in the game.

33. My mother always (prefered, preferred) to save rather than spend everything.

34. The (ex policeman, ex-policeman) was found guilty of perjury.

35. The judge and the attorneys (conferred, confered) for three hours.

36. The athlete (chined, chinned) thirty times on the horizontal bar.

37. The (Pro-Temperance, Pro Temperance) Party won few votes.

38. The poor little bird (flaped, flapped) her wings feebly and then remained still.

39. The (red-cheeked, red cheeked) youngster seemed shy.

40. Some of the guests at the home were over (eighty eight, eighty-eight) years old.

41. Television has been accused of (sub-liminal, subliminal) advertising.

42. The soldier seemed (regretful, regrettful) of his actions.

43. This rouge seems to be the (lowest priced, lowest-priced) in the entire shop.

44. Adolescents are frequently (smitten, smiten) with puppy love.

45. His appearance at the trial was (well-timed, well timed).

46. He was (hiting, hitting) well in that game.

47. The boy kept (running, runing) despite the cries of his mother.

48. Many guards (patroled, patrolled) the prison on the day of the execution.

49. Passengers should be (already, all ready) at 10 P.M.

50. A (run-on, run on) sentence contains more than enough for one complete sentence.

51. We greeted the (senator-elect, senator elect).

52. Rescue boats went back and forth in the (mid Atlantic, mid-Atlantic) area.

53. Her praises were (extoled, extolled) for her amazing performance.

54. Eisenhower's (aide-de-camp, aidedecamp) was later decorated for his contributions.

55. After a little encouragement the guitarist (regaled, regalled) the picnickers with many songs.

56. Vera won first prize, but Stuart was (runner up, runner-up).

57. Mills for (spining, spinning) cotton have long supported the town.

58. A few parts of the story were (omitted, omited) by the defendant.

59. Children frequently (scraped, scrapped) their elbows at the corner.

60. Periods of prosperity have (recurred, recured) with regularity in this state.

61. Their marriage was (annuled, annulled) by mutual consent.

62. The nurse (scrubed, scrubbed) the baby's face until it was gleaming.

63. The crowd (paniced, panicked) after the accident.

64. South America (rebeled, rebelled) against the mother country.

65. Judge Harmon (deferred, defered) sentence until Friday.

Achievement Test 6

Score ____

Chapters 16–17

Underline the word spelled correctly in the parentheses.

1. Many college freshmen (don't, dont) know how to study.

2. This salesman specialized in (mens', men's) shoes.

3. It was (his, his') greatest victory.

4. (Who'se, Who's) there?

5. Dot all the (i's, is) and cross the (ts, t's).

6. "(Youve, You've) won your battle," said the trainer.

7. The shopper specialized in (lady's, ladies') shoes.

8. This was my (brother-in-law's, brother's-in-law's) house.

9. It was the (children's, childrens') ward to which we hurried.

10. This (couldn't, could'nt) have happened to a nicer person.

11. It was once more a conflict between (East, east) and (West, west).

12. The young artists admired the works of (grandma Moses, Grandma Moses).

13. He specialized in the (hindu, Hindu) languages.

14. My uncle belonged to the (elks, Elks).

15. The hit of the week was ("For my Beloved," "For My Beloved").

16. A popular novel is (*A Tale of two Cities*, *A Tale of Two Cities*).

17. They traveled (North, north) for twenty miles.

18. On (Columbus Day, Columbus day), many stores are closed.

19. One of the greatest musical hits is (*My fair Lady*, *My Fair Lady*).

20. He was recently elected to the (house of representatives, House of Representatives).

21. The (boy's, boys') hat was on crooked.

22. ("They're, theyr'e) here," the Captain shouted.

23. The conference passed a resolution against all high (doctor's, doctors') fees.

24. The numerous (teacher's, teachers') contributions were finally rewarded.

25. Count all the (7's, 7s) in this line!

26. We enjoyed (Penn and Teller's, Penn's and Teller's) humor.

27. The sale took place in the (women's, womens') hosiery department.

28. "I never want to touch a penny of (their's, theirs)," she shouted.

29. All the (ts, t's) in this word are left uncrossed.

30. He admired his (lawyer's, lawyers') integrity.

31. The Ivy League colleges are situated mostly in the (east, East).

32. After studying (french, French) literature, he began to appreciate Molière.

33. Higher (Mathematics, mathematics) fascinated Einstein at an early age.

34. (Governor, governor) Rockefeller attempted to balance the state budget.

35. Several (captains, Captains) won their promotions in this campaign.

36. The fiftieth state in the Union is (hawaii, Hawaii).

37. Mrs. Morrow wrote *North to the (Orient, orient)*.

38. There are one hundred members of the U.S. (Senate, senate).

39. On (arbor day, Arbor Day) an interesting ceremony took place.

40. Of all the novels read in high school (*Of Mice and Men, Of mice and Men*) seems to be most popular.

41. Great praise has come recently to (admiral, Admiral) Rickover.

42. A famous personality years ago was (uncle Floyd, Uncle Floyd).

43. This store had good bargains in (boys', boy's) shoes.

44. There are many fine students from the (south, South) in the colleges today.

Achievement Test 7

Score _____

Chapter 19

Select the correctly spelled word from the two in parentheses.

1. Teachers frequently give good (advice, advise) to their students.

2. England and the U.S. have long been (alleys, allies).

3. There is nothing as beautiful as a happy bride walking down the (isle, aisle).

4. My parents said that they were (already, all ready).

5. Frequently one can have an optical (illusion, allusion) after eyestrain.

6. The judge refused to (altar, alter) his decision.

7. (Altogether, All together) there were twelve cents in his pocket.

8. The casket was (borne, born) on the shoulders of the pallbearers.

9. There were several (angles, angels) in this picture by Raphael.

10. We ordered an upper (berth, birth) on the train to Chicago.

11. My father was almost (besides, beside) himself with grief.

12. (Break, Brake) the news gently.

13. The baby's (breath, breathe) came in short spasms.

14. The cowboy grasped the horse by the (bridal, bridle).

15. Ward leaders tried to (canvass, canvas) the district.

16. In Washington we visited the beautiful (Capital, Capitol).

17. The angry principal began to (censure, censor) the students for misbehavior.

18. He could chop several (cords, chords) of wood each day.

19. The salesmen showed me several suits of (clothes, cloths).

20. In college, my brother took the premedical (course, coarse).

21. Don't forget to (complement, compliment) him on his good grades.

22. The German (consul, council) telegraphed to his ambassador in Washington.

23. The cook removed the (corps, core) of the apple.

24. Scientists are often (incredulous, incredible) of new theories.

25. Many authors like to keep (diaries, dairies) when they are young.

26. Justice Oliver Wendell Holmes frequently would (dissent, descent) from his colleagues.

27. After the meal, we had a delicious (dessert, dissert).

28. Da Vinci invented a (devise, device) to hurl cannonballs.

29. Hamilton and Burr fought a (duel, dual) in New Jersey.

30. This spot was (formally, formerly) a cemetery.

31. For several (instance, instants) he remained quiet.

32. Through an (ingenious, ingenuous) trick, the prisoner escaped.

33. Actors like to receive (complements, compliments) for their performances.

34. The (boarder, border) never paid his rent on time.

35. The Dutch (consul, counsel) in New York helped us to obtain a visa.

36. The new president was (formally, formerly) inaugurated.

37. Good food in the barracks will help produce good (moral, morale).

38. A graduate of Harvard was the (personal, personnel) manager of the store.

39. Avogadro's (principal, principle) led to many other important discoveries.

40. This company advertises a fine quality of (stationery, stationary).

41. Standing in line for a token is often a (waste, waist) of valuable time.

42. New inventions (supersede, supercede) old customs.

43. It was an (excedingly, exceedingly) hot day.

44. Nothing (succeeds, suceeds) like success.

45. The parade (proceded, proceeded) without further interruption.

46. The magician created an optical (allusion, illusion) for us.

47. The West will not (accede, acede) to these demands.

48. After the waters (receeded, receded), we returned to our home.

49. The (corps, corpse) was taken to the morgue.

50. The baby liked (it's, its) finger.

51. "It's (later, latter) than you think," the preacher said.

52. Four black-robed monks (led, lead) the way yesterday.

53. After the battle, the general called his (council, counsel) together.

54. Several (lose, loose) shingles fell down.

55. Liquor is not permitted to (minors, miners).

56. A world at (peace, piece) is a world of security.

57. It was as (plane, plain) as the nose on his face.

58. After the hike, the girls were (quite, quiet) starved.

Chapter 25

ANSWER KEY

For Chapters 4–23

Chapter 4

Exercise *Page 17.*
1. su - pər - ′sil - ē - əs
2. ′hyü - mər
3. ′li - kwəd
4. ′in - tri - kə - sē
5. in - ′tim - ə - dāt
6. nä - ′ēv
7. ′güb - ə(r) - nə - ′tor - ē - əl
8. ′far - si - kəl
9. ′der - əd - ən(t)s
10. ri - ′vyü

Chapter 5

Exercise 3 *Page 21.*
1. New York City's *Museum of Modern Art*
2. *National Association of Securities Dealers Automated Quotations* (Over-the-counter stock exchange)
3. *North Atlantic Treaty Organization*
4. *American Society for the Prevention of Cruelty to Animals*
5. *North American Free Trade Agreement*
6. *National Aeronautics and Space Administration*
7. *high definition television*
8. *World Health Organization*

Chapter 6

Exercise 1 *Page 28.*
1. bo·nan·za
2. re·pent
3. fa·tigue
4. pun·ish·ment
5. or·deal
6. rum·mage
7. miss·ing
8. gas·o·line
9. ex·ca·vate
10. ty·ran·ni·cal

Exercise 2 *Page 31.*
1. grammar
2. separate
3. usually
4. C
5. calendar
6. C
7. C
8. until
9. C
10. C
11. C
12. accommodate
13. professor
14. government

15. C

16. across

17. illegible

18. equivalent

19. C

20. C

Exercise 3 *Page 32.*

1. hundred
2. modern
3. perspiration
4. western
5. relevant
6. cavalry
7. children
8. jewelry
9. larynx
10. pattern

Chapter 7

Exercise 1 *Page 34.*
No answers are needed for this exercise since the correct spellings are given.

Exercise 2 *Page 34.*

1. aggrieve
2. brief
3. friend
4. grieve
5. frontier
6. mischief
7. shield
8. shriek
9. wield
10. species
11. relieve
12. leisure
13. handkerchief
14. receipt
15. seize

16. perceive

17. grief

18. niece

19. conceive

Exercise 3 *Page 36.*
The answers to this exercise are incorporated in the sentences.

Exercise 4 *Page 38.*
The answers to this exercise are found in the passage.

Chapter 8

Exercise 1 *Page 42.*

1. dissolve
2. dissimilar
3. misspell
4. disappear
5. mistake

Exercise 2 *Page 42.*
circumscribe—draw limits
transcribe—write a copy
subscribe—sign one's name
describe—represent by words
proscribe—denounce and condemn
pre scribe—dictate directions

Exercise 3 *Pages 42–43.*

1. misstep
2. misunderstood
3. dissimilar
4. restart
5. substandard
6. supersonic
7. pre-Columbian
8. anti-imperialist
9. circumnavigates
10. postoperative

Exercise 4 *Page 44.*

1. persecuted
2. proceed
3. precocious
4. perspective
5. prescribe
6. perforated
7. produce
8. persist
9. perpetual
10. propose

Chapter 9

Exercise 1 *Page 47.*

The answers are contained in the exercise.

Exercise 2 *Page 48.*

The answers are contained in the exercise.

Exercise 3 *Pages 48–49.*

1. accidentally
2. critically
3. elementally
4. equally
5. exceptionally
6. finally
7. generally
8. incidentally
9. intentionally
10. ironically
11. logically
12. mathematically
13. practically
14. professionally
15. really
16. typically
17. usually
18. verbally
19. globally

Exercise 4 *Page 51.*

1. advantageous
2. courageous
3. perilous
4. mountainous
5. beauteous
6. desirous
7. mischievous
8. adventurous
9. bounteous
10. dangerous
11. grievous
12. humorous
13. outrageous
14. libelous
15. poisonous

Exercise 5 *Pages 54–55.*

1. b
2. a
3. a
4. a
5. b
6. a
7. a
8. b
9. b
10. b
11. a
12. b
13. b
14. b
15. b
16. a
17. a
18. a
19. b
20. b
21. a

22. a
23. b
24. b
25. b

Exercise 6 *Page 57.*
1. beggar
2. receiver
3. conductor
4. passenger
5. governor
6. scanner
7. operator
8. dollar
9. supervisor
10. operator

Exercise 7 *Page 59.*
1. compliment
2. remembrance
3. consistent
4. superintendent
5. dependent
6. existence
7. descendant
8. acquaintance
9. grievance
10. permanent
11. magnificent
12. brilliance
13. complimentary or complementary, depending upon meaning
14. convenience
15. abundance
16. guidance
17. conscience
18. coincidence
19. apparent
20. consequential

Exercise 8 *Page 60.*
1. b
2. a
3. b
4. b
5. b
6. a
7. b
8. a
9. b
10. a

Exercise 9 *Page 62.*
1. agonize
2. chastise
3. exercise
4. surprise
5. visualize
6. supervise
7. modernize
8. enterprise
9. fertilize
10. generalize

Chapter 10

Exercise 1 *Pages 66–67.*
1. reproofs
2. reprieves
3. sieves
4. halos or haloes
5. gulfs
6. chiefs
7. albinos
8. shelves
9. puffs
10. muffs
11. sloughs
12. bassos or bassi (Italian)
13. mambos
14. surfs

15. troughs
16. stilettos or stilettoes
17. sheaves
18. radios
19. calves
20. loaves

Exercise 2 *Page 67.*

1. holidays
2. alleys
3. attorneys
4. buoys
5. chimneys
6. donkeys
7. journeys
8. keys
9. pulleys
10. turkeys

Exercise 3 *Page 72.*

1. t's
2. deer
3. anniversaries
4. wives
5. kerchiefs
6. 4's
7. courts-martial
8. lieutenant colonels
9. bays
10. trays
11. flurries
12. sulkies
13. surreys
14. inequities
15. satellites
16. functionaries
17. avocados
18. dynamos

Exercise 4 *Page 72.*

1. groceries
2. things
3. tomatoes
4. potatoes
5. avocados
6. quarts
7. pieces
8. chocolates
9. purchases
10. sopranos or soprani (Italian)
11. altos or alti (Italian)
12. alleys
13. keys
14. days

Chapter 11

Exercise 1 *Page 74.*

1. tourneys
2. allayed
3. volleyed
4. alleys
5. surveyed
6. portraying
7. journeyed
8. relayed
9. delays
10. parlayed

Exercise 2 *Page 76.*

1. C
2. C
3. C
4. attorneys
5. C
6. C
7. C
8. C
9. C
10. icily

Exercise 3 *Page 77.*

1. prettiness
2. pettiness
3. steadying
4. readied
5. bullies
6. airiness
7. pitied
8. tallying
9. buyer
10. dutiful
11. readiness
12. carried
13. hurrying
14. copier
15. sloppiness
16. livelihood

Chapter 12

Exercise 1 *Page 78.*

1. pleasantry
2. artistry
3. portraiture
4. clockwise
5. rocketry
6. jewelry
7. nationality
8. personality
9. dialectical
10. practicality

Exercise 2 *Page 82.*

1. revering
2. lovely
3. purchasable
4. extremely
5. pleasurable
6. largely
7. nudged
8. stated
9. feted
10. fined
11. diving
12. shoved
13. devising
14. deceived
15. relieving
16. procrastinating
17. imagined
18. besieged
19. receiving

Exercise 3 *Page 83.*

1.	benefit	benefiting	benefited
2.	commit	committing	committed
3.	lure	luring	lured
4.	refer	referring	referred
5.	pine	pining	pined
6.	elevate	elevating	elevated
7.	propel	propelling	propelled
8.	fit	fitting	fitted
9.	recur	recurring	recurred
10.	remit	remitting	remitted
11.	open	opening	opened
12.	club	clubbing	clubbed
13.	plunge	plunging	plunged
14.	singe	singeing	singed
15.	pursue	pursuing	pursued
16.	scare	scaring	scared
17.	throb	throbbing	throbbed
18.	trot	trotting	trotted
19.	use	using	used
20.	whip	whipping	whipped

Exercise 4 *Page 88.*

1. agreement
2. amusement
3. careful
4. canoeing
5. coming
6. disagreeable
7. engagement
8. excitement
9. immensity
10. likely
11. safety
12. senseless
13. shining
14. enlargement
15. enticing
16. perceived
17. escaping
18. discharged
19. relieving
20. contrivance

Exercise 5 *Page 88.*
The answers to this exercise are contained in the sentences among the words italicized.

Exercise 6 *Page 89.*

1. scarcely
2. vengeance
3. truly
4. tasty
5. noticeable
6. changeable
7. perspiring
8. retiring
9. awful
10. wisdom
11. assurance
12. insurance
13. outrageous
14. serviceable
15. courageous
16. gorgeous
17. pronounceable

Chapter 13

Exercise 1 *Page 93.*

1. cramping
2. drumming
3. grinning
4. hitting
5. looking
6. nodding
7. paining
8. resting
9. rigging
10. scrubbing

Exercise 2 *Pages 94–95.*

1. deferred
2. reference
3. shopping
4. disapproval
5. nineteen
6. hitting
7. singeing
8. famous
9. controlling
10. repellent
11. desiring
12. tireless
13. truly
14. swimmer
15. trimmer
16. occurrence
17. movable
18. committed
19. equipage
20. excelling

Exercise 3 *Page 95.*

1. adapt	adapting	adapted
2. cramp	cramping	cramped
3. design	designing	designed
4. conceal	concealing	concealed
5. congeal	congealing	congealed
6. blot	blotting	blotted
7. stop	stopping	stopped
8. crush	crushing	crushed
9. excel	excelling	excelled
10. defer	deferring	deferred
11. envelop	enveloping	enveloped
12. extol	extolling	extolled
13. flutter	fluttering	fluttered
14. happen	happening	happened
15. hum	humming	hummed
16. level	leveling	leveled
17. quarrel	quarreling	quarreled
18. rub	rubbing	rubbed
19. signal	signaling	signaled
20. retreat	retreating	retreated

Exercise 4 *Page 96.*

1. witty
2. spinner
3. blotter
4. designer
5. quizzical
6. shutter
7. slipper
8. profiteer
9. meeting
10. dryer
11. inhabitable
12. toiler
13. putter
14. development
15. deferment
16. rubber
17. developer
18. goddess
19. druggist
20. trapper

Exercise 5 *Page 97.*

1. tearfully
2. carefully
3. openness
4. dutifully
5. bountifully
6. commonness
7. mimicked
8. picnicking
9. mimicking
10. panicky

Chapter 14

Exercise 1 *Page 99.*

1. sheep
2. ship
3. cheap
4. chips
5. leave
6. live
7. heat
8. hit
9. sleep
10. slip

Exercise 2 *Page 100.*

1. bet
2. bit
3. lead
4. lid
5. sit
6. set
7. well
8. will
9. fill
10. fell

Exercise 3 *Page 101.*

1. mate
2. met
3. pain
4. pen
5. braids
6. bread
7. break
8. breakfast
9. gate
10. get

Exercise 4 *Page 102.*

1. high
2. hay
3. bay
4. by
5. buy
6. pay
7. pie
8. dye
9. day
10. die

Exercise 5 *Page 103.*

1. bran
2. brain
3. tap
4. tape
5. platter
6. plate
7. bats
8. bait
9. data
10. date

Exercise 6 *Page 104.*

1. Battle
2. bottle
3. gnats
4. knots
5. nuts

6. flop
7. flap
8. cop
9. cap
10. cup

Review Exercise A *Page 105.*

1. beat
2. bet
3. but
4. win
5. whine
6. main
7. men
8. man
9. seem, same
10. been

Exercise 7 *Page 105.*

1. book
2. back
3. hook
4. hocked
5. brook
6. blocks

Exercise 8 *Page 107.*

1. fair
2. for
3. fur
4. store
5. stare
6. torn
7. turn
8. were
9. ore
10. or

Exercise 9 *Pages 107–108.*

1. far
2. four
3. barn

4. born

5. scar

6. score

7. parch

8. porch

9. ardor

10. order

Exercise 10 *Page 109.*

1. coal

2. cool

3. pole

4. pool

5. room

6. roam

7. rule

8. role

9. tools

10. toll

Exercise 11 *Page 110.*

1. allowed

2. aloud

3. alloy

4. oil

5. owl

6. noise

7. now

8. void

9. vowed

10. nouns, avoid

Review Exercise B *Page 110.*

1. carves

2. curves

3. coat

4. cot

5. caught

6. goose

7. goes

8. not

9. note

10. afternoon, none

Exercise 12 *Page 111.*

1. Necessity

2. emotional

3. independence

4. perspires

5. liberal

Exercise 13 *Page 112.*

1. knife, scissors

2. calm, talk

3. psychiatrist, listen

4. heir, reign

5. condemned

Chapter 15

Exercise 1 *Page 118.*

1. C

2. X

3. X

4. C

5. C

6. C

7. C

8. C

9. C

10. C

11. X

12. X

13. X

14. C

15. X

16. X

17. X

18. C

19. C

20. C

Exercise 2 *Page 124.*

1. sister-in-law
2. man-of-war
3. aide-de-camp
4. run-on
5. downstairs
6. antiwar
7. C
8. C
9. C
10. C
11. runner-up
12. drive-in
13. C
14. C
15. trade-in
16. C
17. C
18. built-in
19. C
20. C

Chapter 16

Exercise *Page 128.*

1. The young girl's hat
2. The members' votes
3. The ladies' styles
4. The cats' paws
5. The sailors' decorations
6. The professor's hat
7. The woman's shoe
8. The soprano's voice
9. The dog's tail
10. don't
11. haven't
12. couldn't
13. You're
14. can't
15. It's

16. Let's
17. wouldn't

Chapter 17

Exercise *Page 132.*

1. Hotel Westover
2. Buick
3. Decoration Day
4. North Side High School
5. *The Lion King*
6. Irish
7. English, Bible
8. Uncle
9. Fifth Avenue
10. Washington coffee
11. Britain
12. Bard College, New York
13. *The Taming of the Shrew,* Shakespeare
14. English, French
15. Aunt Emily, West

Chapter 18

Exercise 1 *Page 137.*

1. Sec. or Secy.
2. Treas.
3. C.O.D.
4. A.M.
5. Jr.
6. doz.
7. Aug.
8. M.D.
9. Hon.
10. yr.
11. Sat.
12. R.F.D.
13. R.S.V.P.
14. Esq.
15. Dept.
16. lb.

17. Gov.
18. D.D.S.
19. Rev.
20. Blvd.

Exercise 2 *Page 138.*

1. Doctor of Philosophy
2. Avenue
3. inch
4. et cetera (and so forth)
5. number
6. Brothers
7. Postscript
8. Railroad
9. September
10. Freight on Board
11. Professor
12. Assistant
13. Eastern Standard Time
14. Governor
15. Wednesday
16. assistant
17. Steamship
18. Street
19. received
20. department
21. Doctor of Medicine
22. Treasurer
23. Saturday
24. Honorable
25. Reverend
26. Secretary
27. Doctor of Dental Surgery
28. Captain
29. March
30. post meridiem (after noon)

Chapter 19

Exercise 1 *Page 144.*

1. alter
2. borne

3. brake
4. capital
5. aisle
6. already
7. bridal
8. altogether
9. all ready
10. capital

Exercise 2 *Page 146.*

1. Council
2. complement
3. course
4. dessert
5. It's
6. dissent
7. led
8. counsel
9. core
10. dual

Exercise 3 *Page 150.*

1. minor
2. peace
3. plane—plain
4. principal
5. waist
6. their
7. too
8. stationery
9. whose
10. They're

Exercise 4 *Page 153.*

1. clothes
2. later
3. consul
4. advice
5. beside
6. emigrants
7. formally
8. ingenuous

9. ally

10. allusions

Exercise 5 *Page 155.*

1. morale
2. quite
3. personnel
4. loose
5. than
6. formally
7. lose
8. moral
9. quite
10. than

Chapter 20

Exercise *Page 158.*

1. C
2. C
3. definitive
4. C
5. C
6. C
7. undefinable
8. undesirable
9. pitiless
10. C
11. C
12. C
13. C
14. C
15. C
16. C
17. non-existent
18. preferable
19. C
20. unendurable
21. necessarily
22. C
23. C

24. changeable
25. judgment or judgement
26. accommodate
27. guarantee
28. receipts
29. C
30. C
31. chosen
32. possessed
33. recognized
34. sincerity
35. existence
36. embarrassed
37. C
38. excitable
39. preferred
40. occasion

Chapter 22

Exercise *Page 167.*

1. c
2. a
3. d
4. a
5. a
6. b
7. b
8. c
9. c
10. a
11. a
12. d
13. c
14. c
15. c
16. b
17. d

Chapter 23

Exercise *Page 173.*

1. d
2. d
3. b
4. b
5. a
6. b
7. d
8. a
9. a
10. b
11. c
12. c
13. b
14. d
15. c

For Achievement Tests 1–7

ACHIEVEMENT TEST 1

Chapters 1–4 *Pages 177–179.*

1. T
2. T
3. F
4. F
5. F
6. T
7. T
8. F
9. T
10. F
11. F
12. F
13. F
14. T
15. F
16. F
17. T
18. F
19. T
20. T
21. T
22. T
23. F
24. F
25. F
26. T
27. T
28. T
29. F
30. F
31. F
32. F
33. T
34. T
35. T
36. T
37. T
38. F
39. T
40. T
41. T
42. F
43. T
44. F
45. T
46. T
47. T
48. T
49. T
50. F
51. F
52. F
53. F
54. F
55. F
56. T
57. F

ACHIEVEMENT TEST 2

Chapter 6 *Page 180.*

1. receipt
2. relief
3. shriek
4. yield
5. fiend
6. achievement
7. retrieve
8. friend
9. bier
10. chief
11. receiving
12. deceive
13. achieve
14. perceive
15. neighbors
16. mischievous
17. frontier
18. ceiling

ACHIEVEMENT TEST 3

Chapters 7–8 *Pages 181–183.*

1. disadvantage
2. C
3. misstatement
4. recollect
5. C
6. innovation
7. renovate
8. unnatural
9. C
10. override
11. demoted
12. dissolve
13. pre-eminent
14. antiseptic
15. C
16. interstate
17. interrupt
18. postscript
19. suburban
20. superintendent
21. transient
22. admissible
23. laughable
24. unthinkable
25. eligible
26. invincible
27. legible
28. comfortable
29. perishable
30. demonstrable
31. C
32. recollect
33. C
34. unnoticeable
35. overrated
36. antecedents
37. C
38. C
39. seceded
40. perforated
41. perspective
42. C
43. precocious
44. drinkable
45. inaccessible
46. C
47. eligible
48. C
49. C
50. acquaintance
51. defendant
52. significance
53. hangar
54. C
55. C
56. C
57. radiator
58. C
59. supervisor
60. C

ACHIEVEMENT TEST 4

Chapters 9–11 *Pages 184–185.*

1. buffaloes, buffalos, buffalo
2. vetoes
3. tomatoes
4. pianos
5. lassos, lassoes
6. calves
7. leaves
8. beliefs
9. armies
10. oxen
11. chimneys
12. pulleys
13. volleys
14. salaries
15. tragedies
16. angrily
17. merciful
18. medleys
19. conveyance
20. dignifies
21. dining
22. imaginable
23. judging
24. surprising
25. writing
26. whining
27. desirous
28. density
29. sincerely
30. families
31. dining
32. donkeys
33. encouragement
34. unimaginable
35. casualties
36. busily
37. accompanied
38. worried
39. portrayed
40. sublimity
41. inadvisable
42. singeing
43. vagueness
44. arguing
45. lovely
46. courageous
47. tasteless
48. contrivance
49. anniversaries
50. oxen
51. proofs
52. brothers-in-law
53. besieged
54. likeness
55. gracefully
56. truly
57. mimicking
58. sheep
59. alumni
60. academies
61. curriculum
62. bacilli

ACHIEVEMENT TEST 5

Chapters 12–15 *Pages 186–188.*

1. low-priced
2. best-known
3. thirty-first
4. far-fetched
5. newly born
6. highest priced
7. preelection
8. co-owner
9. ex-Governor
10. Vice-Admiral
11. conferred
12. preference
13. transferred
14. wrappings
15. hopper

16. hitter
17. trimmings
18. controlling
19. excelled
20. regretted
21. low ceiling
22. one half
23. dinning
24. low-necked
25. references
26. hoping
27. occurred
28. hangdog
29. unparalleled
30. twenty-ninth
31. predawn
32. high scorer
33. preferred
34. ex-policeman
35. conferred
36. chinned
37. Pro-Temperance
38. flapped
39. red-cheeked
40. eighty-eight
41. subliminal
42. regretful
43. lowest priced
44. smitten
45. well timed
46. hitting
47. running
48. patrolled
49. all ready
50. run-on
51. senator-elect
52. mid-Atlantic
53. extolled
54. aide-de-camp
55. regaled
56. runner-up
57. spinning
58. omitted
59. scraped
60. recurred
61. annulled
62. scrubbed
63. panicked
64. rebelled
65. deferred

ACHIEVEMENT TEST 6

Chapters 16–17 *Pages 189–190.*

1. don't
2. men's
3. his
4. who's
5. i's, t's
6. you've
7. ladies'
8. brother-in-law's
9. children's
10. couldn't
11. East, West
12. Grandma Moses
13. Hindu
14. Elks
15. "For My Beloved"
16. *A Tale of Two Cities*
17. north
18. Columbus Day
19. *My Fair Lady*
20. House of Representatives
21. boy's
22. They're
23. doctors'
24. teachers'
25. 7's
26. Penn and Teller's
27. women's
28. theirs
29. t's

30. lawyer's
31. East
32. French
33. mathematics
34. Governor
35. captains
36. Hawaii
37. Orient
38. Senate
39. Arbor Day
40. *Of Mice and Men*
41. Admiral
42. Uncle Floyd
43. boys'
44. south

ACHIEVEMENT TEST 7

Chapter 19 *Pages 191–192.*

1. advice
2. allies
3. aisle
4. all ready
5. illusion
6. alter
7. altogether
8. borne
9. angels
10. berth
11. beside
12. break
13. breath
14. bridle
15. canvass
16. Capitol
17. censure
18. cords
19. clothes
20. course

21. compliment
22. consul
23. core
24. incredulous
25. diaries
26. dissent
27. dessert
28. device
29. duel
30. formerly
31. instance
32. ingenious
33. compliments
34. boarder
35. consul
36. formally
37. morale
38. personnel
39. principle
40. stationery
41. waste
42. supersede
43. exceedingly
44. succeeds
45. proceeded
46. illusion
47. accede
48. receded
49. corpse
50. its
51. later
52. led
53. council
54. loose
55. minors
56. peace
57. plain
58. quite

10,000 WORD READY REFERENCE SPELLING LIST

Spelling Reminders

t is not easy to become a good speller; in fact, many people never master the art. Even a computer spell-checker cannot always come to your rescue. English is full of confusing rules, strange spellings (like pneumonia and aerial), and words that sound alike but have different spellings (and you want to write the right word). In this book, you will find rules to help, some words that defy the rules, and common misspellings. Like any other skill, spelling can be improved with practice.

There is no magic formula for learning how to spell. The ability to spell correctly results from persistent study. Here are some useful suggestions for studying the list of words that follows.

1. Use a small notebook exclusively for recording your personal spelling problem words.
2. Each time you discover a problem word, enter it in your notebook. Check a dictionary for the correct syllabification and pronunciation.
3. Look at the word and say it in syllables.
4. Try to apply a rule that will help you to understand *why* the word is spelled as it is.
4. Close your eyes and picture the way the word looks.
6. Write the word. Check it. Rewrite it if necessary.
7. Review words you have already studied until you are absolutely sure that you know how to spell them.

From *Grammar In Plain English,* 4th edition by P. Dutwin and H. Diamond. With permission of Barron's Educational Series, Inc.

Using the 10,000 Words as Practice

The list of 10,000 words is designed to be an ongoing resource for your study of spelling. Go through it in sections. Find the words you're not sure of and use the study tools above to write them, use them, and live with them until you're comfortable about their spelling. You have seen many of them throughout this book. The additional practice will reinforce what you're already learned; you will also notice your progress by finding a word that once was troubling for you, which you can now remember how to spell.

If you have someone to help you by reading some words as you write, it will be easier to identify your trouble spots and those words that will require some practice. However, if you're ready to learn and you don't have a study partner nearby, don't wait. Study what you can; there will be plenty of words left to study when your partner is available.

Like all learning, you won't wake up one day and be a perfect speller; few people are. Even professional writers stumble with troublesome words and keep dictionaries by their sides. However, having gone through this book, you are well on your way to becoming a confident, competent speller. You may already notice the time you save not looking up the same old words and you may, by now, have caught some errors that your spell-checker misses. Continue your study with the 10,000 words to reinforce and strengthen your skills.

How to Use This List

Spelling. The words in this reference list are spelled according to American usage. When two spellings are valid, both are listed:

dem·a·gogue, dem·a·gog

Dividing words at the end of a line. Centered dots indicate division points at which a hyphen may be put at the end of a line of typing or writing. For example, *baccalaureate (bac·ca·lau·re·ate)* may be ended on one line with

bac-

bacca-

baccalau-

baccalaure-

and continued on the next line, respectively, with

-calaureate

-laureate

-reate

-ate

Note, however, that a single initial letter or a single terminal letter is not cut off. The following words, for example, are not hyphenated:

abound   icy   o'clock   seamy

Plurals. Most English nouns form their plural by adding *s*. These regular plurals are not shown in the reference list. Irregular plurals are shown:

la·bo·ra·to·ry (–ries)   las·so (las·sos *or* las·soes)
knife (knives)   la·tex (la·ti·ces *or* la·tex·es)
lar·nyx (la·ryn·ges *or* lar·ynx·es)   oc·to·pus (–pus·es *or* –pi)

Definitions. Brief definitions of confusing pairs of words are given:

> arc (something arched or curved; see *ark*)
> ark (a boat; a repository for Torah scrolls, see *arc*)
>
> af·fect (to influence; see *effect*)
> ef·fect (to accomplish; see *affect*)

Brief definitions of commonly used foreign words and phrases are also given:

> a la carte (French: each item is priced separately)
> cul-de-sac (French: street closed at one end)

10,000 Words

A

aback
aba·cus (–cus·es)
aban·don
aban·don·ment
abase
abase·ment
abash
abate·ment
ab·bey
ab·bot
ab·bre·vi·ate
ab·bre·vi·a·tion
ab·di·cate
ab·di·ca·tion
ab·do·men
ab·dom·i·nal
ab·duct
ab·duc·tion
ab·er·ra·tion
abet
abet·ted
ab·hor
ab·hor·rence
abide
abil·i·ty (–ties)
ab·ject
ab·jur·ing
able·bod·ied
ab·lu·tion
ably
ab·nor·mal·i·ty (–ties)

ab·nor·mal·ly
aboard
abol·ish
ab·o·li·tion
abom·i·na·ble
abort
abor·tion
abound
about·face
abra·sive
abreast
abridge
abridg·ment, abridge·ment
abroad
ab·ro·gate
abrupt
ab·scess
ab·scond
ab·sence
ab·so·lute
ab·so·lute·ly
ab·solve
ab·sorb
ab·sor·bent
ab·stain
ab·strac·tion
abun·dant
abut·ment
abys·mal
abyss
ac·a·dem·i·cal·ly
ac·cede
ac·cel·er·ate
ac·cent

ac·cept (to receive; see *except*)
ac·ces·so·ry, ac·ces·sa·ry (–ries)
ac·ces·si·ble
ac·ci·dent
ac·ci·den·tal
ac·claim
ac·cli·mate
ac·cli·ma·tize
ac·co·lade
ac·com·mo·date
ac·com·mo·da·tion
ac·com·pa·nist
ac·com·pa·ny
ac·com·plice
ac·com·plish
ac·cord
ac·cost
ac·count
ac·coun·tant
ac·cru·al
ac·cu·mu·late
ac·cu·ra·cy
ac·cu·sa·tion
ac·cuse
ac·e·tate
acet·y·lene
achieve
achieve·ment
ac·knowl·edge
acous·tics
ac·quain·tance
ac·qui·esce
ac·quire
ac·qui·si·tion

ac·quit·tal
acre
acre·age
ac·ri·mo·ni·ous
across
ac·tiv·i·ty (–ties)
ac·tu·al
ac·tu·ar·i·al
ac·tu·ary
acu·punc·ture
acu·punc·tur·ist
ad·ap·ta·tion
ad·dict
ad·dic·tive
ad·di·tion·al
ad·dress·ee
ad·duce
ad·e·noid
ad·e·quate
ad·here
ad·he·sive
ad hoc (Latin: pertaining to the
    case at hand)
ad ho·mi·nem (Latin: argument
    based on personality)
adieu (adieus or adieux)
    (French: farewell)
ad in·fi·ni·tum (Latin: without end)
ad·ja·cent
ad·jec·tive
ad·join·ing
ad·journ
ad·journ·ment
ad·ju·di·cate
ad·junct
ad·just·able
ad-lib (Latin: without preparation)
ad·min·is·ter
ad·min·is·trate
ad·min·is·tra·tion
ad·min·is·tra·tor
ad·mi·ra·ble
ad·mi·ra·tion
ad·mis·si·ble
ad nau·se·am (Latin: to a
    sickening degree)
ad·o·les·cent
adopt
adop·tion
ad·re·nal
adren·a·line
adroit
ad·u·la·tion
ad·van·ta·geous

ad·ven·tur·ous
ad·ver·sary (–sar·ies)
ad·ver·si·ty (–ties)
ad·ver·tise·ment
ad·vice (recommendation; see
    advise)
ad·vis·able
ad·vise (to give advice; see
    advice)
ad·vis·er, ad·vi·sor
ad·vo·cate
aer·ate
ae·ri·al (relating to the air)
aer·i·al (antenna)
aer·o·bics
aero·dy·nam·ics
aero·nau·tics
aero·sol
aes·thet·ics
af·fa·ble
af·fect (to influence; see effect)
af·fec·tion·ate
af·fi·da·vit
af·fil·i·ate
af·fin·i·ty (–ties)
af·fir·ma·tive
af·flic·tion
af·flu·ent
af·ford
af·fray
af·front
af·ghan
afore·men·tioned
afraid
af·ter·ward, af·ter·wards
again
agen·cy (–cies)
agen·da
agent
ag·glom·er·ate
ag·gran·dize·ment
ag·gra·vate
ag·gres·sion
ag·gres·sive
ag·grieved
aghast
ag·ile
agil·i·ty (–ties)
ag·i·tate
ag·i·ta·tor
ag·nos·tic
ag·on·ize
agrar·i·an
agree·able

ag·ri·cul·ture
agron·o·my
aid (to give assistance, a subsidy;
    see aide)
aide (military assistant; see aid)
air·con·di·tion
air con·di·tion·er
air force
air·line
air·port
aisle
ajar
a la carte (French: each item is
    priced separately)
alac·ri·ty
al·ba·tross
al·bu·men
al·che·my
al·co·hol
al·ge·bra
al·ga (al·gae)
alias
al·i·bi
alien·ate
align·ment, aline·ment
al·i·men·ta·ry
al·i·mo·ny (–nies)
alive
al·ka·li (–lies or –lis)
al·lay (relieve; see alley, ally)
al·le·ga·tion
al·lege
al·le·giance
al·le·go·ry (–ries)
al·ler·gy (–gies)
al·le·vi·ate
al·ley (narrow passage; see allay,
    ally)
al·li·ance
al·li·ga·tor
al·lit·er·ate
al·lit·er·a·tion
al·lo·cate
al·lo·path·ic
al·lot
al·lot·ment
al·low
al·low·able
al·low·ance
al·loy
all right
al·lude (to refer; see elude)
al·lure
al·lu·sion

al·ly (an associate; see *allay, alley*)
al·ma·nac
al·mond
al·most
alo·ha
alone
aloud
al·pha·bet
al·pha·bet·ize
al·ready
al·tar (structure used in religious ceremonies; see *alter*)
al·ter (to change; see *altar*)
al·ter·ation
al·ter·ca·tion
al·ter·nate
al·ter·na·tive
al·though
al·tim·e·ter
al·ti·tude
al·to·geth·er
al·tru·ism
al·um
alu·mi·num
alum·na (–nae)
alum·nus (–ni)
al·ways
amal·gam
amal·gam·ate
am·a·teur
am·a·to·ry
amaze
am·bas·sa·dor
am·bi·dex·trous
am·bi·ence, am·bi·ance
am·bi·gu·ity (–ties)
am·big·u·ous
am·bi·tious
am·biv·a·lence
am·bu·lance
am·bu·la·to·ry
ame·lio·rate
ame·na·ble
amend·ment
ame·ni·ty (–ties)
am·e·thyst
ami·a·ble
am·i·ca·ble
am·mo·nia
am·mu·ni·tion
am·ne·sia
am·nes·ty (–ties)

am·nio·cen·te·sis
amoe·ba (–bas *or* –bae)
among
amor·al
am·o·rous
amor·phous
am·or·ti·za·tion
amor·tize
amount
am·phet·amine
am·phib·i·an
am·phi·the·ater
am·pli·fy
am·pu·tate
amuse·ment
anach·ro·nism
an·al·ge·sic
an·a·log
anal·o·gous
anal·o·gy
anal·y·sis
an·a·lyst
an·a·lyze
an·ar·chy
anat·o·my
an·ces·tor
an·ces·try
anchor
an·cho·vy (–vies)
an·cient
an·cil·lary
an·ec·dote
an·es·the·sia
an·eu·rysm, an·eu·rism
an·gel (heavenly messenger; see *angle*)
an·gle (geometric figure; see *angel*)
angst
an·gu·lar
an·guish
an·i·mate
an·i·ma·tion
an·i·ma·tor
an·i·mos·i·ty (–ties)
an·nals
an·nex (noun), an·nex (verb)
an·ni·hi·late
an·ni·ver·sa·ry (–ries)
an·no·tate
an·nounce·ment
an·nounc·er
an·noy

an·nu·al
an·nu·ity (–ities)
an·nul
an·nun·ci·ate
anoint
anom·a·ly (–lies)
anon·y·mous
an·swer
ant (insect; see *aunt*)
an·tag·o·nize
an·te·ced·ent
an·te·date
an·te·lope
an·ten·na
an·te·ri·or
an·te·room
an·them
an·thol·o·gy (–gies)
an·thra·cite
an·thro·pol·o·gy
an·ti·bi·ot·ic
an·tic
an·tic·i·pate
an·ti·cli·max
an·ti·de·pres·sant
an·ti·dote
an·ti·his·ta·mine
an·ti·ox·i·dant
an·ti·pas·to
an·tip·a·thy (–thies)
an·ti·pol·lu·tion
an·ti·quar·i·an
an·tique
an·tiq·ui·ty (–ties)
an·ti·sep·tic
an·ti·so·cial
an·tith·e·sis (–e·ses)
ant·onym
anx·i·ety (–eties)
anx·ious
aor·ta
apart·heid
apart·ment
ap·a·thy
aper·i·tif
ap·er·ture
apex
aph·o·rism
aph·ro·dis·i·ac
aplomb
apoc·a·lypse
apoc·ry·phal
apo·gee

apol·o·gize
apol·o·gy (–gies)
ap·o·plec·tic
ap·o·plexy
apos·tro·phe
apo·the·o·sis (–ses)
ap·pall, ap·pal
ap·pa·ra·tus (–tus·es *or* –tus)
ap·par·el
ap·par·ent
ap·pa·ri·tion
ap·peal
ap·pear·ance
ap·pease
ap·pel·lant
ap·pe·late
ap·pend·age
ap·pen·dec·to·my (–mies)
ap·pen·di·ci·tis
ap·pen·dix (–dix·es *or* –di·ces)
ap·per·tain
ap·pe·tite
ap·pe·tiz·er
ap·plaud
ap·plause
ap·pli·ance
ap·pli·ca·ble
ap·pli·ca·tion
ap·pli·ca·tor
ap·plied
ap·ply
ap·point·ment
ap·por·tion
ap·pose
ap·praise
ap·pre·ci·ate
ap·pre·hend
ap·pren·tice
ap·prise
ap·proach
ap·pro·ba·tion
ap·pro·pri·ate
ap·pro·pri·a·tion
ap·prov·al
ap·prox·i·mate
apri·cot
ap·ti·tude
apt·ly
aquar·i·um
aquat·ic
aq·ue·duct
ar·bi·ter
ar·bi·trary

ar·bi·trate
ar·bi·tra·tor
ar·bor
arc (curved line; see *ark*)
ar·cade
arch
ar·chae·ol·o·gy
ar·cha·ic
ar·chery
ar·che·type
ar·chi·tect
ar·chi·tec·tur·al
ar·chi·tec·ture
ar·chive
arc·tic
ar·dent
ar·dor
ar·du·ous
ar·ea
are·na
ar·gue
ar·id
ar·is·toc·ra·cy (–cies)
aris·to·crat
arith·me·tic
ark (boat; see *arc*)
ar·ma·ment
ar·ma·ture
ar·mi·stice
ar·moire
ar·mor
ar·my (ar·mies)
aro·ma
aro·ma·ther·a·py
ar·o·mat·ic
arouse
ar·raign
ar·range
ar·ray
ar·rears
ar·rest
ar·riv·al
ar·rive
ar·ro·gance
ar·se·nic
ar·son
ar·te·ri·al
ar·te·rio·scle·ro·sis
ar·tery (–ter·ies)
art·ful
arth·ri·tis
ar·ti·choke
ar·ti·cle

ar·tic·u·late
ar·ti·fact
ar·ti·fice
ar·ti·fi·cial
ar·ti·san
ar·tis·tic
ar·tis·ti·cal·ly
as·bes·tos
as·cend
as·cen·sion
as·cent (climb; see *assent*)
as·cer·tain
as·cet·ic
as·cribe
asep·tic
askew
as·par·a·gus (–gus·es)
as·pect
as·per·i·ty (–ties)
as·per·sion
as·phalt
as·phyx·i·ate
as·pire
as·pi·rin
as·sail
as·sas·sin
as·sas·si·na·tion
as·sault
as·sem·ble
as·sem·bly (–blies)
as·sent (to agree; see *ascent*)
as·sert
as·sess·ment
as·set
as·sid·u·ous
as·sign·ment
as·sim·i·late
as·sis·tant
as·so·ci·a·tion
as·so·nance
as·sort·ment
as·suage
as·sump·tion
as·sur·ance
as·ter·isk
as·ter·oid
asth·ma
as·trin·gent
as·trol·o·gy
as·tro·naut
as·tron·o·mer
as·tro·nom·i·cal, as·tro·nom·ic
as·tron·o·my (–mies)

as·tute
asun·der
asy·lum
asym·met·ric, asym·met·ri·cal
athe·ist
ath·lete
ath·let·ic
at·mo·sphere
atom·ic
atone·ment
atro·cious
at·ro·phy
at·tach
at·ta·ché
at·tach·ment
at·tack
at·tain
at·tempt
at·ten·dance
at·ten·tive
at·ten·u·ate
at·test
at·tic
at·tire
at·ti·tude
at·tor·ney
at·trac·tive
at·tri·bute
at·tri·tion
at·tor·ney
at·tune
atyp·i·cal
au·burn
auc·tion·eer
au·da·cious
au·dac·i·ty (–ties)
au·di·ble
au·di·ence
au·dio·vi·su·al
au·dit
au·di·tion
au·di·to·ri·um
aug·ment
auld lang syne (Scottish: the
    good old times)
aunt (relative; see *ant*)
au·ral (relating to the ear; see
    oral)
au re·voir (French: good·bye)
au·ri·cle
aus·pic·es
aus·pi·cious
aus·tere

aus·ter·i·ty (–ties)
au·then·tic
au·then·ti·cate
au·then·tic·i·ty
au·thor
au·thor·i·ta·tive
au·thor·i·ty (–ties)
au·tho·ri·za·tion
au·tho·rize
au·tism
au·to·bio·graph·i·cal,
    au·to·bio·graph·ic
au·to·bi·og·ra·phy (–phies)
au·toc·ra·cy (–cies)
au·to·crat
au·to·graph
au·to·mat·ed
au·to·mat·ic
au·to·mat·i·cal·ly
au·to·ma·tion
au·tom·a·ton
au·to·mo·bile
au·to·mo·tive
au·ton·o·mous
au·ton·o·my (–mies)
au·top·sy (–sies)
au·to·sug·ges·tion
au·tumn
aux·il·ia·ry (–ries)
avail·abil·i·ty (–ties)
avail·able
av·a·lanche
av·a·rice
av·a·ri·cious
avenge
av·e·nue
av·er·age
averse
aver·sion
avert
avi·ary (–ar·ies)
avi·a·tion
avi·a·tor
av·id
av·o·ca·do (–dos *or* –does)
av·o·ca·tion
avoid·able
avoid·ance
av·oir·du·pois (French: weight)
await
awake
awak·en·ing
award

aware
away
awe·some
aw·ful
awhile
awk·ward
aw·ning
awoke
ax·i·al
ax·i·om
ax·is (ax·es)
ax·le
ay·ur·ve·dic
aza·lea
azure

B

bab·ble
bab·bling
ba·by (ba·bies)
ba·boon
bac·ca·lau·re·ate
bach·e·lor
ba·cil·lus (–li)
back·bone
back·fire
back·ground
back·log
back·stop
back·ward
ba·con
bac·te·ri·al
bac·te·ri·ol·o·gy
bac·te·ri·um (–ria)
bad·ger
bad·min·ton
baf·fle
bag·gage
bail (security for due appearance;
    see *bale*)
bai·liff
bai·li·wick
bak·ery (–er·ies)
bak·ing
bal·ance
bal·co·ny (–nies)
bale (large bundle; see *bail*)
balk
bal·lad
bal·last
bal·le·ri·na

bal·let
bal·lis·tics
bal·loon
bat·lot
balm
ba·lo·ney, bo·lo·ney
bal·sa
bam·boo
ba·nal
ba·nana
ban·dage
ban·dan·na
ban·di·try
band·width
bane·ful
ban·ish
ban·is·ter
bank·rupt
bank·rupt·cy (–cies)
ban·ner
ban·quet
ban·ter
bar·be·cue
bare (exposed; see *bear)*
bar·gain
ba·rom·e·ter
ba·ron (a lord of the realm; see
    barren)
bar·rack
bar·rel
bar·ren (not reproducing; see
    baron)
bar·rette (hair pin; see *beret)*
bar·ri·cade
bar·ri·er
bar·room
base (bottom; see *bass)*
bash·ful
ba·sic
ba·si·cal·ly
ba·sil·i·ca
ba·sis (ba·ses)
bas·ket·ry (–ries)
bass (a deep tone; see *base)*
bas·si·net
bas·soon
baste
bas·tion
bathe
bat·tal·ion
bat·tle
bau·ble
bay·o·net

bay·ou
ba·zaar (market; see *bizarre)*
beach (shore; see *beech)*
bea·con
beady
bear (an animal, to endure, to
    give birth; see *bare)*
beard
beast
beau
beau·ti·ful
beau·ti·fy
beau·ty (–ties)
be·cause
beech (tree; see *beach)*
beer (alcoholic beverage; see
    bier)
be·fore
be·fud·dle
beg·gar
be·gin·ning
be·go·nia
be·grudge
be·guile
be·hav·ior
be·he·moth
be·hest
be·hold·en
be·hoove
beige
be·ing
be·la·bor
be·lat·ed
bel·fry (–fries)
be·lie
be·lief
be·lieve
bell (chime; see *belle)*
belle (beauty; see *bell)*
bel·lig·er·ent
bel·lows
be·neath
bene·fac·tor
be·nef·i·cence
ben·e·fi·cial
ben·e·fi·cia·ry (–ries)
be·nev·o·lence
be·nev·o·lent
be·nign
ben·zene, ben·zine
be·queath
be·quest
be·reave

be·ret (woolen cap; see
    barrette)
ber·serk
berth (place; see *birth)*
be·siege
bes·tial
be·stow
be·tray
be·tween
bev·el
bev·er·age
bevy (bev·ies)
be·wail
bi·an·nu·al
bi·as (–es)
bi·ble
bib·li·cal
bib·li·og·ra·phy (–phies)
bi·car·bon·ate
bi·cen·ten·ni·al
bi·ceps
bi·cy·cle
bi·en·ni·al
bi·fo·cal
big·a·my
big·ot
big·ot·ry (–ries)
bi·ki·ni
bi·lat·er·al
bi·lin·ear
bi·lin·gual
bill·board
bil·liards
bil·lion
bil·lion·aire
bi·na·ry
bin·au·ral
bind·ery (–er·ies)
bin·oc·u·lar
bio·chem·is·try
bio·de·grad·able
bio·feed·back
bio·graph·i·cal
bi·og·ra·phy (–phies)
bi·o·log·i·cal
bi·ol·o·gy
bi·on·ic
bi·op·sy
bi·par·ti·san
bi·ra·cial
birth (originate; see *berth)*
bis·cuit
bi·son

bisque

bit·ter

bit·ter·ness

bi·zarre (out of the ordinary; see *bazaar*)

black·mail

blar·ney

bla·sé

blas·phe·my (—mies)

bla·tant

bla·zon

blem·ish

blight

blind·ly

bliz·zard

bloc (group; see *block*)

block (hinder; see *bloc*)

block·ade

blog

blog·ger

blos·som

blotch

blown

blud·geon

blue

blurb

boar (wild pig; see *bore*)

board (a piece of wood; see *bored*)

bod·ily

bo·gey

bog·gle

bo·lo·gna, bo·lo·ney,

bol·ster

bom·bard

bona fide (Latin: in good faith)

bo·nan·za

bond·age

bon·fire

bo·nus

bon voy·age (French: farewell)

book·keep·ing

boo·mer·ang

boor·ish

bo·rax

bor·der

bore (to drill; past of bear; dull person; see *boar*)

bored (past of *bore*; see *board*)

born (from birth; see *borne*)

borne (past participle of *bear*; see *born*)

bor·ough (town; see *borrow*)

bor·row (to receive with intention of returning; see *borough*)

borscht (Russian: soup of beets and sour cream)

bo·som

bos·sy

bot·a·ny

bot·tle

bot·tom

bou·doir (French: bedroom, private sitting room)

bough (tree limb; see *bow*)

bouil·la·baisse (French: fish stew)

bouil·lon

boul·der

bou·le·vard

bound·ary (—aries)

boun·te·ous

bou·quet

bour·bon

bou·ton·niere (French: flower worn in buttonhole)

bo·vine

bow (to bend; see *bough*)

bow·el

boy·cott

brace·let

braid

braille

braise

brake (to stop; see *break*)

bram·ble

bras·siere

bra·va·do

brav·ery

bra·vo (bra·vos)

brawny

bra·zen

breach

breadth

break (to tear; see *brake*)

break·fast

breath

breathe

breath·less

breech·es

breeze

breth·ren

bre·via·ry (—ries)

brev·i·ty

brib·ery

bric-a-brac

brid·al (relating to a bride; see *bridle*)

bridge

bri·dle (horse's headgear; see *bridal*)

brief

bri·gade

brig·a·dier

brig·and

bright

bril·liant

brine

bri·quette, bri·quet

bris·tle

brit·tie

broach (to open up a subject for discussion; see *brooch*)

broad·band

broad·cast

bro·cade

bro·co·li, broc·o·li

bro·chure

bro·ker·age

bro·mide

bron·chi·al

brooch (ornament; see *broach*)

broth·er·ly

brow·beat

browse

bruise

brun·et, brun·ette

brusque

bru·tal

bub·ble

buc·ca·neer

buck·et

bu·col·ic

bud·get

buf·fa·lo

buf·fet

buf·foon

bug·a·boo

bu·gle

build

bul·le·tin

bul·lion

bump·kin

bump·tious

bun·ga·low

bun·gle

buoy·an·cy

bur·den

bu·reau
bu·reau·cra·cy (–cies)
bu·reau·crat
bur·geon
bur·glar
buri·al
bur·lesque
bur·ly
burnt
bur·ro (donkey; see *burrow*)
bur·row (a hole made in the
    ground by an animal; see
    burro)
bur·sar
bush·el
busi·ness
bus·tle
busy
butch·er
but·ter·fly
but·tock
but·ton
but·tress
bux·om
buy (purchase; see *by, bye)*
buzz
buz·zard
by (near; see *buy, bye)*
bye
by·pass
by·pro·duct
by·stand·er
byte (computer term)
by·way

C

ca·ba·na
cab·a·ret
cab·bage
cab·i·net
ca·ble
ca·boose
cache
ca·chet
ca·coph·o·ny (–nies)
cac·tus
ca·dav·er
ca·dence
caf·e·te·ria
caf·feine
ca·gey

ca·jole
ca·lam·i·ty (–ties)
cal·ci·fy
cal·ci·um
cal·cu·late
cal·cu·la·tor
cal·cu·lus (–lus·es)
cal·en·dar
cal·i·ber, cal·i·bre
cal·i·brate
cal·i·co
cal·is·then·ics
cal·lig·ra·pher
cal·lig·ra·phy
cal·lous (feeling no emotion; see
    callus)
cal·lus (hard, thickened area of
    skin; see *callous*)
ca·lo·ric
cal·o·rie, cal·o·ry (–ries)
ca·lyp·so
ca·ma·ra·de·rie
ca·mel·lia, ca·me·lia
cam·eo (cam·eos)
cam·i·sole
cam·ou·flage
cam·paign
cam·phor
ca·nal
ca·nard
ca·nas·ta
can·cel
can·cel·la·tion, can·cel·ation
can·cer
can·des·cence
can·di·da·cy (–cies)
can·di·date
can·dle
can·dor
ca·nine
can·is·ter
can·ker
can·ni·bal
can·non (gun; see *canon*)
can·not
ca·noe
canon (dogma; see *cannon*)
can·o·py (–pies)
can·ta·loupe
can·tan·ker·ous
can·ta·ta
can·teen
can·ti·cle

can·vas (closely woven cloth; see
    canvass)
can·vass (examine votes; see
    canvas)
can·yon
ca·pa·bil·i·ty (–ties)
ca·pa·ble
ca·pa·cious
ca·pac·i·ty (–ties)
ca·per
cap·il·lary (–lar·ies)
cap·i·tal (seat of government; see
    capitol)
cap·i·tal·ism
cap·i·tol (building in which
    legislature meets; see
    capital)
ca·pit·u·late
ca·pon
ca·price
ca·pri·cious
cap·sule
cap·tain
cap·tion
cap·ti·vate
car·a·mel
car·at, kar·at (unit of weight; see
    caret, carrot)
car·a·van
car·bine
car·bo·hy·drate
car·bon
car·bun·cle
car·bu·re·tor
car·cass
car·cin·o·gen
car·ci·no·gen·ic
car·di·ac
car·di·gan
car·di·nal
car·dio·gram
car·di·ol·o·gist
ca·reen
ca·reer
care·ful
ca·ress
car·et (printing symbol; see *carat,*
    carrot)
car·go
car·i·ca·ture
car·ies
car·il·lon
car·nage

car·nal
car·ni·val
car·niv·o·rous
car·ol
car·pen·ter
carp·ing
car·riage
car·ri·er
car·ri·on
car·rot (vegetable; see *carat, caret*)
carte blanche (French: full discretionary power)
car·tog·ra·pher
car·ton
car·toon
car·tridge
cas·cade
case·work
cash·ier
cash·mere
ca·si·no
cas·ket
cas·se·role
cas·sette, ca·sette
cas·sock
cast (direct; see *caste*)
cas·ta·net
caste (class; see *cast*)
cas·ti·gate
cas·tle
cas·tor
ca·su·al·ty (–ties)
cat·a·clysm
cat·a·comb
cat·a·lep·sy (–sies)
cat·a·log, cat·a·logue
cat·a·lyst
cat·a·pult
cat·a·ract
ca·tas·tro·phe
cata·ton·ic
cat·e·chism
cat·e·go·rize
cat·e·go·ry (–ries)
ca·ter
cat·er·cor·ner, kit·ty-cor·ner
cat·er·pil·lar
ca·thar·sis
ca·the·dral
cath·e·ter
cat·sup, ketch·up
cau·cus

caught
caul·dron
cau·li·flow·er
caulk
caus·al
caus·tic
cau·tion
cau·tious
cav·a·lier
cav·al·ry (–ries)
cav·i·ar
cav·il
cav·i·ty (–ties)
ca·vort
cease
ce·dar
cede
ceil·ing
cel·e·brate
ce·leb·ri·ty (–ties)
cel·ery (–er·ies)
ce·les·tial
cel·i·ba·cy
cell (microscopic mass; see *sell*)
cel·lar (basement; see *seller*)
cel·lo
cel·lo·phane
cel·lu·lar
cel·lu·loid
ce·ment
cem·e·tery (–ter·ies)
cen·ser (incense burner; see *censor*)
cen·sor (supervisor of conduct and morals; see *censer*)
cen·sure
cen·sus
cent (monetary unit; see *sent*)
cen·te·na·ry (–ries)
cen·ten·ni·al
cen·ter·piece
cen·ti·grade
cen·ti·me·ter
cen·trif·u·gal
cen·trip·e·tal
cen·tu·ry (–ries)
ce·phal·ic
ce·ram·ic
ce·re·al (prepared grain; see *serial*)
cer·e·bel·lum
ce·re·bral

cer·e·mo·ny (–nies)
ce·rise
cer·tain
cer·tif·i·cate
cer·ti·fy
cer·ti·tude
ces·sa·tion
ces·sion
cess·pool
chafe
chaff
cha·grin
chair·man
cha·let
chal·ice
chalk
chal·lenge
chal·lis (chal·lises)
cham·ber·lain
cham·bray
cha·me·leon
cham·ois
cham·pagne
cham·pi·on
chan·cel·lor
chan·cery (–cer·ies)
chan·de·lier
change
chan·nel
chan·tey, chan·ty (chan·teys, chan·ties)
cha·os
cha·pel
chap·er·on, chap·er·one
chap·lain
chap·ter
char·ac·ter
cha·rade
char·coal
charge
char·i·ot
cha·ris·ma
char·i·ty (–ties)
char·la·tan
char·treuse
chary
chasm
chas·sis
chaste
chas·tise
chas·ti·ty
châ·teau (French: mansion)
chat·tel

chat·ty
chauf·feur
chau·vin·ism
check
chee·tah
chef
chem·i·cal
che·mise
chem·is·try
che·mo·ther·a·py
che·nille
cher·ish
cher·ub
chess
che·va·lier
chev·ron
chic
chic·o·ry (–ries)
chief
chif·fon
child (chil·dren)
chime
chim·ney
chim·pan·zee
chin·chil·la
chintz
chi·ro·prac·tic
chi·ro·prac·tor
chis·el
chiv·al·ry (–ries)
chlo·rine
chlo·ro·form
chlo·ro·phyll
choc·o·late
choir
chol·era
cho·les·ter·ol
cho·ral
chord
cho·re·og·ra·phy (–phies)
chorus
chor·tle
chris·ten
chro·mat·ic
chrome
chro·mo·some
chron·ic
chron·i·cle
chro·no·log·i·cal
chro·nol·o·gy (–gies)
chry·san·the·mum
church
chute

ci·gar
cig·a·rette, cig·a·ret
cin·der
cin·e·ma
cin·na·mon
ci·pher
cir·cle
cir·cuit
cir·cu·lar
cir·cu·la·tion
cir·cum·cise
cir·cum·fer·ence
cir·cum·lo·cu·tion
cir·cum·scribe
cir·cum·spect
cir·cum·stance
cir·cum·stan·tial
cir·cum·vent
cir·rho·sis
cis·tern
ci·ta·tion
cite (to quote; see *site*)
cit·i·zen
city
civ·ic
civ·il
civ·il·ian
ci·vil·i·ty (–ties)
civ·i·li·za·tion
claim
claim·ant
clair·voy·ance
clam·my
clam·or
clan·des·tine
clan·gor
claque
clar·et
clar·i·fy
clar·i·net
clar·i·on
clar·i·ty
clas·sic
clas·si·cal
clas·si·cist
clas·si·fied
class·less
clause
claus·tro·pho·bia
clav·i·chord
clav·i·cle
cleanse
clear·ance

cleave
clef
cleft
clem·en·cy (–cies)
cler·i·cal
cli·ché (French: trite expression)
click (slight sharp noise; see *clique*)
cli·en·tele
cliff
cli·mate
climb
clin·ic
clique (exclusive group; see *click*)
clob·ber
clois·ter
clos·et
cloth
clothe
cloud
clout
clus·ter
clutch
co·ag·u·late
co·alesce
co·a·li·tion
coarse (rough; see *course*)
coax
co·bra
co·caine
cock·ney
co·coa
co·co·nut
co·coon
cod·dle
co·de·fen·dant
co·deine
cod·ger
cod·i·cil
cod·i·fy
co·ed·u·ca·tion
co·ef·fi·cient
co·erce
cof·fers
cof·fin
co·gent
cog·i·tate
co·gnac
cog·ni·tion
cog·ni·zant
co·here
co·he·sive·ness

coif·fure
co·in·cide
col·an·der
col·ic
col·i·se·um
col·lab·o·rate
col·lapse
col·laps·ible
col·late
col·lat·er·al
col·league
col·lec·tive
col·lege
col·lide
col·lie
col·li·sion
col·lo·qui·al
col·lo·quy (–quies)
col·lu·sion
co·logne
co·lon
col·o·nel (army officer; see
    kernel)
co·lo·nial
col·on·nade
col·o·ny (–nies)
col·or
co·los·sal
col·umn
col·um·nist
co·ma
comb
com·bat n., com·bat vb.
com·bi·na·tion
co·me·di·an
com·e·dy (–dies)
com·et
come·up·pance
com·fort·able
com·ma
com·man·deer
com·mand·ment
com·man·do
com·mem·o·rate
com·mem·o·ra·tive
com·mence
com·mend
com·men·da·tion
com·men·su·rate
com·men·tary (–tar·ies)
com·men·ta·tor
com·merce
com·mer·cial

com·min·gle
com·mis·er·ate
com·mis·sar
com·mis·sary (–sar·ies)
com·mis·sion
com·mit
com·mit·tee
com·mode
com·mo·di·ous
com·mod·i·ty (–ties)
com·mo·dore
com·mon
com·mo·tion
com·mu·nal
com·mune
com·mu·ni·ca·ble
com·mu·ni·cate
com·mun·ing
com·mu·nion
com·mu·ni·qué
com·mu·nism
com·mu·nist
com·mu·ni·ty (–ties)
com·mute
com·mut·ing
com·pa·ny (–nies)
com·pan·ion
com·pa·ra·ble
com·par·a·tive
com·pas·sion·ate
com·pat·i·bil·i·ty
com·pat·i·ble
com·pel
com·pen·sate
com·pete
com·pe·tence
com·pe·ti·tion
com·pet·i·tor
com·pi·la·tion
com·pla·cent (self-satisfied; see
    complaisant)
com·plain
com·plais·ant (obliging; see
    complacent)
com·ple·ment (something that
    completes; see *compliment*)
com·ple·men·ta·ry
com·plete
com·plex·ion
com·plex·i·ty (–ties)
com·pli·ant
com·pli·cate
com·plic·i·ty (–ties)

com·pli·ment (expression of
    praise; see *complement*)
com·pli·men·ta·ry
com·ply
com·po·nent
com·pos·ite
com·po·si·tion
com·pos·i·tor
com·pound
com·pre·hend
com·pre·hen·sive
com·press
com·prise
com·pro·mise
comp·trol·ler, con·trol·ler
com·pul·sion
com·punc·tion
com·put·er
com·put·er·ize
com·rade
con·ceal
con·cede
con·ceit
con·ceive
con·cen·trate
con·cen·tric
con·cept
con·cep·tu·al
con·cern
con·cert
con·cer·to
con·ces·sion
con·cil·i·ate
con·cise
con·clude
con·coct
con·cord
con·course
con·crete
con·cu·bine
con·cu·pis·cent
con·cur
con·cur·rent
con·cus·sion
con·dem·na·tion
con·dense
con·de·scend
con·di·ment
con·di·tion·al
con·do·lence
con·do·min·i·um
con·done
con·du·cive

con·duct
con·duit
con·fer
con·fer·ence
con·ferred
con·fes·sion
con·fet·ti
con·fi·dant (one to whom secrets are entrusted; see *confident)*
con·fi·dante (a female confidant)
con·fi·dence
con·fi·dent (assured; see *confidant)*
con·fig·u·ra·tion
con·fine
con·firm
con·fis·cate
con·fla·gra·tion
con·flict
con·form
con·frere
con·fron·ta·tion
con·fu·sion
con·geal
con·ge·nial
con·gest
con·glom·er·ate
con·grat·u·late
con·gre·gate
con·gres·sio·nal
con·gru·ent
con·ic
co·ni·fer
con·jec·ture
con·ju·gal
con·ju·gate
con·junc·tion
con·jure
con·nect
con·nec·tion
con·nive
con·nois·seur
con·no·ta·tion
con·nu·bi·al
con·quer
con·quis·ta·dor (Spanish: one that conquers)
con·science
con·sci·en·tious
con·scious
con·script
con·se·crate
con·sec·u·tive

con·sen·sus
con·sent
con·se·quence
con·ser·va·tion
con·ser·va·tive
con·ser·va·to·ry (–ries)
con·sid·er
con·sign
con·sis·tent
con·sole
con·sol·i·date
con·som·mé
con·so·nance
con·spic·u·ous
con·spir·a·cy (–cies)
con·spir·a·tor
con·spire
con·sta·ble
con·stab·u·lary
con·stant
con·stel·la·tion
con·ster·na·tion
con·sti·pa·tion
con·stit·u·ent
con·sti·tute
con·sti·tu·tion
con·sti·tu·tion·al·i·ty
con·strain
con·strict
con·struc·tive
con·strue
con·sul
con·sul·ta·tion
con·sume
con·sum·er
con·sum·mate
con·sump·tion
con·tact
con·ta·gious
con·tain·er
con·tam·i·na·tion
con·tem·plate
con·tem·po·ra·ne·ous
con·tem·po·rary
con·tempt·ible
con·temp·tu·ous
con·tend
con·tent (noun), con·tent (verb, adjective)
con·tes·tant
con·text
con·tig·u·ous
con·ti·nence

con·ti·nent
con·tin·gen·cy (–cies)
con·tin·u·al
con·tin·u·ous
con·tin·u·um
con·tort
con·tour
con·tra·band
con·tra·cep·tion
con·trac·tion
con·trac·tu·al
con·tra·dict
con·tral·to
con·trary (–trar·ies)
con·trast (noun), con·trast (verb)
con·trib·ute
con·trite
con·trive
con·trolled
con·trol·ler, comp·trol·ler
con·tro·ver·sial
con·tro·ver·sy (–sies)
con·tro·vert
con·tu·sion
co·nun·drum
con·va·lesce
con·vene
con·ven·tion
con·ve·nience
con·verge
con·ver·sa·tion
con·ver·sion
con·vert·er
con·vey
con·vic·tion
con·vince
con·viv·ial
con·vo·ca·tion
con·vo·lu·tion
con·vulse
co·op·er·ate
co·or·di·nate
co·pi·ous
cop·u·late
cor·dial
cor·don
cor·do·van
cor·du·roy
cor·nea
cor·ner
cor·net
cor·nu·co·pia
cor·ol·lary (–lar·ies)

cor·o·nary
cor·o·na·tion
cor·o·ner
cor·po·ral
cor·po·rate
cor·po·ra·tion
cor·po·re·al
corps (group; see *corpse*)
corpse (dead body; see *corps*)
cor·pu·lent
cor·pus·cle
cor·pus de·lic·ti (New Latin: fact
    necessary to prove a crime)
cor·ral
cor·rect
cor·rec·tion
cor·re·late
cor·re·la·tion
cor·re·spon·dence
cor·ri·dor
cor·rob·o·rate
cor·rode
cor·ro·sion
cor·rupt
cor·sage
cor·set
cor·ti·sone
co·sign·er
cos·met·ic
cos·mo·pol·i·tan
cos·mos
cos·tume
cost·ly
cot·tage
cou·gar
could
coun·cil (advisory group; see
    counsel)
coun·sel (advice; see *council*)
coun·sel·or, coun·sel·lor
coun·te·nance
coun·ter·feit
coun·ter·part
coun·ter·point
coun·ter·pro·duc·tive
coun·try
coup
coupe
cou·ple
cou·pon
cou·ra·geous
cou·ri·er

course (direction, customary
    procedure; see *coarse*)
cour·te·ous
cous·in
cou·tu·ri·er
cov·er·age
co·vert
co·work·er
coy·ote
crab·by
cra·dle
cra·ni·al
cra·vat
cray·on
crease
cre·a·tion
cre·ativ·i·ty
crea·ture
cre·dence
cre·den·tial
cred·i·bil·i·ty
cred·i·ble
cred·it
cre·do
cre·du·li·ty
cre·du·lous
cre·mate
cre·ole
crepe, crêpe
cre·scen·do
cres·cent
cre·tin
cre·vasse
crev·ice
cri·er
crim·i·nal
crim·i·nol·o·gy
cringe
crin·kle
crip·ple
cri·sis (–ses)
cris·py
cri·te·ri·on (–ria *or* –rions)
crit·i·cal
crit·i·cism
crit·i·cize
cri·tique
cro·chet
crotch·ety
crock·ery
croc·o·dile
cro·cus
crois·sant

cro·ny (–nies)
cro·quet
cross·road
crouch
crou·ton
crowd
cru·cial
cru·ci·fix (–fix·es)
cru·el
cruise
cru·sade
crus·ta·cean
crutch
crux
cry
cryp·tic
crys·tal
crys·tall·ize
cu·bi·cal (shaped like a cube; see
    cubicle)
cu·bi·cle (sleeping compartment;
    see *cubical*)
cud·dle
cue
cui·sine
cul-de-sac (culs-de-sac) (French:
    street closed at one end)
cu·li·nary
cul·mi·nate
cul·pa·ble
cul·ti·vate
cul·tur·al
cum·ber·some
cu·mu·la·tive
cun·ning
cup·board
cu·po·la
cu·rate
cu·ra·tor
cur·few
cu·ri·ous
cur·rant (berry; see *current*)
cur·ren·cy (–cies)
cur·rent (present; see *currant*)
cur·ric·u·lum
cur·so·ry
cur·tail·ment
cur·tain
cur·te·sy (–sies)
curt·sy, curt·sey (curt·sies *or*
    curt·seys)
cur·va·ture
curve

cush·ion
cus·tard
cus·to·di·an
cus·to·dy (–dies)
cus·tom
cus·tom·ary
cus·tom·er
cu·ti·cle
cut·lery
cy·ber·space
cy·cle
cy·clic, cy·cli·cal
cy·clone
cyl·in·der
cym·bal
cyn·ic
cy·press
cyst

D

dab·ble
dad·dy (daddies)
daf·fo·dil
dag·ger
dai·ly
dai·ry
dai·sy (daisies)
dam·age
dam·ask
dam·sel
dance
dan·de·li·on
dan·druff
dan·ger·ous
dan·gle
dash·board
da·ta
da·ta·base
date
daugh·ter
daunt·less
daw·dle
day·care
daz·zle
dear (expensive; expression of
    endearment; see *deer*)
de·ba·cle
de·base·ment
de·bat·able
de·bil·i·tate
deb·it

deb·o·nair
de·brief
de·bris (plural also debris)
debt
debt·or
de·bug
de·but
de·cade
dec·a·dence
de·caf·fein·ate
de·cal
de·cap·i·tate
de·cath·lon
de·cay
de·ceased
de·cree
de·ceit
de·ceive
de·cen·cy
de·cent
de·cen·tral·iza·tion
de·cep·tion
deci·bel
de·cide
de·cid·u·ous
dec·i·mal
dec·i·mate
de·ci·pher
de·ci·sion
dec·la·ma·tion
dec·la·ra·tion
de·clas·si·fy
de·cliv·i·ty (–ties)
de·code
de·com·pose
de·con·tam·i·nate
de·cor, dé·cor (French:
    decoration)
dec·o·rate
dec·o·rous
de·co·rum
de·coy (noun), de·coy (verb)
de·crease
de·crep·it
de·cry
ded·i·cate
de·duct·ible
de·duc·tion
deer (an animal; see *dear*)
de·fac·to (New Latin: in reality)
def·a·ma·tion
de·fault
de·fec·tive

de·fen·dant
de·fense
de·fen·sive
def·er·ence
de·fi·ance
de·fi·cien·cy (–cies)
def·i·cit
de·fine
def·i·nite
def·i·ni·tion
de·fo·li·ant
de·for·mi·ty (–ties)
de·fraud
de·fray
deft
de·fy
de·gen·er·ate
de·gree
de·hy·drate
de·i·fy
deign
de·i·ty (–ties)
de·lay
de·lec·ta·ble
del·e·gate
del·e·ga·tion
de·lete
del·e·te·ri·ous
de·lib·er·ate
del·i·cate
de·li·cious
de·light
de·lin·eate
de·lin·quent
de·lir·i·ous
de·liv·ery (–er·ies)
de·lude
del·uge
de·lu·sion
de·luxe
dem·a·gogue, dem·a·gog
de·mand
de·mean·or
de·mil·i·ta·rize
de·mise
demi·tasse
de·moc·ra·cy (–cies)
de·mol·ish
dem·on·strate
de·mor·al·ize
de·mur
de·mure
de·ni·al

den·i·grate
den·im
de·nom·i·na·tion
de·nom·i·na·tor
de·nounce
dense
den·tal
den·tist·ry
de·odor·ant
de·part·ment
de·par·ture
de·pen·dent
de·pict
de·plete
de·plor·able
de·ploy
de·por·ta·tion
de·pos·it
de·pos·i·to·ry (–ries)
de·pot
dep·re·cate
de·pre·ciate
dep·re·da·tion
de·pres·sion
de·pri·va·tion
depth
dep·u·ty (–ties)
de·reg·u·la·tion
der·e·lict
der·i·va·tion
de·riv·a·tive
der·ma·tol·o·gy
de·rog·a·to·ry
de·scend·ant, de·scend·ent
de·scen·sion
de·scent
de·scribe
de·scrip·tion
des·e·crate
de·seg·re·ga·tion
de·sert (arid barren tract; see
    dessert)
des·ic·cate
de·sign
des·ig·nate
de·sir·able
de·sist
des·o·la·tion
des·per·ate
de·spi·ca·ble
de·spise
de·spite
de·spon·dent

des·pot
des·sert (course served at end of
    meal; see *desert*)
des·ti·ny (–nies)
des·ti·tute
de·stroy
de·struc·tion
de·sue·tude
des·ul·to·ry
de·tach
de·tail
de·tect
de·ter·gent
de·te·ri·o·rate
de·ter·mi·na·tion
de·ter·rent
det·o·na·tion
de·tour
de·tox
de·tox·i·fy
de·tract
det·ri·ment
deuce
de·val·u·a·tion
dev·as·tate
de·vel·op
de·vel·op·ment
de·vi·ate
de·vice (mechanism; see
    devise)
de·vi·ous
de·vise (to invent; see *device*)
de·void
de·vour
de·vout
dew (moisture; see *due*)
dex·ter·i·ty (–ties)
di·a·be·tes
di·a·bol·ic
di·ag·no·sis (–no·ses)
di·ag·o·nal
di·a·gram·ing, di·a·gram·ming
di·a·lect
di·a·logue
di·am·e·ter
di·a·mond
di·a·per
di·a·phragm
di·ar·rhea
di·a·ry (–ries)
di·a·tribe
di·chot·o·my (–mies)
dic·tate

dic·ta·tion
dic·ta·tor
dic·tio·nary (–nar·ies)
dic·tum (dic·ta, dic·tums)
di·dac·tic
die (to expire; see *dye*)
die·sel
di·etary
dif·fer·ence
dif·fer·en·tial
dif·fi·cult
dif·fi·dence
dif·fuse
di·gest·ible
dig·it
dig·i·tal
dig·i·tal·is
dig·ni·fy
dig·ni·tary (–tar·ies)
di·gress
di·lap·i·dat·ed
di·late
dil·a·tory
di·lem·ma
dil·et·tante
dil·i·gence
dil·ly·dal·ly
di·lute
di·men·sion
di·min·ish
di·min·u·tive
din·er (restaurant; see *dinner*)
di·nette
din·ghy (dinghies)
din·gy
din·ner (meal; see *diner*)
di·no·saur
di·ora·ma
diph·the·ria
diph·thong
di·plo·ma
di·plo·ma·cy
di·rec·tion
di·rec·tor·ate
dirge
dis·abil·i·ty
dis·ad·van·tage
dis·agree
dis·al·low
dis·ap·pear
dis·ap·pear·ance
dis·ap·point
dis·ap·prove

dis·ar·ma·ment
dis·arm·ing
dis·ar·range
dis·ar·ray
dis·as·so·ci·ate
dis·as·ter
dis·as·trous
dis·avow
dis·burse
disc, disk
dis·cern
dis·cern·ible, dis·cern·able
dis·ci·ple
dis·ci·pline
dis·claim·er
dis·clo·sure
dis·com·fort
dis·con·cert·ing
dis·con·nect
dis·con·so·late
dis·con·tin·ue
dis·cor·dant
dis·count
dis·cour·age
dis·cour·te·ous
dis·cov·ery (–er·ies)
dis·creet (showing
     discernment in speech; see
     discrete)
dis·crep·an·cy (–cies)
dis·crete (individually distinct; see
     discreet)
dis·cre·tion
dis·crim·i·nate
dis·cus (disk; see *discuss*)
dis·cuss (to talk about; see
     discus)
dis·cus·sion
dis·dain
dis·ease
dis·em·bark
dis·en·chant
dis·en·fran·chise
dis·en·gage
dis·en·tan·gle
dis·grace
dis·guise
dis·gust·ing
dis·har·mo·ny
dis·heart·en
di·shev·el
dis·hon·es·ty
dis·il·lu·sion

dis·in·cline
dis·in·fec·tant
dis·in·her·it
dis·in·te·grate
disk, disc
dis·lodge
dis·mal
dis·miss
dis·obe·di·ent
dis·obey
dis·or·ga·nized
dis·par·age
dis·pa·rate
dis·pas·sion·ate
dis·patch
dis·pel
dis·pens·able
dis·pen·sa·ry (–ries)
dis·pen·sa·tion
dis·perse
dis·plea·sure
dis·pose
dis·pos·sess
dis·pute
dis·pro·por·tion
dis·re·gard
dis·re·pair
dis·re·pute
dis·rupt
dis·sat·is·fy
dis·sect
dis·sem·ble
dis·sem·i·nate
dis·sen·sion, dis·sen·tion
dis·sent
dis·ser·ta·tion
dis·ser·vice
dis·si·dent
dis·sim·i·lar
dis·sim·u·late
dis·si·pate
dis·so·ci·ate
dis·so·lute
dis·solve
dis·so·nance
dis·suade
dis·tain
dis·tance
dis·taste·ful
dis·tem·per
dis·tinct
dis·tin·guish
dis·tor·tion

dis·tract
dis·traught
dis·tress
dis·tri·bu·tion
dis·tur·bance
dis·uni·ty
di·verge
di·verse
di·ver·si·fy
di·ver·si·ty
div·i·dend
di·vine
di·vis·i·ble
di·vi·sion
di·vi·sive
di·vorce
div·ot
di·vulge
doc·ile
dock·et
doc·tor
doc·trine
doc·u·ment
dod·der·ing
dodge
doe (female deer; see *dough*)
dog·ger·el
dog·ma
doi·ly
dole·ful
dol·lar
do·lor·ous
dol·phin
do·main
do·mes·tic
dom·i·nance
dom·i·neer
do·min·ion
dom·i·no
do·nate
don·key
do·nor
doo·dle
dor·mant
dor·mi·to·ry (–ries)
dor·sal
dos·age
dos·sier
dou·ble
doubt
doubt·ful
dough (flour mixture; money; see
     doe)

dough·nut

dour

douse, dowse

dow·a·ger

down·load

down·load·a·ble

down·ward

dow·ry (dowries)

dox·ol·o·gy (–gies)

doz·en

draft

drag·net

drag·on

drain

dra·ma

dra·mat·ic

dra·mat·i·cal·ly

drap·ery (–er·ies)

drawl

drea·ry

dredge

driv·el

driz·zle

droll

droop·ing

drop·ping

drought

drowsy

drudge

drug·gist

drunk·ard

dry

du·al (two parts; see *duel*)

du·bi·ous

duc·tile

dud·geon

due (owing; see *dew*)

du·el (combat; see *dual*)

du·et

duf·fel, duf·fle

dul·cet

dul·ci·mer

dumb·bell

dumb·found, dum·found

dun·ga·ree

dun·geon

du·plex

du·pli·cate

du·plic·i·ty (–ties)

du·ra·ble

du·ra·tion

du·ress

du·ti·ful

dwarf

dwin·dle

dye (color; see *die*)

dy·nam·ic

dy·na·mite

dy·nas·ty (–ties)

dys·en·tery (–ter·ies)

dys·lex·ia

E

ea·ger

ea·gle

ear·ache

ear·li·er

early

ear·nest

earn·ings

ear·piece

ear·ring

earth

earth·quake

ea·sel

ease·ment

eas·i·ly

east·ern

easy

eau de co·logne (French: cologne)

eaves·drop

eb·o·ny

ebul·lient

ec·cen·tric

ec·cen·tri·ci·ty

ech·e·lon

echo (ech·oes)

éclair

eclec·tic

eclipse

ecol·o·gy

eco·nom·ic

eco·nom·i·cal

eco·sys·tem

ec·sta·sy (–sies)

ec·stat·ic

ec·ze·ma

edge

edgy

ed·i·ble

edict

ed·i·fi·ca·tion

ed·i·fice

edi·tion

ed·i·tor

ed·i·to·ri·al·ize

ed·u·ca·tion

ee·rie

ef·face

ef·fect (to accomplish; see *affect*)

ef·fem·i·nate

ef·fer·ves·cence

ef·fi·ca·cious

ef·fi·ca·cy (–cies)

ef·fi·cien·cy (–cies)

ef·fi·gy (–gies)

ef·fort·less

ef·fron·tery

ef·fu·sion

egal·i·tar·i·an

ego·cen·tric

ego·tist

egre·gious

eighth

ei·ther

ejac·u·late

elab·o·rate

elapse

elas·tic

ela·tion

el·bow

el·der·ly

elec·tion

elec·tor·al

elec·tric

elec·tro·car·dio·gram

elec·tro·cute

elec·trode

elec·trol·y·sis

elec·tro·mag·net·ic

elec·tron

elec·tron·ic

el·e·gance

el·e·gy (–gies)

el·e·men·ta·ry

el·e·phant

el·e·va·tion

elev·en

elic·it (draw out; see *illicit*)

el·i·gi·ble

elim·i·nate

elite

elix·ir

el·lipse

el·o·cu·tion

elon·gate
elope
el·o·quence
elu·ci·date
elude (avoid; see *allude*)
elu·sive
ema·ci·at·ed
e-mail
em·a·nate
eman·ci·pate
emas·cu·late
em·bar·go
em·bar·ka·tion
em·bar·rass
em·bas·sy (–sies)
em·bel·lish
em·ber
em·bez·zle
em·bit·ter
em·bla·zon
em·blem
em·body
em·brace
em·broi·der
em·broi·dery (–der·ies)
em·broil
em·bryo
em·bry·ol·o·gy
em·bry·on·ic
em·cee (also M.C.)
em·er·ald
emerge
emer·gen·cy (–cies)
emer·i·tus (–ti)
em·ery (–er·ies)
em·i·grate (to leave one's
    country; see *immigrate*)
émi·gré, emi·gré
em·i·nence
em·is·sary
emis·sion
emol·lient
emol·u·ment
emo·ti·con
emo·tion
em·pa·thet·ic
em·pa·thy
em·per·or
em·pha·sis
em·pha·size
em·phat·ic
em·pire
em·pir·i·cal

em·ploy·able
em·ploy·ee
em·ploy·ment
em·po·ri·um
emp·ty
em·u·late
emul·si·fy
en·able
en·act·ment
enam·el
en·camp·ment
en·ceph·a·li·tis
    (en·ceph·a·lit·i·des)
en·chant
en·cir·cle
en·close, in·close
en·clo·sure
en·code
en·com·pass
en·core
en·coun·ter
en·cour·age
en·croach
en·cum·ber
en·cum·brance
en·cyc·li·cal
en·cy·clo·pe·dia
en·dan·ger
en·dear·ment
en·deav·or
en·dem·ic
en·dive
end·less
en·do·crine
en·do·cri·nol·o·gy
en·dorse
en·dow·ment
en·dur·ance
en·dure
en·e·ma
en·e·my (–mies)
en·er·get·ic
en·er·gize
en·er·gy
en·er·vate
en·fran·chise
en·gage
en·gage·ment
en·gen·der
en·gi·neer
en·grave
en·gross
en·gulf

en·hance
enig·ma
en·join
en·joy·ment
en·large·ment
en·light·en·ment
en·list
en·liv·en
en masse
en·mesh
en·mi·ty (–ties)
en·no·ble
enor·mous
enough
en·plane
en·rage
en·rap·ture
en·rich
en·roll·ment
en route
en·sem·ble
en·shrine
en·sign
en·slave
en·sue
en·tail
en·tan·gle
en·ter·prise
en·ter·tain
en·thrall
en·throne
en·thu·si·asm
en·tice
en·tire·ly
en·tire·ty (–ties)
en·ti·tle
en·ti·ty (–ties)
en·tomb
en·to·mol·o·gy
en·tou·rage
en·trails
en·trance
en·trant
en·treat
en·trée, en·tree
en·trench
en·tre·pre·neur
en·tre·pre·neur·ial
en·trust
en·try
en·twine
enu·mer·ate
enun·ci·ate

enun·ci·a·tion

en·vel·op (enclose completely; see *envelope*)

en·ve·lope (container for letter; see *envelop*)

en·vi·able

en·vi·ous

en·vi·ron·ment

en·vi·ron·men·tal

en·vi·ron·men·tal·ism

en·vi·rons

en·vi·sion

en·voy

en·vy

en·zyme

eon

ephem·er·al

ep·ic

ep·i·cure

ep·i·dem·ic

epi·der·mis

ep·i·gram

ep·i·gram·mat·ic

ep·i·lep·sy

ep·i·logue

ep·i·sode

ep·i·taph

ep·i·thet

epit·o·me

equa·ble

equal

equal·ize

equa·nim·i·ty (–ties)

equate

equa·tion

equa·tor

eques·tri·an

equi·dis·tant

equi·lat·er·al

equi·lib·ri·um

equine

equi·noc·tial

equi·nox

equip

equip·ment

eq·ui·ta·ble

eq·ui·ty (–ties)

equiv·a·lent

equiv·o·cate

era

erad·i·cate

eras·er (a device to remove marks; see *erasure*)

era·sure (act of erasing; see *eraser*)

er·go (Latin: therefore, hence)

er·mine

erode

erog·e·nous

ero·sion

erot·ic

err

er·rand

er·rant

er·rat·ic

er·ro·ne·ous

er·ror

er·u·dite

erup·tion

es·ca·late

es·ca·la·tor

es·ca·pade

es·cape

es·ca·role

es·chew

es·cort

es·crow

esoph·a·gus

es·o·ter·ic

es·pe·cial·ly

es·pi·o·nage

es·pla·nade

es·pouse

espres·so

es·quire

es·say (noun), es·say (verb)

es·sence

es·sen·tial

es·tab·lish

es·tate

es·teem

es·thet·ic

es·ti·ma·ble

es·ti·mate

es·trange

es·tu·ary (–ar·ies)

et cet·era (Latin: and so forth)

etch·ing

eter·nal

eter·ni·ty (–ties)

ether

ethe·re·al

Ether·net

eth·i·cal

eth·ics

eth·nic

ethos

eth·yl

eti·ol·o·gy

et·i·quette

étude

et·y·mol·o·gy (–gies)

eu·ca·lyp·tus (–ti)

eu·chre

eu·gen·ic

eu·lo·gy (–gies)

eu·nuch

eu·phe·mism

eu·phon·ic

eu·pho·ria

eu·re·ka

eu·tha·na·sia

evac·u·ate

evade

eval·u·ate

ev·a·nes·cence

evan·ge·list

evap·o·rate

eva·sion

even·tu·al·i·ty (–ties)

ev·ery·where

evict

ev·i·dent

evil

evis·cer·ate

evoc·a·tive

evoke

evo·lu·tion

evo·lu·tion·ary

evolve

ex·ac·er·bate

ex·act

ex·act·ly

ex·ag·ger·ate

ex·alt

ex·am·i·na·tion

ex·am·ple

ex·as·per·ate

ex·ca·va·tion

ex·ceed

ex·cel

ex·cel·lent

ex·cel·si·or

ex·cept (leave out; see *accept*)

ex·cep·tion·al

ex·cerpt

ex·cess

ex·ces·sive

ex·change

ex·che·quer
ex·cise
ex·cite·ment
ex·claim
ex·cla·ma·tion
ex·clude
ex·clu·sive
ex·com·mu·ni·cate
ex·cre·ment
ex·cru·ci·at·ing
ex·cur·sion
ex·cus·ably
ex·e·cute
ex·e·cut·able
ex·ec·u·tive
ex·ec·u·tor
ex·em·pla·ry
ex·em·pli·fy
ex·empt
ex·emp·tion
ex·er·cise
ex·ert
ex·ha·la·tion
ex·haust
ex·haus·tion
ex·hib·it
ex·hil·a·rate
ex·hume
ex·i·gen·cy (—cies)
ex·ile
ex·is·tence
ex·is·ten·tial·ism
ex·it
ex·o·dus
ex·on·er·ate
ex·or·bi·tant
ex·or·cise
ex·o·ter·ic
ex·ot·ic
ex·pand
ex·pand·able
ex·panse
ex·pa·tri·ate
ex·pec·tan·cy (—cies)
ex·pec·to·rate
ex·pe·di·en·cy (—cies)
ex·pe·dite
ex·pe·di·tion
ex·pe·di·tious
ex·pel
ex·pend·able
ex·pen·di·ture
ex·pense

ex·pe·ri·ence
ex·per·i·ment
ex·per·i·men·tal
ex·pert
ex·per·tise
ex·pi·ate
ex·pi·ra·tion
ex·plain
ex·plan·a·tory
ex·ple·tive
ex·pli·ca·ble
ex·plic·it
ex·plode
ex·ploi·ta·tion
ex·plore
ex·plor·a·to·ry
ex·plo·sion
ex·po·nent
ex·port (noun), ex·port (verb)
ex·pose (to disclose; see *exposé*)
ex·po·sé (a statement; see
    expose)
ex·po·si·tion
ex·pos·tu·late
ex·po·sure
ex·pound
ex·press
ex·pres·sion
ex·press·way
ex·pro·pri·ate
ex·pul·sion
ex·punge
ex·pur·gate
ex·qui·site
ex·tant
ex·tem·po·ra·ne·ous
ex·tem·po·rize
ex·tend
ex·ten·sion
ex·ten·sive
ex·tent
ex·ten·u·ate
ex·te·ri·or
ex·ter·mi·nate
ex·ter·nal
ex·tinct
ex·tin·guish
ex·tir·pate
ex·tol
ex·tort
ex·tra
ex·tract
ex·tra·cur·ric·u·lar

ex·tra·dite
ex·tra·mar·i·tal
ex·tra·ne·ous
ex·tra·or·di·nary
ex·trap·o·late
ex·tra·sen·so·ry
ex·tra·ter·res·tri·al
ex·trav·a·gance
ex·treme
ex·trem·i·ty (—ties)
ex·tri·cate
ex·trin·sic
ex·tro·vert, ex·tra·vert
ex·u·ber·ance
ex·u·ber·ant
ex·ude

F

fa·ble
fab·ric
fab·ri·cate
fab·u·lous
fa·cade
face
fac·et
fa·ce·tious
fa·cial
fac·ile
fa·cil·i·tate
fa·cil·i·tat·or
fa·cil·i·ty (—ties)
fac·sim·i·le
fac·tion
fac·to·ry (—ries)
fac·tu·al
fac·ul·ty (—ties)
Fahr·en·heit
fail·ure
faint (lose consciousness; see
    feint)
fairy
fait ac·com·pli (French:
    accomplished fact)
faith·ful
fak·er
fal·con
fall
fal·la·cious
fal·la·cy (—cies)
fal·li·ble
fal·low

false·ly
fal·set·to
fal·si·fy
fal·ter
fa·mil·iar
fa·mil·iar·ity
fa·mil·iar·ize
fam·i·ly (–lies)
fam·ine
fam·ish
fa·mous
fa·nat·ic
fa·nat·i·cism
fan·ci·ful
fan·fare
fan·tasm, phan·tasm
fan·tas·tic
fan·ta·sy (–sies)
farce
far·ci·cal
fare·well
farm·er
far·ther
fas·ci·nate
fas·cism
fash·ion·able
fas·ten
fas·tid·i·ous
fa·tal
fate
fa·ther
fath·om
fa·tigue
fat·ten
fau·cet
fault·less
faun (mythological being; see *fawn*)
fau·na
faux (French: fake)
faux pas (French: a social blunder)
fa·vor·able
fawn (young deer; see *faun*)
fear·ful
fea·si·ble
feast
feat (deed; see *feet*)
feath·er
fea·ture
fed·er·al
fee·ble
feet (plural of foot; see *feat*)

feign
feint (something feigned; see *faint*)
fe·line
fel·low·ship
fel·o·ny
fe·male
fem·i·nine
fence
fe·ral
fer·ment
fe·ro·cious
fer·ret
fer·ry (–ries)
fer·tile
fer·til·ize
fer·vent
fer·vid
fer·vor
fes·ti·val
fes·toon
fe·tal
fet·id
fe·tus
feud
feu·dal
fe·ver
few
fi·an·cé (French: engaged man)
fi·an·cée (French: engaged woman)
fi·as·co
fi·ber·glass
fi·bro·my·al·gic
fick·le
fic·tion
fic·ti·tious
fid·dle
fi·del·i·ty (–ties)
fid·get
fi·du·cia·ry (–ries)
field
fiend
fierce
fi·ery
fi·es·ta
fifth
fif·ti·eth
fight
fig·ment
fig·ure
fig·u·rine
fil·a·ment

fil·ial
fil·i·bus·ter
fil·i·gree
fil·let, fi·let
fil·ly (fillies)
film
fil·ter
fi·nal
fi·na·le
fi·nance
fi·nan·cier
fi·nesse
fin·ger·print
fi·nis (French: end)
fin·ish
fi·nite
fir·ma·ment
first
fis·cal
fis·sure
fix·ture
flac·cid
flag·pole
fla·grant
flair (natural aptitude; see *flare*)
flam·boy·ant
fla·min·go
flam·ma·ble
flan·nel
flap·per
flare (unsteady glaring light; see *flair*)
flat·tery (–ter·ies)
flaunt
fla·vor
flaw·less
flax·en
flea (insect; see *flee*)
fledg·ling
flee (to run from; see *flea*)
fleece
flew (past tense of fly; see *flue, flu*)
flex·i·ble
fli·er
flight
flir·ta·tion
float·ing
floc·cu·lent
flock
flog
flood·light
floor·board

flor·al
flo·res·cence
flo·ri·cul·ture
flor·id
flo·rist
flo·ta·tion
flo·til·la
flot·sam
flounce
floun·der
flour (from grain; see *flower*)
flour·ish
flow·chart
flow·er (blossom; see *flour*)
fluc·tu·ate
flu
flue (air channel; see *flew*)
flu·ent
flu·id
flu·o·res·cent
flu·o·ri·date
flu·o·ri·nate
flu·o·ro·scope
flute
fly (flies)
fo·cal
fo·cus (–cus·es *or* –ci)
foe
foi·ble
fold·er
fo·liage
fo·lio
folk
fol·li·cle
fol·low
fol·ly (follies)
fo·ment
fon·dle
fon·due
food
fool·ish
foot·age
foot·note
for·age
for·ay
for·bear·ance
for·bid·den
force
for·ceps
forc·ible
fore·bear, for·bear
fore·cast
fore·clo·sure

fore·ground
for·eign
fore·man
fore·most
fo·ren·sic
for·est·ry
fore·word (preface; see *forward*)
for·ev·er
for·feit
forg·ery (–ies)
for·get·ful
for·give·ness
for·giv·ing
for·go, fore·go
for·got·ten
fork
for·lorn
form·al·de·hyde
for·mal·i·ty (–ties)
for·mal·ly (following established
    custom; see *formerly*)
for·mat
for·ma·tion
for·ma·tive
for·mer·ly (at an earlier time; see
    formally)
for·mi·da·ble
for·mu·la (–las *or* –lae)
for·mu·late
for·syth·ia
fort (fortified place; see *forte*)
forte (one's strong point; see *fort*)
forth (forward; see *fourth*)
forth·right
for·ti·eth
for·ti·fi·ca·tion
for·tis·si·mo
for·ti·tude
fort·night
for·tress
for·tu·i·tous
for·tu·nate
fo·rum
for·ward (in front; see *foreword*)
fos·sil
fos·sil·ize
fos·ter
foul (offensive to the senses; see
    fowl)
foun·da·tion
found·ry (–ries)
foun·tain
four

fourth (numeric order; see *forth*)
fowl (bird; see *foul*)
foy·er
frac·tion
frac·ture
frag·ile
frag·ment
fra·grant
frail
fran·chise
frank·fur·ter
frank·in·cense
fran·tic
frap·pe, frap·pé
fra·ter·ni·ty (–ties)
fraud
fraud·u·lent
fraught
free·dom
free·lance
freeze (turn into ice; see *frieze*)
freight
fre·net·ic, phre·net·ic
fren·zy (fren·zies)
fre·quent (adjective), fre·quent
    (verb)
fresh·man (–men)
Freud·ian
fri·ar (monk; see *fryer*)
fric·as·see
fric·tion
friend
frieze (architectural decoration;
    see *freeze*)
frig·ate
fright·en
fringe
frisky
frit·ter
friv·o·lous
frol·ic
front·age
fron·tier
fron·tis·piece
fro·zen
fru·gal
fru·i·tion
fruit·ful
frus·trate
fry·er (something intended for
    frying; see *friar*)
fuch·sia
fu·el

fu·gi·tive
fugue
ful·crum
ful·fill, ful·fil
ful·some
fu·mi·gate
func·tion·al
fun·da·men·tal
fu·ner·al
fu·ne·re·al
fun·nel
fu·ri·ous
furl
fur·lough
fur·nace
fur·ni·ture
fu·ror
fur·ri·er
fur·row
fur·ther
fur·tive
fuse
fu·se·lage
fus·ible
fu·sion
fu·tile
fu·til·i·ty (–ties)
fu·ture
fu·tur·is·tic

G

gab·er·dine
gad·get
gai·ety (–eties)
gain·ful·ly
gait (manner of walking; see *gate*)
gala
gal·axy (gal·ax·ies)
gal·lant
gal·lery (–ries)
gal·ley
gall·ing
gal·lon
gal·lop
ga·lore
ga·losh (–es)
gal·lows
gal·va·nize
gam·bit
gam·ble

game·keep·er
gam·ut
gan·der
gan·gli·on (gan·glia)
gan·grene
ga·rage
gar·bage
gar·ble
gar·den·er
gar·de·nia
gar·gan·tuan
gar·goyle
gar·ish
gar·land
gar·ment
gar·ner
gar·nish
gar·nish·ee
gar·ri·son
gas·eous
gas·ket
gas·o·line
gas·tric
gas·tron·o·my
gate (opening in wall *or* fence; see *gait*)
gath·er·ing
gauche
gaudy
gauge
gaunt
gaunt·let
gauze
gav·el
ga·ze·bo
ga·zelle
ga·zette
gei·sha
gel·a·tin
gene
ge·ne·al·o·gy (–gies)
gen·er·al·i·ty (–ties)
gen·er·ate
gen·er·a·tion
gen·er·a·tor
gen·er·ic
gen·er·ous
genes
gen·e·sis (–e·ses)
ge·net·ic
ge·net·i·cal·ly
ge·nial
gen·i·tal

ge·nius (–nius·es *or* –nii)
gen·o·cide
genre
gen·teel
gen·tile
gen·til·i·ty (–ties)
gen·tle·man (–men)
gen·try
gen·u·flect
gen·u·ine
ge·og·ra·phy (–phies)
ge·ol·o·gy
ge·om·e·try (–tries)
ge·ra·ni·um
ge·ri·at·rics
ger·mane
ger·mi·cide
ger·mi·na·tion
ger·on·tol·o·gy
gest
ges·ta·tion
ges·tic·u·late
ges·ture
gey·ser
ghast·ly
ghet·to (ghettos *or* ghettoes)
ghoul·ish
gi·ant
gib·ber·ish
gibe
gib·lets
gift
gi·gan·tic
gig·o·lo
gild (to overlay with a thin covering of gold or something similar; see *gilt*)
gilt (covered with gold, or with something that resembles gold; see *gild*)
gim·mick
gin·ger
gi·raffe
gird·er
gir·dle
girth
gist
giz·zard
gla·cial
gla·cier
glad·i·a·tor
glad·i·o·la
glam·or·ous

glam·our, glam·or
glan·du·lar
glass·ware
glau·co·ma
gla·zier
glib
glim·mer
glimpse
glis·ten
glitch
glob·al
glob·al·i·za·tion
glob·u·lar
gloomy
glo·ri·ous
glos·sa·ry (–ries)
glossy (gloss·ies)
glove
glu·cose
glue
glut·ton
glyc·er·in
gnarl
gnash
gnat
gnaw
gnome
gnu (African antelope; see *knew* and *new*)
goal
gob·let
gog·gles
goi·ter
gold·en
golf (a game; see *gulf*)
gon·do·la
good·will
go·pher
gor·geous
go·ril·la (an ape; see *guerrilla*)
gos·sa·mer
gos·sip
gouge
gou·lash
gourd
gour·met
gout
gov·ern·ment
gov·er·nor
gra·cious
gra·da·tion
gra·di·ent
grad·u·al

grad·u·ate
grad·u·a·tion
graph·ics
grain
gram·mar
gram·mat·i·cal·ly
gra·na·ry (–ries)
gran·deur
grand·fa·ther
gran·di·ose
grand·mo·ther
gran·ite
grant
gran·u·late
graph·ic
graph·ite
grap·ple
grate (rasp noisily; see *great*)
grate·ful
grat·i·fy
grat·i·tude
gra·tu·itous
gra·tu·ity (–i·ties)
grav·i·tate
grav·i·ty (–ties)
great (large; see *grate*)
greedy
gre·gar·i·ous
grem·lin
gre·nade
gren·a·dine
grey·hound
grid·dle
grid·iron
griev·ance
griev·ous
gri·mace
grime
grippe
gris·ly (inspiring horror; see *grizzly*)
griz·zly (bear; see *grisly*)
groan
gro·cery (–cer·ies)
gro·tesque
grot·to (–toes)
group
grouse (grouse *or* grouses)
grov·el
grudge
gru·el
gruel·ing
grue·some

grum·ble
grun·gy
guar·an·tee (assurance of quality; see *guaranty*)
guaranty (something given as security; see *guarantee*)
guard
guard·ian
gu·ber·na·to·ri·al
guer·ril·la (one who engages in irregular warfare; see *gorilla*)
guess
guest
guid·ance
guild
guile
guil·lo·tine
guilt
guise
gui·tar
gulf (part of an ocean, a chasm; see *golf*)
gul·li·ble
gul·ly (–lies)
gur·gle
gu·ru
gut·tur·al
guz·zle
gym·na·si·um
gym·nast
gy·ne·col·o·gy
gyp·sum
gyp·sy
gy·rate
gy·ro·scope

H

ha·be·as cor·pus (Latin: legal writ to bring a person before a court)
hab·er·dash·ery (–er·ies)
hab·it·able
hab·i·tat
ha·bit·u·al
hack·ney
had·dock
hag·gard
hag·gle
hail (greet; see *hale*)
hair (threadlike outgrowth on skin; see *hare*)

hal·cy·on
hale (free from disease; see *hail*)
half
hal·i·but
hal·i·to·sis
hal·low
Hal·low·een
hal·lu·ci·na·tion
hal·lu·ci·no·gen
halve
ham·burg·er
ham·mer
ham·mock
ham·per
hand·i·cap
hand·i·craft
hand·ker·chief
han·dle
hand·some (pleasing appear-
    ance; see *hansom*)
handy
han·gar (place for housing
    aircraft; see *hanger*)
hang·er (device on which
    something is hung; see
    hangar)
han·som (cab; see *handsome*)
hap·haz·ard
hap·pen
hap·pi·ness
hap·py
ha·rangue
ha·rass
har·bin·ger
har·bor
hard·ly
hard·ship
har·dy
hard·ware
hare (animal resembling rabbit;
    see *hair*)
har·em
harm·less
har·mon·ic
har·mo·ni·ous
har·mo·ny (–nies)
har·ness
har·poon
harp·si·chord
har·row·ing
har·ry
har·vest
hash·ish

has·sock
hatch·et
hate·ful
ha·tred
haugh·ty
haul
haunch
haunt
ha·ven
hav·oc
haw·thorn
haz·ard·ous
haze
ha·zel
head·ache
head·quar·ters
head·set
heal (restore to health; see *heel*)
heal·er
health·ful
healthy
hear (listen; see *here*)
hear·ken
hearse
heart
heart·ache
hearth
heart·i·ly
heat
heath
heath·er
heav·en
heavy
heck·le
hec·tic
hedge
he·do·nism
heed·less
heel (part of foot; see *heal*)
hefty
heif·er
height
hei·nous
heir
heir·loom
heist
he·li·cop·ter
he·li·um
help·ful
hemi·sphere
hem·lock
he·mo·phil·ia
hem·or·rhage

hem·or·rhoid
hence·forth
hen·na
hep·a·ti·tis
her·ald
herb
herb·al
herb·al·ist
Her·cu·le·an
here (in this place; see *hear*)
he·red·i·tary
her·e·sy (–sies)
her·e·tic
her·i·tage
her·maph·ro·dite
her·met·ic
her·mit
her·nia
her·o·in (drug; see *heroine*)
her·o·ine (central figure in drama;
    see *heroin*)
her·on
her·ring·bone
hes·i·tate
het·ero·dox
het·er·o·ge·neous
het·ero·sex·u·al
hew (to cut by blows; see *hue*)
hexa·gon
hex·am·e·ter
hi·a·tus
hi·ba·chi
hi·ber·nate
hi·bis·cus
hic·cough, hic·cup
hid·eous
hi·er·ar·chy (–chies)
hi·ero·glyph·ic
high·er (more elevated, taller; see
    hire)
hi·jack
hi·lar·i·ous
hin·drance
hinge
hip·po·drome
hip·po·pot·a·mus (–mus·es *or*
    –mi)
hire (employ, wage; see *higher*)
his·ta·mine
his·to·ri·an
his·tor·i·cal
his·to·ry (–ries)
his·tri·on·ic

hith·er·to

hives

hoard

hoarse

hoax

hob·ble

hock·ey

ho·cus-po·cus

hodge·podge

hoe

hoist

ho·li·ness

ho·lis·tic

hol·lan·daise

hol·low

ho·lo·caust

ho·lo·gram

ho·lo·graph

hol·ster

hom·age

home·ly

ho·meo·path

ho·me·op·a·thy

ho·mi·cide

hom·i·ly (–lies)

ho·mo·ge·neous

ho·mog·e·nize

hom·onym

ho·mo·sex·u·al

hon·es·ty (–ties)

hon·ey

hon·or

hon·o·rar·i·um

hon·or·ary (–ar·ies)

hood·lum

hoo·li·gan

hope

hop·ing (longing for; see *hopping*)

hop·ping (jumping; see *hoping*)

horde

ho·ri·zon

hor·i·zon·tal

hor·mone

horo·scope

hor·ren·dous

hor·ri·ble

hor·rid

hor·ror

hors d'oeuvre (French: appetizers)

horse

hor·ti·cul·ture

ho·siery

hos·pi·tal

hos·tage

hos·tel

host·ess

hos·tile

ho·tel

hour (time; see *our*)

house·hold

hov·el

hov·er

howl

huck·le·ber·ry (–ries)

huck·ster

hue (complexion, see *hew*)

huge

hu·mane

hu·man·i·tar·i·an

hu·man·i·ty

hu·man·ize

hum·ble

hu·mid

hu·mi·dor

hu·mil·i·ate

hu·mil·i·ty

hu·mor

hu·mor·ous

hu·mus

hun·dredth

hun·ger

hur·dle

hurl

hur·ri·cane

hur·ried

hur·tle

hus·band

hus·ky (–kies)

hus·tle

hy·a·cinth

hy·brid

hy·dran·gea

hy·drant

hy·drate

hy·drau·lic

hy·dro·chlo·ric

hy·dro·elec·tric

hy·dro·gen

hy·drom·e·ter

hy·dro·pho·bia

hy·drox·ide

hy·giene

hy·gien·ic

hy·men

hymn

hy·per·bo·le

hy·per·ten·sion

hy·per·ven·ti·la·tion

hy·phen

hy·phen·ate

hyp·no·sis (–ses)

hyp·no·tism

hy·po·chon·dria

hy·poc·ri·sy (–sies)

hy·po·crite

hy·po·der·mic

hy·pot·e·nuse, hy·poth·e·nuse

hy·poth·e·sis (–ses)

hy·poth·e·size

hy·po·thet·i·cal

hys·ter·ec·to·my (–mies)

hys·te·ria

I

ice·berg

ice floe

ici·cle

ic·ing

icy

icon

icon·o·clast

idea

ide·al

iden·ti·cal

iden·ti·fi·ca·tion

iden·ti·fy

ide·ol·o·gy, ide·al·o·gy (–gies)

id·i·o·cy (–cies)

id·i·om

id·i·om·at·ic

id·io·syn·cra·sy (–sies)

id·i·ot

idle (not occupied; see *idol, idyll*)

idol (symbolic object of worship; see *idle, idyll*)

idol·a·try (–tries)

idol·ize

idyll, idyl (narrative poem; see *idle, idol*)

ig·loo

ig·ne·ous

ig·nite

ig·ni·tion

ig·no·ble

ig·no·min·i·ous

ig·no·rance

ig·nore
igua·na
il·le·gal
il·leg·i·ble
il·le·git·i·mate
ill·got·ten
il·lib·er·al
il·lic·it (not permitted; see *elicit*)
il·lit·er·ate
ill·ness
il·log·i·cal
il·lu·mi·na·tion
il·lu·sion (misleading
   image; see *allusion*)
il·lu·so·ry
il·lus·trate
il·lus·tra·tion
il·lus·tri·ous
im·age
imag·in·able
imag·i·na·tive
imag·ine
im·bal·ance
im·be·cile
im·bibe
im·bue
im·i·ta·tion
im·i·ta·tive
im·mac·u·late
im·ma·nent (inherent; see
   imminent)
im·ma·te·ri·al
im·ma·ture
im·mea·sur·able
im·me·di·ate
im·me·mo·ri·al
im·mense
im·merse
im·mer·sion
im·mi·grate (to come into a
   country; see *emigrate*)
im·mi·nent (ready to take place;
   see *immanent*)
im·mo·bile
im·mod·er·ate
im·mod·est
im·mo·late
im·mor·al
im·mor·tal
im·mov·able
im·mune
im·mu·ni·ty (–ties)
im·pact (noun), im·pact (verb)
im·pair

im·pale
im·pal·pa·ble
im·par·tial
im·pass·able
im·passe
im·pas·sioned
im·pas·sive
im·pa·tience
im·peach
im·pec·ca·ble
im·pede
im·ped·i·ment
im·pel
im·pend·ing
im·pen·e·tra·ble
im·per·a·tive
im·per·cep·ti·ble
im·per·fect
im·pe·ri·al
im·pe·ri·ous
im·per·ish·able
im·per·ma·nence
im·per·me·able
im·per·mis·si·ble
im·per·son·al
im·per·son·ate
im·per·ti·nent
im·per·vi·ous
im·pet·u·ous
im·pe·tus
im·pi·ety (–eties)
im·pinge
im·pi·ous
imp·ish
im·pla·ca·ble
im·plant
im·plau·si·ble
im·ple·ment
im·pli·cate
im·pli·ca·tion
im·plic·it
im·plore
im·ply
im·po·lite
im·pol·i·tic
im·pon·der·a·ble
im·port
im·por·tance
im·pose
im·po·si·tion
im·pos·si·bil·i·ty (–ties)
im·pos·si·ble
im·pos·tor, im·pos·ter
im·pos·ture

im·po·tent
im·pound
im·pov·er·ish
im·prac·ti·ca·ble
im·prac·ti·cal
im·pre·cate
im·pre·cise
im·preg·na·ble
im·pre·sa·rio
im·press
im·pres·sive
im·pri·ma·tur
im·print
im·pris·on·ment
im·prob·a·ble
im·promp·tu
im·prop·er
im·pro·pri·ety (–eties)
im·prove·ment
im·prov·i·dent
im·pro·vise
im·pru·dent
im·pu·dent
im·pugn
im·pulse
im·pu·ni·ty (–ties)
im·pu·ri·ty (–ties)
in·abil·i·ty (–ties)
in ab·sen·tia
in·ac·ces·si·ble
in·ac·cu·ra·cy (–cies)
in·ac·tive
in·ad·e·qua·cy (–cies)
in·ad·e·quate
in·ad·mis·si·ble
in·ad·ver·tent
in·ad·vis·able
in·alien·able
in·al·ter·able
inane
in·an·i·mate
in·ap·pli·ca·ble
in·ap·pro·pri·ate
in·ar·tic·u·late
in·ar·tis·tic
in·at·ten·tive
in·au·di·ble
in·au·gu·ral
in·au·gu·rate
in·aus·pi·cious
in·born
in·cal·cu·la·ble
in·can·des·cent
in·can·ta·tion

in·ca·pa·ble
in·ca·pac·i·tate
in·car·cer·ate
in·car·nate
in·cau·tious
in·cen·di·ary (–ar·ies)
in·cense
in·cen·tive
in·cep·tion
in·ces·sant
in·ci·den·tal·ly
in·cin·er·ate
in·cip·i·ent
in·cise
in·ci·sion
in·ci·sive
in·cite (to stir up; see *insight*)
in·clem·ent
in·cli·na·tion
in·cline
in·close, en·close
in·clude
in·cog·ni·to
in·co·her·ent
in·com·bus·ti·ble
in·come
in·com·men·su·ra·ble
in·com·pa·ra·ble
in·com·pat·i·ble
in·com·pe·tence
in·com·plete
in·com·pre·hen·si·ble
in·con·ceiv·able
in·con·clu·sive
in·con·gru·ous
in·con·se·quen·tial
in·con·sid·er·ate
in·con·sist·tent
in·con·sol·able
in·con·spic·u·ous
in·con·stant
in·con·test·able
in·con·tro·vert·ible
in·con·ve·nient
in·cor·por·ate
in·cor·rect
in·cor·ri·gi·ble
in·cor·rupt·ible
in·crease
in·creas·ing·ly
in·cred·i·ble
in·cred·i·bly
in·cre·du·li·ty
in·cred·u·lous

in·cre·ment
in·crim·i·nate
in·cu·bate
in·cu·ba·tor
in·cu·bus (–bus·es *or* –bi)
in·cul·cate
in·cum·bent
in·cur
in·cur·able
in·debt·ed
in·de·cent
in·de·ci·pher·able
in·de·ci·sion
in·de·fen·si·ble
in·de·fin·able
in·def·i·nite
in·del·i·ble
in·del·i·cate
in·dem·ni·fy
in·den·ta·tion
in·de·pen·dent
in·de·scrib·able
in·de·struc·ti·ble
in·de·ter·min·able
in·dex (in·dex·es *or* in·di·ces)
in·di·cate
in·dict (charge with offence; see
     indite)
in·dif·fer·ent
in·dig·e·nous
in·di·gent
in·di·gest·ible
in·di·ges·tion
in·dig·nant
in·dig·ni·ty (–ties)
in·di·go (–gos *or* –goes)
in·di·rect
in·dis·creet
in·dis·cre·tion
in·dis·crim·i·nate
in·dis·pens·able
in·dis·pose
in·dis·put·able
in·dis·sol·u·ble
in·dis·tinct
in·dis·tin·guish·able
in·dite (to put down in writing; see
     indict)
in·di·vid·u·al
in·di·vid·u·al·i·ty
in·di·vis·i·ble
in·doc·tri·nate
in·do·lence
in·dom·i·ta·ble

in·du·bi·ta·ble
in·duce
in·duct
in·dulge
in·dul·gence
in·dus·tri·al·ist
in·dus·try (–tries)
ine·bri·ate
in·ed·i·ble
in·ef·fa·ble
in·ef·fec·tive
in·ef·fec·tu·al
in·ef·fi·cien·cy (–cies)
in·elas·tic
in·el·i·gi·ble
in·ept
in·ep·ti·tude
in·equal·i·ty (–ties)
in·eq·ui·ta·ble
in·eq·ui·ty
in·ert
in·er·tia
in·es·cap·able
in·es·ti·ma·ble
in·ev·i·ta·ble
in·ex·cus·able
in·ex·haust·ible
in·ex·o·ra·ble
in·ex·pe·di·ent
in·ex·pen·sive
in·ex·pe·ri·enced
in·ex·pert
in·ex·pli·ca·ble
in·ex·press·ible
in·ex·tin·guish·able
in·ex·tri·ca·ble
in·fal·li·ble
in·fa·mous
in·fan·cy (–cies)
in·fan·tile
in·fan·try (–tries)
in·fat·u·a·tion
in·fec·tion
in·fec·tious
in·fer
in·fer·ence
in·fe·ri·or·i·ty (–ties)
in·fer·nal
in·fer·no
in·ferred
in·fer·tile
in·fi·del·i·ty (–ties)
in·field
in·fil·trate

in·fi·nite
in·fin·i·tes·i·mal
in·fin·i·tive
in·fin·i·ty (–ties)
in·fir·ma·ry (–ries)
in·fir·mi·ty (–ties)
in·flame
in·flam·ma·ble
in·flam·ma·tion
in·flate
in·fla·tion
in·flec·tion
in·flex·i·ble
in·flict
in·flu·ence
in·flu·en·za
in·flux
in·for·mal
in·for·ma·tion
in·form·er
in·frac·tion
in·fra·red
in·fra·struc·ture
in·fre·quent
in·fringe
in·fu·ri·ate
in·fuse
in·fu·sion
in·ge·nious (clever; see
    ingenuous)
in·ge·nu·ity (–ities)
in·gen·u·ous (showing childlike
    simplicity; see *ingenious*)
in·gest
in·glo·ri·ous
in·got
in·grained
in·grate
in·gra·ti·ate
in·grat·i·tude
in·gre·di·ent
in·gress
in·hab·it
in·hab·it·ant
in·ha·la·tion
in·hale
in·her·ent
in·her·i·tance
in·hib·it
in·hi·bi·tion
in·hos·pi·ta·ble
in·hu·man
in·hu·mane
in·im·i·cal

in·im·i·ta·ble
in·iq·ui·ty (–ties)
ini·tial
ini·tiate
ini·tia·tive
in·jec·tion
in·ju·di·cious
in·junc·tion
in·jure
in·ju·ri·ous
in·ju·ry (–ries)
in·jus·tice
in·kling
in·land
in·let
in·mate
in me·mo·ri·am
in·nate
in·ning
in·no·cent
in·noc·u·ous
in·no·vate
in·no·va·tor
in·nu·en·do (–dos *or* –does)
in·nu·mer·able
in·oc·u·late
in·of·fen·sive
in·op·er·a·ble
in·op·er·a·tive
in·op·por·tune
in·or·di·nate
in·or·gan·ic
in·quest
in·quire
in·qui·si·tion
in·quis·i·tive
in·road
in·sane
in·san·i·ty (–ties)
in·sa·tia·ble
in·scribe
in·scrip·tion
in·scru·ta·ble
in·sec·ti·cide
in·se·cure
in·sem·i·na·tion
in·sen·sate
in·sen·si·ble
in·sen·si·tive
in·sep·a·ra·ble
in·sert
in·side
in·sid·i·ous

in·sight (act of apprehending inner
    nature of things; see *incite*)
in·sig·nia, in·sig·ne (–nia *or*
    –ni·as)
in·sig·nif·i·cant
in·sin·cere
in·sin·u·ate
in·sip·id
in·sist
in·sis·tence
in·sole
in·so·lent
in·sol·u·ble
in·solv·able
in·sol·vent
in·som·nia
in·spec·tor
in·spi·ra·tion
in·sta·bil·i·ty
in·stall, in·stal
in·stant
in·stan·ta·neous
in·stead
in·step
in·sti·gate
in·stinct
in·sti·tute
in·struct
in·stru·ment
in·sub·or·di·nate
in·sub·stan·tial
in·suf·fer·able
in·suf·fi·cient
in·su·lar
in·su·late
in·su·lin
in·sult
in·su·per·a·ble
in·sup·port·able
in·sup·press·ible
in·sur·ance
in·sur·gent
in·sur·mount·able
in·sur·rec·tion
in·tact
in·tan·gi·ble
in·te·ger
in·te·gral
in·te·grate
in·teg·ri·ty
in·tel·lect
in·tel·li·gence
in·tel·li·gent·sia
in·tel·li·gi·ble

in·tem·per·ate
in·tend
in·tense
in·ten·tion·al
in·ter
in·ter·ac·tion
in·ter·cede
in·ter·cept
in·ter·ces·sion
in·ter·change·able
in·ter·com·mu·ni·ca·tion
in·ter·con·nect
in·ter·course
in·ter·de·part·men·tal
in·ter·dict
in·ter·est
in·ter·fere
in·ter·fer·ence
in·ter·im
in·te·ri·or
in·ter·ject
in·ter·line
in·ter·lin·ear
in·ter·lock
in·ter·lop·er
in·ter·lude
in·ter·mar·ry
in·ter·me·di·ary (–ar·ies)
in·ter·me·di·ate
in·ter·mez·zo (–zi or –zos)
in·ter·mi·na·ble
in·ter·mis·sion
in·ter·mit·tent
in·ter·mix
in·tern (noun), in·tern (verb)
in·ter·nal
in·ter·nal·ize
in·ter·na·tion·al
in·tern
In·ter·net
in·tern·ment
in·ter·pose
in·ter·pret
in·ter·pre·tive
in·ter·ra·cial
in·ter·ro·gate
in·ter·rupt
in·ter·sect
in·ter·ses·sion
in·ter·sperse
in·ter·state
in·ter·stel·lar
in·ter·stice
in·ter·val

in·ter·vene
in·ter·view
in·tes·tine
in·ti·ma·cy (–cies)
in·ti·mate
in·tim·i·date
in·tol·er·a·ble
in·tol·er·ant
in·to·na·tion
in·tox·i·cate
in·trac·ta·ble
in·tra·mu·ral
in·tran·si·gent
in·tran·si·tive
in·tra·ve·nous
in·trep·id
in·tri·ca·cy (–cies)
in·tri·cate
in·trigue
in·trin·sic
in·tro·duce
in·tro·spec·tion
in·tro·ver·sion
in·tro·vert
in·tru·sion
in·tu·ition
in·tu·itive
in·un·date
in·val·id
in·valu·able
in·vari·able
in·va·sion
in·vec·tive
in·veigh
in·ven·tion
in·ven·to·ry (–ries)
in·verse
in·ver·te·brate
in·ves·ti·ga·tor
in·ves·ti·ture
in·ves·tor
in·vet·er·ate
in·vig·o·rate
in·vin·ci·ble
in·vi·o·la·ble
in·vis·i·ble
in·vi·ta·tion
in·vo·ca·tion
in·voice
in·voke
in·vol·un·tary
in·volve
in·vul·ner·a·ble
in·ward

io·dine
ion
io·ta
iras·ci·ble
irate
ire
ir·i·des·cence
iris (iris·es or iri·des)
irk·some
iron
ir·ra·di·a·tion
ir·ra·tio·nal
ir·rec·on·cil·able
ir·re·cov·er·able
ir·re·deem·able
ir·re·duc·ible
ir·re·fut·able
ir·reg·u·lar
ir·rel·e·van·cy (–cies)
ir·rel·e·vant
ir·rep·a·ra·ble
ir·re·place·able
ir·re·proach·able
ir·re·sist·ible
ir·res·o·lute
ir·re·spec·tive
ir·re·spon·si·ble
ir·re·triev·able
ir·rev·er·ent
ir·re·vers·ible
ir·rev·o·ca·ble
ir·ri·gate
ir·ri·ta·ble
ir·ri·tate
is·land
isle
iso·late
isos·ce·les
iso·tope
is·sue
ital·ic
item·ize
itin·er·ary (–ar·ies)
it's
its
ivo·ry (–ries)
ivy (ivies)

J

jab·ber
jack·et
jade

jag·ged
jag·uar
jail·er, jail·or
ja·lopy (jalopies)
jam·bo·ree
jan·gle
jan·i·tor
jar·gon
jas·mine
jaun·dice
jaunt
jav·e·lin
jeal·ous
jeans (denim pants; see *genes*)
jeer
jel·ly (jel·lies)
jeop·ar·dize
jer·sey
jest
jet·pro·pelled
jet·ti·son
jet·ty (jetties)
jew·el·ry
jibe, gibe
jig·ger
jit·ney
jock·ey
joc·u·lar
jog·ging
join·ing
joint
jos·tle
jour·nal
jour·nal·ism
jour·ney
joust
jo·vial
joy·ful
joy·ous
ju·bi·lant
ju·bi·lee
judge
judg·ment, judge·ment
ju·di·ca·ture
ju·di·cial
ju·di·cia·ry
ju·di·cious
jug·gler
jug·u·lar
juicy
ju·jit·su, ju·jut·su
juke·box
ju·lep
ju·li·enne

jum·ble
jum·bo
jump
junc·tion
junc·ture
jun·gle
ju·nior
ju·ni·per
jun·ket
jun·ta
ju·ris·dic·tion
ju·ris·pru·dence
ju·rist
ju·ror
jus·tice
jus·ti·fi·able
jus·ti·fi·ca·tion
ju·ve·nile
jux·ta·pose

K

ka·lei·do·scope
kan·ga·roo
kar·a·kul
kar·at, car·at
ka·ra·te
kay·ak
kayo
keel
keen
keen·ness
keep·sake
kelp
ken·nel
kept
ker·chief
ker·nel (inner part of a seed; see *colonel*)
ker·o·sene, ker·o·sine
ketch·up, cat·sup
ket·tle
kha·ki
ki·bosh
kid·nap
kid·nap·per
kid·ney
kiln
ki·lo·gram
kilo·li·ter
ki·lo·me·ter
kilo·watt
kil·ter

ki·mo·no
kin·der·gar·ten
kin·dle
kind·li·ness
kin·dling
kin·dred
kin·e·scope
kin·es·thet·ic
ki·net·ic
ki·osk
kitch·en·ette
klep·to·ma·ni·ac
knack
knap·sack
knave (tricky fellow; see *nave*)
knead (press into a mass; see *need*)
knee
kneel
knell
knew (past tense of know; see *gnu, new*)
knife (knives)
knight (feudal nobleman; see *night*)
knob
knoll
knot
knowl·edge
knowl·edge·able
knuck·le
ko·ala
ko·sher
ku·dos
kum·quat

L

la·bel
la·bor
lab·o·ra·to·ry (–ries)
la·bo·ri·ous
lab·y·rinth
lac·er·ate
lack·ey
lack·lus·ter
la·con·ic
lac·quer
lad·der
la·den
lad·ing
la·dle
la·ger

lag·gard

la·gniappe

la·goon

lair

lais·sez-faire (French: doctrine of individual freedom)

la·ity

lam·baste, lam·bast

lame (cripple; see *lamé*)

lamé (fabric; see *lame*)

la·men·ta·ble

lam·i·nate

lamp·light

lam·poon

lance

land·lord

lan·guage

lan·guid

lan·guish

lan·guor

lan·o·lin

lan·tern

lan·yard

la·pel

lap·i·dary (—dar·ies)

lapse

lar·ce·ny (—nies)

large

lar·gess, lar·gesse

lar·i·at

lar·va (—vae)

lar·yn·gi·tis

lar·ynx (lar·ynxes)

la·sa·gna

las·civ·i·ous

la·ser

las·si·tude

las·so (las·sos *or* las·soes)

la·tent

lat·er·al

la·tex (la·ti·ces *or* la·tex·es)

lath (thin strip of wood; see *lathe*)

lathe (shaping machine; see *lath*)

lat·i·tude

la·trine

lat·ter

laud

lau·da·to·ry

laugh

laugh·able

launch

laun·der

laun·dry (—dries)

lau·re·ate

lau·rel

lav·a·to·ry (—ries)

lav·en·der

lav·ish

law·ful

law·ful·ly

lawn

law·yer

lax·a·tive

lax·ity

lay·ette

lay·person

la·zy

leach (to dissolve out; see *leech*)

lead

lead·er

leaf·let

league

leak (to escape through an opening; see *leek*)

lean (to incline; see *lien*)

learn

lease

leash

least

leath·er

leave

leav·en

lech·er

lech·er·ous

lec·tern

lec·ture

led·ger

leech (bloodsucking worm; see *leach*)

leek (herb; see *leak*)

leer

leery

lee·ward

lee·way

left

leg·a·cy (—cies)

le·gal

le·gal·i·ty (—ties)

leg·ate

le·ga·to

leg·end

leg·end·ary

leg·gy

leg·horn

leg·i·ble

le·gion

le·gion·naire

leg·is·late

leg·is·la·tive

leg·is·la·ture

le·git·i·ma·cy

le·git·i·mate

le·gume

lei·sure

lem·ming

length

length·en

le·nient

len·til

leop·ard

le·o·tard

lep·er

lep·re·chaun

lep·ro·sy

les·bi·an

le·sion

les·see

les·son

les·sor

le·thal

le·thar·gic

let·ter

let·tuce

leu·ke·mia

lev·ee (embankment; see *levy*)

lev·el

lev·i·ty

levy (assessment; see *levee*)

lewd

lex·i·cog·ra·phy

lex·i·con

li·a·ble

li·ai·son

li·ar

li·ba·tion

li·bel

lib·er·al

lib·er·ate

lib·er·tar·i·an

lib·er·ty (—ties)

li·brar·i·an

li·brary (—brar·ies)

li·bret·to (—tos *or* —ti)

li·cense, li·cence

li·cen·tious

li·chen

lic·o·rice

lie (untruth; see *lye*)

lien (payment of debt; see *lean*)

lieu

lieu·ten·ant

life (lives)

lig·a·ment
lig·a·ture
light·ning
like·li·hood
li·lac
lily (lil·ies)
limb
lim·bo
lime·light
lim·er·ick
lim·i·ta·tion
lim·ou·sine
lim·pid
lin·eal
lin·ear
lin·ge·rie
lin·go (lingoes)
lin·gual
lin·guis·tic
lin·i·ment
lin·ing
li·no·leum
lin·seed
lin·tel
liq·ue·fy
li·queur
liq·ui·date
li·quor
lis·ten
lit·a·ny (—nies)
li·ter
lit·er·a·cy
lit·er·al
lit·er·al·ly
lit·er·ary
lit·er·ate
lit·er·a·ture
litho·graph
lit·i·gant
lit·i·gate
lit·i·ga·tion
lit·mus
lit·tle
li·tur·gi·cal
lit·ur·gy (—gies)
liv·able
live·li·hood
live·li·ness
live·ly
liv·er
liv·er·wurst
live·stock
liv·id
liz·ard

lla·ma
loan
loath (unwilling, reluctant; see
    loathe)
loathe (dislike greatly; see *loath*)
lob·by (lobbies)
lob·ster
lo·cal (not general or widespread;
    see *locale*)
lo·cale (place related to a particu-
    lar event; see *local*)
lo·cate
lock·et
lo·co·mo·tion
lo·cust
lodge
log·a·rithm
log·i·cal
lo·gis·tics
lo·gy, log·gy
loi·ter
lol·li·pop, lol·ly·pop
lone·li·ness
lone·ly
lone·some
lon·gev·i·ty
lon·gi·tude
lore
loose
loot (something taken by force;
    see *lute*)
lop·sid·ed
lo·qua·cious
lose
lo·tion
lot·tery (—ter·ies)
lo·tus, lo·tos
loud
lounge
lou·ver, lou·vre
lov·able, love·able
love·ly
loy·al
loz·enge
lu·bri·cate
lu·cid
lu·cid·i·ty
luck·i·ly
lu·cra·tive
lu·di·crous
lug·gage
lull
lum·ba·go
lum·ber

lu·mi·nary (—nar·ies)
lum·mox
lu·na·cy (—cies)
lu·nar
lu·na·tic
lun·cheon
lun·cheon·ette
lunge
lurch
lu·rid
lurk
lus·cious
lus·trous
lute (musical instrument; see
    loot)
lux·u·ri·ous
lux·u·ry (—ries)
ly·ce·um
lymph
lynch
lynx (lynx *or* lynx·es)
lyre
lyr·ic

M

ma·ca·bre
mac·ad·am
mac·a·ro·ni
mac·a·roon
mac·er·ate
ma·chete
mach·i·na·tion
ma·chine
ma·chin·ery
ma·chin·ist
mack·er·el
mack·i·naw
mac·ro·bi·ot·ic
mac·ro·cosm
mac·ro·scop·ic
mad·am, ma·dame
mad·den·ing
ma·de·moi·selle (ma·de·moi·
    selles *or* mes·de·moi·selles)
ma·dras
mad·ri·gal
mael·strom
mae·stro (mae·stros *or* mae·stri)
mag·a·zine
ma·gen·ta
mag·got
mag·i·cal

ma·gi·cian
mag·is·trate
mag·nan·i·mous
mag·nate (person of rank and
    power; see *magnet*)
mag·ne·sia
mag·ne·sium
mag·net (something that attracts;
    see *magnate*)
mag·net·ic
mag·nif·i·cent
mag·ni·fy
mag·ni·tude
mag·no·lia
mag·pie
ma·hog·a·ny (−nies)
maid·en
mail (letters; see *male*)
maim
main (chief; see *mane*)
main·tain
main·te·nance
mai·tre d' (maitre d's)
maize (Indian corn; see *maze*)
ma·jes·tic
ma·jor·i·ty (−ties)
mal·ad·just·ment
mal·a·dy (−dies)
mal·aise (French: indefinite
    feeling of ill health)
ma·lar·ia
mal·con·tent
male (masculine; see *mail*)
ma·lev·o·lent
mal·fea·sance
mal·formed
mal·func·tion
mal·ice
ma·li·cious
ma·lign
ma·lig·nan·cy (−cies)
ma·lin·ger
ma·lin·ger·er
mall
mal·lard
mal·lea·ble
mal·let
mal·nour·ished
mal·nu·tri·tion
mal·prac·tice
malt
mam·mal
mam·moth
man·age·able

man·age·ment
man·da·mus
man·da·rin
man·date
man·da·to·ry
man·di·ble
man·do·lin, man·do·line
mane (long, heavy hair on neck
    of horses; see *main*)
ma·neu·ver
man·gle
man·go (man·gos *or* man·goes)
mangy
ma·nia
ma·ni·ac
man·ic
ma·ni·cot·ti
man·i·cure
man·i·fest
man·i·fes·to
man·i·fold
ma·nip·u·late
man·li·ness
man·ne·quin
man·ner
man·or
man·sion
man·tel (shelf; see *mantle*)
man·tle (cloak; see *mantel*)
man·u·al
man·u·fac·ture
man·u·mit
ma·nure
manu·script
mar·a·schi·no
mar·a·thon
ma·raud·er
mar·ble
mare
mar·ga·rine
mar·gin
mar·gin·al
mari·gold
mar·i·jua·na
ma·rim·ba
mar·i·nate
ma·rine
mar·i·o·nette
mar·i·tal
mar·i·time
mar·jo·ram
mar·ket·able
mar·lin
mar·ma·lade

ma·roon
mar·quee
mar·quise
mar·qui·sette
mar·riage
mar·row
mar·shal, mar·shall (officer; see
    martial)
marsh·mal·low
mar·su·pi·al
mar·tial (relating to war; see
    marshall)
mar·ti·net
mar·tyr
mar·vel
mar·vel·ous, mar·vel·lous
mar·zi·pan
mas·cara
mas·cot
mas·cu·line
mas·och·ism
mas·och·ist
ma·son·ry (−ries)
mas·quer·ade
mas·sa·cre
mas·sage
mas·seur
mas·seuse
mas·sive
mas·ter·piece
mast·head
mas·ti·cate
mas·toid
mat·a·dor
ma·te·ri·al (substance; see
    matériel)
ma·te·ri·al·ism
ma·té·ri·el, ma·te·ri·el (equipment
    and supplies; see *material*)
ma·ter·nal
ma·ter·ni·ty (−ties)
math·e·mat·ics
mat·i·nee
ma·tri·arch
ma·tric·u·late
mat·ri·mo·ny
ma·trix (ma·tri·ces *or* ma·trix·es)
ma·tron·ly
mat·ter
mat·tress
ma·ture
ma·tu·ri·ty
maud·lin
maul

mau·so·le·um (mau·so·le·ums *or* mau·so·lea)
mauve
mav·er·ick
max·i·mum (–ma *or* –mums)
may·hem
may·on·naise
may·or·al·ty
maze (network of passages; see *maize*)
mead·ow
mea·ger, mea·gre
me·an·der
mean·ing·ful
mean·while
mea·sles
mea·sure
meat (flesh of domestic animals; see *meet*)
me·chan·ic
me·chan·i·cal
mech·a·nism
med·al (metal disk; see *meddle, metal*)
med·dle (interfere; see *medal*)
me·dia (–di·ae)
me·di·an
me·di·ate
me·di·a·tion
med·i·cal
med·i·ca·tion
me·dic·i·nal
med·i·cine
me·di·eval, me·di·ae·val
me·di·o·cre
me·di·oc·ri·ty (–ties)
med·i·tate
med·i·ta·tion
me·di·um (me·di·ums *or* me·dia)
med·ley
meet
mega·cy·cle
mega·phone
mega·ton
mel·an·choly (–chol·ies)
me·lee (French: fight)
mel·lif·lu·ent
mel·lif·lu·ous
mel·low
me·lo·di·ous
melo·dra·ma
mel·o·dy (–dies)
mem·ber·ship
mem·brane

me·men·to
mem·oir
mem·o·ra·bil·ia
mem·o·ra·ble
mem·o·ran·dum
me·mo·ri·al
mem·o·ry (–ries)
men·ace
me·nag·er·ie
me·nial
meno·pause
men·stru·ate
men·su·ra·tion
men·tal
men·thol
men·tion
men·tor
menu
mer·ce·nary (–nar·ies)
mer·chan·dise
mer·chant
mer·ci·ful
mer·cy (mer·cies)
mer·e·tri·cious
merge
merg·er
me·rid·i·an
me·ringue
mer·i·to·ri·ous
mer·maid
mes·dames
mes·mer·ize
mes·sage
mes·sag·ing
mes·sen·ger
me·tab·o·lism
me·tal·ic
meta·mor·pho·sis (–ses)
met·a·phor
meta·phys·ics
mete (allot; see *meat* and *meet*)
me·te·or·ic
me·te·or
me·te·or·ite
me·ter
meth·a·done, meth·a·don
meth·od
meth·od·ol·o·gy (–gies)
me·tic·u·lous
met·ric
met·ro·nome
me·trop·o·lis
met·ro·pol·i·tan

met·tle
mez·za·nine
mez·zo-so·pra·no
mi·as·ma (–mas *or* –ma·ta)
mi·ca
mi·cro·anal·y·sis
mi·crobe
mi·cro·cosm
mi·crom·e·ter
mi·cro·phone
mi·cro·scope
mid·dle
mid·night
mid·riff
midst
mien
might (power; see *mite*)
mi·graine
mi·grate
mi·gra·to·ry
mil·dew
mile·age
mi·lieu (mi·lieus *or* mi·lieux)
mil·i·tan·cy
mil·i·ta·rist
mil·i·tary
mil·i·tate
mi·li·tia
mil·len·ni·um
mil·li·gram
mil·li·li·ter
mil·li·me·ter
mil·li·nery
mil·lion
mil·lion·aire
mim·eo·graph
mim·ic
minc·ing·ly
mind·less
min·er (mine worker; see *minor*)
min·er·al·o·gy
min·gle
min·ia·ture
min·i·mum
min·i·mize
min·is·cule, mi·nus·cule
min·is·te·ri·al
mi·nor (comparatively unimportant; see *miner*)
mi·nor·i·ty (–ties)
min·strel
min·u·et
mi·nus·cule, min·is·cule
min·ute (space of time)

mi·nute (of small importance)
minx
mi·rac·u·lous
mi·rage
mire
mir·ror
mirth·ful
mis·al·li·ance
mis·an·thrope
mis·car·riage
mis·cel·la·neous
mis·cel·la·ny (–nies)
mis·chie·vous
mis·con·ceive
mis·con·strue
mis·de·mean·or
mis·er·a·ble
mi·ser·ly
mis·for·tune
mis·han·dle
mis·in·ter·pret
mis·judge
mis·man·age
mis·no·mer
mis·rep·re·sent
mis·shap·en
mis·sile
mis·sion·ary (–ar·ies)
mis·sive
mis·spell
mis·state
mis·take
mis·tle·toe
mis·tress
mis·tri·al
mite (small object or creature;
    see *might*)
mit·i·gate
mix·ture
mne·mon·ic
moat (trench; see *mote*)
mo·bile
mo·bi·li·za·tion
moc·ca·sin
mod·el
mod·er·ate
mod·er·a·tor
mod·ern·i·za·tion
mod·es·ty
mod·i·fi·er
mod·ish
mod·u·late
mo·gul

mo·hair
moist·en
mo·lar
mo·las·ses
mo·lec·u·lar
mol·e·cule
mol·li·fy
mol·ten
mo·men·tary
mo·men·tum
mon·arch
mon·as·tery (–ter·ies)
mon·e·tary
mon·ey (moneys *or* mon·ies)
Mon·gol·oid
mon·grel
mon·i·tor
mon·key
mono·chro·mat·ic
mon·o·cle
mo·nog·a·my
mono·gram
mono·logue, mono·log
mono·logu·ist, mo·no·lo·gist
mo·nop·o·ly (–lies)
mono·syl·lab·ic
mono·the·ism
mono·tone
mo·not·o·nous
mon·soon
mon·stros·i·ty (–ties)
mon·strous
mon·tage
month·ly
mon·u·men·tal
moon·light
mor·al
mo·rale
mo·rass
mor·a·to·ri·um (mor·a·to·ri·ums *or*
    mor·a·to·ria)
mor·bid
mor·dant
more·over
mo·res
morgue
mor·i·bund
morn·ing (time from sunrise to
    noon; see *mourning*)
mor·phine
mor·sel
mor·tal·i·ty
mort·gage

mor·ti·cian
mor·ti·fy
mor·tu·ary (–ar·ies)
mo·sa·ic
mosque
mos·qui·to (–tos *or* –toes)
mote (speck; see *moat*)
mo·tif
mo·tion
mo·ti·va·tion
mo·tor
mot·tled
mot·to (mot·tos *or* mot·toes)
moun·tain·ous
mourn
mourn·ing (act of sorrowing; see
    morning)
mouse
mousse
mouth·ful
mov·able, move·able
mov·ie
moz·za·rel·la
mu·ci·lage
mu·cous
mug·ger
mug·gy
mul·ber·ry (–ries)
mul·ti·cul·tur·al
mul·ti·eth·nic
mul·ti·fac·et·ed
mul·ti·far·i·ous
mul·ti·lat·er·al
mul·ti·me·dia
mul·ti·mil·lion·aire
mul·ti·na·tion·al
mul·ti·ple
mul·ti·tude
mum·ble
mum·bo jum·bo
mum·my (mummies)
mun·dane
mu·nic·i·pal
mu·ni·tion
mu·ral
mur·der·ous
mus·cle (body tissue; see
    mussel)
mus·cu·lar
muse
mu·se·um
mu·si·cal
mu·si·cian

mus·ke·teer
musk·rat
mus·lin
mus·sel (mollusk; see *muscle*)
mus·tache
mus·tard
mu·ta·ble
mu·ta·tion
mu·ti·late
mu·ti·neer
mut·ter
mut·ton
mu·tu·al
muz·zle
my·o·pic
myr·i·ad
myrrh
myr·tle
mys·te·ri·ous
mys·tery (–ter·ies)
mys·tic
mys·ti·cal
mys·ti·cism
mys·tique
myth
myth·i·cal
my·thol·o·gy (–gies)

N

na·ive
na·ive·té
na·ked·ness
na·palm
nap·kin
nar·cis·sism
nar·cis·sus
nar·cot·ic
nar·rate
nar·ra·tor
nar·row
na·sal·i·ty (–ties)
na·scent
nas·ty
na·tion·al·i·ty (–ties)
na·tive
na·tiv·i·ty (–ties)
nat·u·ral·ize
na·tu·ro·path
naugh·ti·ness
nau·se·ate
nau·seous

nau·ti·cal
na·val (relating to ships; see *navel*)
nave (church aisle; see *knave*)
na·vel (depression in abdomen; see *naval*)
nav·i·gate
nav·i·ga·tor
near·by
neb·u·lous
nec·es·sary
ne·ces·si·tate
neck·lace
nec·tar·ine
nee·dle·work
ne'er-do-well
ne·far·i·ous
ne·gate
neg·a·tive
ne·glect
neg·li·gee, neg·li·gé
neg·li·gent
neg·li·gi·ble
ne·go·ti·a·tion
neigh
neigh·bor
neigh·bor·hood
nei·ther
nem·e·sis (–ses)
ne·on
neo·na·tal
neo·phyte
neph·ew
nep·o·tism
ner·vous
ner·vous·ness
nes·tle
net·ting
net·tle
net·work
neu·ral·gia
neu·ron
neu·ro·sis (–ses)
neu·rot·ic
neu·ro·tox·in
neu·ter
neu·tral·ize
neu·tron
new (recent; see *gnu* and *knew*)
news·group
news·stand
nib·ble
nice·ty (–ties)

niche
nick·el, nick·le
nick·nack, knick·knack
nic·o·tine
niece
night (time from dusk to dawn; see *knight*)
night·in·gale
night·mare
nim·ble
nine·teen
nine·ty (nineties)
ninth
nip·ple
ni·trate
ni·tro·gen
ni·tro·glyc·er·in, ni·tro·glyc·er·ine
no·bil·i·ty
no·ble
noc·tur·nal
noc·turne
nod·ule
noi·some
noisy
no·mad
nom de plume (French: pen name, pseudonym)
no·men·cla·ture
nom·i·nal
nom·i·nate
nom·i·na·tion
nom·i·nee
non·al·co·hol·ic
non·be·liev·er
non·bel·lig·er·ent
non·cha·lance
non·com·ba·tant
non·com·mis·sioned
non·com·mit·tal
non·com·pli·ance
non·con·duc·tor
non·con·form·ist
non·de·script
non·en·ti·ty (–ties)
non·es·sen·tial
non·fic·tion
non·in·ter·ven·tion
non·pa·reil (French: having no equal)
non·par·ti·san
non·poi·son·ous
non·pro·duc·tive
non·prof·it

non·re·new·able
non·sec·tar·i·an
non·sense
non se·qui·tur
non·tax·able
non·vi·o·lence
noo·dle
noose
nor·mal
north·ern
nose
nos·tal·gia
nos·tril
nos·trum
no·ta·bly
no·ta·rize
no·ta·ry public (no·ta·ries public
     or no·ta·ry publics)
no·ta·tion
notch
note·wor·thy
no·tice·able
no·ti·fy
no·tion
no·to·ri·ety (—eties)
no·to·ri·ous
nou·gat
nought
noun
nour·ish·ment
nov·el·lette
nov·el·ty (—ties)
nov·ice
nox·ious
noz·zle
nu·ance
nu·bile
nu·cle·ar
nu·cle·us (—clei or —cle·us·es)
nu·di·ty
nug·get
nui·sance
nul·li·fy
numb
number
nu·mer·al
nu·mer·a·tor
nu·mer·ous
nu·mis·mat·ic
nup·tial
nurse
nurs·ery (—er·ies)
nur·ture
nu·tri·ent

nu·tri·tion
nu·tri·tious
nuz·zle
ny·lon

O

oa·sis (—ses)
oath
oat·meal
obe·di·ence
obe·lisk
obese
obe·si·ty
obey
ob·fus·cate
obit·u·ary (—ar·ries)
ob·jec·tion
ob·jec·tive
ob·jec·tor
ob·li·gate
ob·li·ga·tion
oblig·a·to·ry
oblige
oblique
oblit·er·ate
obliv·i·on
obliv·i·ous
ob·long
ob·lo·quy (—quies)
ob·nox·ious
oboe
obo·ist
ob·scene
ob·scen·i·ty (—ties)
ob·scure
ob·scu·ri·ty (—ties)
ob·se·qui·ous
ob·se·quy (—quies)
ob·ser·vant
ob·ser·va·to·ry (—ries)
ob·ses·sion
ob·so·les·cence
ob·so·lete
ob·sta·cle
ob·ste·tri·cian
ob·stet·rics
ob·sti·nate
ob·struc·tion
ob·tain
ob·tru·sive
ob·tuse
ob·vi·ate

ob·vi·ous
oc·ca·sion
oc·cip·i·tal
oc·clu·sion
oc·cult
oc·cu·pan·cy (—cies)
oc·cu·pant
oc·cu·pa·tion
oc·cu·py
oc·cur
oc·curred
oc·cur·rence
ocean
ocean·og·ra·phy
oc·ta·gon
oc·tag·o·nal
oc·tane
oc·tave
oc·tet
oc·to·ge·nar·i·an
oc·to·pus (—pus·es or —pi)
odd·i·ty (—ties)
odd·ly
odi·ous
odom·e·ter
odor·ant
odor·ous
od·ys·sey
of·fend·er
of·fense, of·fence
of·ferred
off·hand
of·fi·cer
of·fi·cial
of·fi·ci·ate
of·fi·cious
off·set
off·spring (off·spring or
     off·springs)
ohm
oil·er
oily
oint·ment
okra
old·fash·ioned
old·ster
ole·ag·i·nous
ol·fac·to·ry
oli·gar·chy (—chies)
ol·ive
olym·pi·ad
olym·pic
om·elet, om·elette
om·i·nous

omis·sion
omit
om·ni·bus
om·nip·o·tence
om·ni·science
om·niv·o·rous
on·col·o·gy
on·com·ing
oner·ous
on·ion
on·line
on·o·mato·poe·ia
on·set
on·shore
on·side
on·slaught
on·tol·o·gy
onus
on·ward, on·wards
on·yx
oo·long
opal·es·cent
opaque
open
op·er·a·ble
op·er·ate
op·er·at·ic
op·er·a·tion
op·er·et·ta
oph·thal·mol·o·gist
opi·ate
opin·ion
opin·ion·at·ed
opi·um
opos·sum
op·po·nent
op·por·tune
op·por·tu·nis·tic
op·por·tu·ni·ty (–ties)
op·po·site
op·pres·sion
op·ti·cal
op·ti·cian
op·ti·mism
op·ti·mum (–ma *or* –mums)
op·tion
op·tom·e·trist
op·tom·e·try
op·u·lent
opus (opera *or* opus·es)
or·a·cle
oral (relating to the mouth; see
    aural)
or·ange

orate
or·a·to·ry (–ries)
or·bit·al
or·chard
or·ches·tra
or·chid
or·dain
or·deal
or·der
or·di·nance
or·di·nary
or·di·nari·ly
or·di·na·tion
ord·nance
ore
oreg·a·no
or·gan
or·gan·ic
or·gan·ism
or·ga·ni·za·tion
or·ga·niz·er
or·gasm
or·gi·as·tic
or·gy (or·gies)
ori·en·tal
ori·en·ta·tion
or·i·fice
orig·i·nal·i·ty
orig·i·na·tor
ori·ole
or·na·men·tal
or·na·men·ta·tion
or·nate
or·nery
or·ni·thol·o·gy (–gies)
or·phan·age
orth·odon·tist
or·tho·dox
or·tho·pe·dic, or·tho·pae·dic
os·cil·late
os·mo·sis
os·prey
os·si·fi·ca·tion
os·si·fy
os·ten·si·ble
os·ten·ta·tious
os·teo·path
os·tra·cize
os·trich
ot·to·man
ought
ounce
our (relating to us; see *hour*)
oust

out·age
out·break
out·dis·tance
out·fit·ter
out·land·ish
out·pour·ing
out·put
out·ra·geous
out·ward
out·weigh
out·wit
oval
ova·ry (–ries)
ova·tion
over·alls
over·bear·ing
over·board
over·cast
over·con·fi·dent
over·dose
over·draft
over·ex·pose
over·haul
overjoyed
over·lap
over·rate
over·seas
over·seer
over·sight
overt
over·ture
over·whelm
over·wrought
ow·ing
own·er
ox·i·da·tion
ox·ide
ox·i·dize
ox·tail
ox·y·gen
ox·y·gen·ate
oys·ter
ozone

P

pace·mak·er
pac·er
pa·cif·ic
pac·i·fi·er
pack·age
pack·et
pact

pad·ding
pad·dle
pad·dock
pad·lock
pa·gan
page
pag·eant·ry
pag·i·nate
pa·go·da
paid
pail (container; see *pale*)
pain (suffering; see *pane*)
pains·tak·ing
paint
pair (two; see *pare, pear*)
pa·ja·mas
pal·ace
pal·at·able
pal·ate (roof or mouth; see *palette*)
pa·la·tial
pale (deficient in color; see *pail*)
Pa·leo·lith·ic
pal·ette (painter's board; see *palate*)
pal·in·drome
pal·i·sade
pal·la·di·um (–la·dia)
pall·bear·er
pal·met·to
palm·ist
pal·o·mi·no
pal·pa·ble
pal·pi·tate
pal·sy (palsies)
pal·try
pam·per
pam·phlet
pan·a·cea
pan·cre·as
pan·da
pan·de·mo·ni·um
pan·der
pane (sheet of glass; see *pain*)
pan·el
pan·han·dle
pan·ic
pan·icked
pan·o·ply (–plies)
pan·ora·ma
pan·sy (pansies)
pan·the·ism
pan·ther

pant·ing
pan·to·mime
pan·try (pantries)
pa·pa·cy (–cies)
pa·pal
pa·pa·ya
pa·pier-mâ·ché
pa·pri·ka
pa·py·rus (pa·py·rus·es *or* pa·py·ri)
par·a·ble
pa·rab·o·la
para·chute
pa·rade
par·a·digm
par·a·dise
par·a·dox
par·af·fin
par·a·gon
para·graph
par·a·keet
par·al·lel
par·al·lel·o·gram
pa·ral·y·sis
par·a·lyt·ic
par·a·lyze
pa·ram·e·ter
par·a·mount
par·amour
para·noia
para·noid
par·a·pet
par·a·pher·na·lia
para·phrase
para·ple·gic
par·a·site
para·sol
para·troop·er
par·boil
par·cel
parch
parch·ment
par·don·able
pare (shave off; see *pear, pair*)
pa·ren·tal
pa·ren·the·sis (–ses)
par·en·thet·i·cal·ly
pa·ri·etal
pa·rish·io·ner
par·i·ty (–ties)
par·ka
park·way

par·lay (two or more bets in advance; see *parley*)
par·ley (conference; see *parlay*)
par·lia·ment
par·lia·men·ta·ry
par·lor
par·mi·gia·na, par·mi·gia·no
pa·ro·chi·al
par·o·dy (–dies)
pa·role
par·quet (French: type of flooring)
par·rot
par·ry
parse
par·si·mo·ni·ous
pars·ley
pars·nip
par·son·age
par·terre
par·tial
par·tic·i·pate
par·ti·cip·i·al
par·ti·ci·ple
par·ti·cle
par·tic·u·lar·ly
par·ti·san, par·ti·zan
par·ti·tion
par·ti·tive
part·ner
par·tridge
par·ve·nu (French: one with new wealth, lacking social standing)
pas·chal
pass·able
pas·sage
pas·sé (French: behind the times)
pas·sen·ger
pass·er·by (pass·ers·by)
pas·sion·ate
pas·sive
pass·port
past
paste
pas·tel
pas·teur·ize
pas·tille, pas·til
pas·time
pas·to·ral
past·ry (pastries)
pas·ty (pasties)
patch·work
patchy
pat·ent

pa·ter·nal·ism
pa·ter·ni·ty
pa·thet·ic
pa·thol·o·gy (–gies)
pa·thos
path·way
pa·tience
pa·tient
pa·ti·na (–nas or –nae)
pa·tio
pa·tois (plural also pa·tois)
pa·tri·arch
pa·tri·cian
pat·ri·cide
pat·ri·mo·ny
pa·tri·ot·ic
pa·trol
pa·tron
pa·tron·age
pat·ter
pat·tern
paunch
pau·per
pause
pave·ment
pa·vil·ion
pawn
pay·able
peace (state of tranquillity; see *piece*)
peace·ful
peachy
pea·cock
peak (sharp or pointed end; see *peek, pique*)
peal (loud ringing of bells; see *peel*)
pea·nut
pear (fruit; see *pair, pare*)
pearl
peas·ant·ry
peb·ble
pe·can
pec·ca·dil·lo
pec·to·ral
pe·cu·liar·i·ty (–ties)
pe·cu·ni·ary
ped·a·gogue, ped·a·gog
ped·a·go·gy
ped·al (foot lever; see *peddle*)
pe·dan·tic
ped·dle (travel with wares to sell; see *pedal*)

ped·es·tal
pe·des·tri·an
pe·di·a·tri·cian
pe·di·at·rics
ped·i·cure
ped·i·gree
ped·i·ment
pe·dom·e·ter
peek (look furtively; see *peak, pique*)
peel (strip off; see *peal*)
peer (equal; see *pier*)
peer·age
pee·vish
pei·gnoir
pe·jo·ra·tive
pe·koe
pe·lag·ic
pel·i·can
pel·let
pel·vic
pel·vis (pel·vis·es or pel·ves)
pe·nal·ize
pen·al·ty (–ties)
pen·ance
pen·chant
pen·ciled
pen·dant, pen·dent
pen·du·lum
pen·e·trate
pen·guin
pen·i·cil·lin
pen·in·su·la
pen·i·tence
pen·i·ten·tia·ry (–ries)
pen·man·ship
pen·nant
pen·ni·less
pen·sion
pen·ta·gon
pent·house
pe·o·ny (–nies)
peo·ple
pep·per
per·cale
per cap·i·ta
per·ceive
per·cent
per·cent·age
per·cen·tile
per·cept
per·cep·ti·ble
per·cep·tive

per·cep·tu·al
perch
per·chance
per·cip·i·ent
per·co·late
per·co·la·tor
per·cus·sion
per di·em
per·di·tion
pe·remp·to·ry
pe·ren·ni·al
per·fect
per·fec·ta
per·fo·rate
per·force
per·for·mance
per·fume
per·func·to·ry
per·haps
per·il·ous
pe·rim·e·ter
pe·ri·od·ic
pe·riph·er·al
pe·riph·ery (–er·ies)
peri·scope
per·ish·able
peri·to·ni·tis
per·i·win·kle
per·jure
per·ju·ry
per·ma·frost
per·ma·nent
per·me·able
per·me·ate
per·mis·si·ble
per·mis·sion
per·mit·ted
per·mu·ta·tion
per·ni·cious
per·ora·tion
per·ox·ide
per·pen·dic·u·lar
per·pe·tra·tor
per·pet·u·al
per·pe·tu·ity (–ities)
per·plex
per·se·cu·tion
per·se·ver·ance
per·sis·tence
per·snick·e·ty
per·son·able
per·son·age

per·son·al (private, relating to a person; see *personnel*)
per·son·al·i·ty (–ties)
per·so·na non gra·ta (Latin: being unwelcome)
per·son·i·fi·ca·tion
per·son·nel (body of employees; see *personal*)
per·spec·tive
per·spi·ca·cious
per·spi·ra·tion
per·sua·sion
per·tain
per·ti·nent
pe·ruse
per·vade
per·verse
per·vert
pes·si·mism
pes·ter
pes·ti·lence
pes·tle
pet·al
pe·tit (French: small)
pe·ti·tion
pe·trel (sea bird; see *petrol*)
pet·ri·fy
pet·rol (gasoline; see *petrel*)
pe·tro·leum
pet·ti·coat
pet·ti·ness (–ness·es)
pet·ty
pet·u·lant
pe·tu·nia
pew·ter
pha·lanx (pha·lanx·es *or* pha·lan·ges)
phan·tasm, fan·tasm
phan·tas·ma·go·ria
phan·tom
phar·ma·ceu·ti·cal
phar·ma·cist
phar·ma·cy (–cies)
phar·ynx (pha·rynx·es *or* pha·ryn·ges)
phase
pheas·ant
phe·nom·e·nal
phe·nom·e·non
phi·lan·der·er
phi·lan·thro·py (–pies)
philo·den·dron
phi·lol·o·gy
phi·los·o·pher

phi·los·o·phi·cal
phlegm
phleg·mat·ic
pho·bia
phoe·nix
pho·nate
pho·net·ics
pho·nics
pho·no·graph
phony, phoney (phonies)
phos·phate
phos·pho·res·cent
pho·to·copy (–cop·ies)
pho·to·elec·tric
pho·to·graph·ic
pho·to·stat
phot·to·syn·the·sis
phrase
phrase·ol·o·gy (–gies)
phre·net·ic, fre·net·ic
phre·nol·o·gy
phys·i·cal
phy·si·cian
phys·i·cist
phys·ics
phys·i·ol·o·gy
phys·io·ther·a·py
phy·sique
pi·a·nist
pi·az·za
pi·ca
pic·ca·lil·li
pic·co·lo
pick·et
pick·le
pic·nic
pic·nicked
pic·to·graph
pic·to·ri·al
pic·ture (painting, drawing or pho·tograph; see *pitcher*)
pic·tur·esque
piece (part of a whole; see *peace*)
pièce de ré·sis·tance (pièces de ré·sis·tance) (French: out·standing item)
pier (dock; see *peer*)
pierce
pi·ety (pi·eties)
pi·geon
pig·ment
Pi·la·tes
pil·fer

pil·grim·age
pil·ing
pil·lage
pil·lar
pil·low
pi·lot
pi·men·to
pim·ple
pin·afore
pin·cer
pin·cush·ion
pine·ap·ple
pin·na·cle
pi·noch·le
pi·o·neer
pi·ous
pipe
pip·ing
pique (to wound vanity; see *peak, peek*)
pi·ra·cy
pir·ou·ette (French: ballet turn)
pis·ta·chio
pis·til (plant organ; see *pistol*)
pis·tol (gun; see *pistil*)
pitch·er (container for liquids; see *picture*)
pitch·fork
pit·e·ous
pit·fall
pithy
piti·able
piti·ful
piti·less
pit·tance
piv·ot·al
pix·el
pix·ie, pixy (pix·ies)
pix·i·lat·ed
piz·ze·ria
plac·ard
pla·cate
pla·ce·bo
place·ment
plac·id
plack·et
pla·gia·rize
plague
plaid
plain (level country; lacking orna·ment; see *plane*)
plain·tiff
plane (tool; geometric surface; see *plain*)

plan·et
plan·e·tar·i·um
plan·tain
plan·ta·tion
plaque
plas·ma
plas·ter
plas·tic
plas·ti·cize
pla·teau
plat·form
plat·i·num
plat·i·tude
pla·ton·ic
pla·toon
plat·ter
plau·si·ble
play·mate
play·wright
pla·za
plead
pleas·ant·ry (–ries)
plea·sure
pleat
plebe
ple·be·ian
pledge
ple·na·ry
pleni·po·ten·tia·ry (–ries)
plen·te·ous
plen·ti·ful
pli·able
pli·ers
plight
plow, plough
plow·share
plum·age
plumb·er
plume
plum·met
plump
plun·der
plunge
plu·ral
plu·ral·i·ty (–ties)
plu·toc·ra·cy (–cies)
plu·to·ni·um
ply·wood
pneu·mat·ic
pneu·mo·nia
poach·er
pock·et·book
po·di·a·trist
po·di·um

po·em
po·et·ic
poi·gnan·cy (–cies)
poi·gnant
poin·set·tia
point
poi·son·ous
po·lar·i·ty (–ties)
po·lar·i·za·tion
po·lar·ize
pole (long slender object; see *poll*)
po·lem·ic
po·lice (plural also po·lice)
pol·i·cy (–cies)
po·lio
pol·ish
po·lit·bu·ro
po·lit·i·cal
pol·i·ti·cian
pol·i·tics
pol·ka
poll (receive and record votes; see *pole*)
pol·len
pol·li·nate
pol·lu·tion
poly·es·ter
po·lyg·a·my
poly·gon
pol·yp
poly·tech·nic
poly·ure·thane
pome·gran·ate
pom·pos·i·ty (–ties)
pomp·ous
pon·cho
pon·der
pon·tiff
pon·tif·i·cal
pon·toon
po·ny·tail
poo·dle
pop·corn
pop·lar (tree; see *popular*)
pop·py (pop·pies)
pop·u·lace
pop·u·lar (commonly liked; see *poplar*)
pop·u·la·tion
pop·u·list
por·ce·lain
por·cu·pine
por·nog·ra·phy

po·rous
por·poise
por·ridge
por·ta·ble
por·tend
por·tent
por·ten·tous
por·ter·house
port·fo·lio
por·ti·co (–coes *or* –cos)
por·tion
por·trait
por·tray
pos·it
po·si·tion
pos·i·tive·ly
pos·se
pos·sess·or
pos·ses·sion
pos·si·bil·i·ty (–ties)
post·age
pos·te·ri·or
pos·ter·i·ty
post·hu·mous
post·mor·tem
post·pone
post·script
pos·tu·late
pos·tur·ing
po·ta·ble
po·ta·to (–toes)
po·ten·cy (–cies)
po·tent
po·ten·tial
po·tion
pot·pour·ri
pot·shot
pot·tery
poul·tice
poul·try
pounce
pound
pov·er·ty
pow·der
pow·er·ful
prac·ti·cal
prac·tice
prac·ti·tio·ner
prag·mat·ic
prai·rie
prat·tle
prayer·ful
preach
preachy

pre·am·ble
pre·ar·range
pre·car·i·ous
pre·cau·tion
pre·cede
pre·ce·dence
pre·ce·dent
pre·cept
pre·cinct
pre·cious
prec·i·pice
pre·cip·i·tate
pre·cise
pre·ci·sion
pre·clude
pre·co·cious
pre·con·ceive
pre·con·cep·tion
pre·con·di·tion
pre·cur·sor
pred·a·tor
pre·de·cease
pre·des·ti·na·tion
pre·de·ter·mine
pre·dic·a·ment
pred·i·cate
pre·dict
pre·di·lec·tion
pre·dis·pose
pre·doc·tor·al
pre·dom·i·nant
pre·em·i·nence
pre·empt
preen
pre·fab·ri·cate
pref·ace
pref·a·to·ry
pre·fect
pre·fer
pref·er·a·ble
pref·er·ence
pre·fig·ure
preg·na·ble
preg·nan·cy (—cies)
preg·nant
pre·heat
pre·his·tor·ic
pre·in·duc·tion
prej·u·dice
pre·lim·i·nary (—nar·ies)
pre·lude
pre·mar·i·tal
pre·ma·ture

pre·mier (prime minister; see *premiere*)
pre·miere (first public perform-ance; see *premier*)
pre·mise
pre·mi·um
pre·mo·ni·tion
pre·oc·cu·pa·tion
prep·a·ra·tion
pre·pa·ra·to·ry
pre·pared·ness
pre·pon·der·ance
prep·o·si·tion
pre·pos·sess
pre·pos·ter·ous
pre·req·ui·site
pre·scribe
pre·scrip·tion
pre·sent·able
pre·sen·ta·tion
pre·sent·ly
pres·er·va·tion·ist
pre·ser·va·tive
pre·shrunk
pres·i·den·cy (—cies)
pres·sure
pres·sur·ize
pres·tige
pres·ti·gious
pre·sume
pre·sump·tion
pre·sump·tu·ous
pre·tend·er
pre·ten·sion
pre·ten·tious
pre·ter·nat·u·ral
pre·test
pre·text
pret·ti·ness
pret·ty
pret·zel
pre·vail
prev·a·lent
pre·var·i·cate
pre·vent·able
pre·ven·tive, pre·ven·ta·tive
pre·view
pre·vi·ous
prey
prick·ly
pri·ma·cy
pri·ma don·na
pri·ma fa·cie

pri·mar·i·ly
pri·mate
prime
prim·er
pri·me·val
prim·ing
prim·i·tive
pri·mor·di·al
prim·rose
prince·ly
prin·ci·pal (head of school; see *principle*)
prin·ci·ple (fundamental law; see *principal*)
print·able
pri·or
prism
pris·mat·ic
pris·on·er
pris·tine
pri·va·cy (—cies)
pri·vate
pri·va·tion
priv·et
priv·i·lege
prize
prob·a·bil·i·ty (—ties)
prob·a·ble
pro·bate
pro·ba·tion·er
prob·lem·at·ic
pro·ce·dur·al
pro·ce·dure
pro·ceed
pro·cess (pro·cess·es)
pro·ces·sion
pro·ces·sor
pro·claim
proc·la·ma·tion
pro·cliv·i·ty (—ties)
pro·cras·ti·nate
pro·cre·ate
pro·crus·te·an
proc·tor
proc·u·ra·tor
pro·cure·ment
prod·i·gal
pro·di·gious
prod·i·gy (—gies)
pro·duce (noun), pro·duce (verb)
pro·duc·tion
pro·fan·i·ty (—ties)
pro·fes·sion

pro·fes·sor
pro·fi·cien·cy (–cies)
pro·file
prof·it (gain; see *prophet*)
prof·li·ga·cy (–cies)
pro·found
pro·fun·di·ty (–ties)
pro·fuse·ly
prog·e·ny (–nies)
prog·no·sis
prog·nos·tic
prog·nos·ti·cate
pro·gram
pro·gram·mer
pro·gres·sion
pro·gres·sive
pro·hib·it
pro·hi·bi·tion
proj·ect
pro·jec·tile
pro·jec·tion
pro·lif·er·ate
pro·lif·ic
pro·logue
pro·long
prom·e·nade
prom·i·nence
pro·mis·cu·ity (–ities)
prom·is·ing
prom·is·so·ry (–ries)
prom·on·to·ry (–ries)
pro·mot·er
pro·mo·tion
prompt·ness
pro·mul·gate
pro·nate
pro·noun
pro·nounce·ment
pro·nun·ci·a·tion
pro·pa·gan·da
prop·a·gate
pro·pane
pro·pel
pro·pen·si·ty (–ties)
prop·er·ly
prop·er·ty (–ties)
proph·e·cy (–cies) (inspired dec-
    laration; see *prophesy*)
proph·e·sy (to predict; see
    prophecy)
prophet (one who foretells the
    future; see *profit*)
pro·phet·ic

pro·phy·lac·tic
pro·pi·tious
pro·por·tion
pro·pose
prop·o·si·tion
pro·pri·etary (–etar·ies)
pro·pri·etor
pro·pul·sion
pro·rate
pro·sa·ic
pro·scribe
pro·scrip·tion
pros·e·cute
pros·e·cu·tor
pros·e·ly·tize
pro·spect
pro·spec·tive
pro·spec·tus
pros·tate (gland; see *prostrate*)
pros·trate (prone; see *prostate*)
pro·tag·o·nist
pro·tec·tive·ly
pro·tec·tion
pro·té·gé
pro·tein
pro·test·er, pro·test·or
pro·tes·ta·tion
pro·to·col
pro·ton
pro·to·type
pro·to·zo·an
pro·trac·tor
pro·trude
pro·tru·sion
pro·tu·ber·ant
prove
prov·en·der
pro·ver·bi·al
prov·i·dence
prov·i·den·tial
pro·vin·cial
pro·vi·sion·al
pro·vi·so
prov·o·ca·tion
pro·voc·a·tive
pro·vo·lo·ne (Italian: a kind of
    cheese)
pro·vost
prow·ess
prowl
prox·i·mate
prox·im·i·ty
proxy (prox·ies)

pru·dence
pru·ri·ence
pry·ing
psalm·ist
psal·tery, psal·try (psal·ter·ies *or*
    psal·tries)
pseud·onym
psy·che·del·ic
psy·chi·a·trist
psy·chi·a·try
psy·chic
psy·cho·anal·y·sis
psy·cho·log·i·cal
psy·chol·o·gist
psy·cho·path
psy·cho·so·mat·ics
psy·cho·ther·a·py
pto·maine
pu·ber·ty
pu·bes·cent
pu·bic
pub·lic
pub·li·can
pub·lic·i·ty
pub·lic·ly
pub·lish·er
puck·er
pud·ding
pud·dle
pug·na·cious
pul·ley
pul·mo·nary
pulp
pul·pit
pul·sar
pul·sate
pulse
pul·ver·ize
pu·ma
pum·ice
pum·mel
pump·er
pum·per·nick·el
pump·kin
punch
punc·tu·al
punc·tu·ate
punc·tu·a·tion
punc·ture
pun·dit
pun·gen·cy
pun·gent
pun·ish·able

pu·ni·tive
pun·ster
punt·er
pup·pet
pup·pe·teer
pur·chase
pu·rée (French: to strain cooked food)
purge
pu·ri·fi·ca·tion
pu·ri·fy
pur·ist
pu·ri·tan·i·cal
pur·loin
pur·ple
pur·port
pur·pose
pur·pose·ly
pur·su·ance
pur·sue
pur·suit
pur·vey·or
pur·view
pushy
pus·tu·lar
pus·tule
pu·tre·fy
pu·trid
put·ter
put·ty (putties)
puz·zling
pyg·my (pygmies)
py·or·rhea
pyr·a·mid
pyre
py·ro·tech·nics
py·thon
pyx·ie

Q

quack·ery
quad·rant
qua·dren·ni·al
quad·ri·lat·er·al
qua·dru·ple
quaff
quag·mire
quail
quaint·ly
quake
qual·i·fi·ca·tion

qual·i·fied
qual·i·fy
qual·i·ta·tive
qual·i·ty (–ties)
qualm
quan·da·ry (–ries)
quan·ti·fy
quan·ti·ta·tive
quan·ti·ty (–ties)
quan·tum (–ta)
quar·an·tine
quar·rel
quar·rel·some
quar·ry (quar·ries)
quar·ter
quar·ter·back
quar·tet, quar·tette
quar·to
quartz
qua·sar
quash
qua·train
quay
quea·sy, quea·zy
queen
queen·size
queer
quell
quench
quer·u·lous
que·ry (que·ries)
quest
ques·tion
ques·tion·able
ques·tion·naire
queue (ordered list, see *cue*)
quib·ble
quick·en
qui·et (free from noise; see *quite*)
qui·etus
quilt
quince
qui·nine
quin·tes·sence
quin·tet, quin·tette
quin·tile
quin·tu·plet
quip
quirk
quirky
quit
quite (completely; see *quiet*)
quit·ter

quiv·er
quix·ot·ic
quiz (quiz·zes)
quiz·zi·cal
quo·rum
quo·ta
quot·able
quo·ta·tion
quote
quo·tient

R

rab·bit (rab·bit *or* rab·bits)
rabble
ra·bid
ra·bies (plural also ra·bies)
rac·coon (rac·coon *or* rac·coons)
race·way
ra·cial
rac·ism
rack·et, rac·quet
racy
ra·dar
ra·di·al
ra·di·ance
ra·di·ate
ra·di·a·tor
rad·i·cal
rad·i·cal·ly
ra·dio·ac·tive
rad·ish
ra·di·um
ra·di·us (ra·di·us·es *or* ra·dii)
raff·ish
raf·fle
raf·ter
rag·ged
rag·gle-tag·gle
rag·ing
ra·gout
raid·er
rail·road
rain (water falling in drops from the atmosphere; see *reign, rein*)
rain·bow
rainy
raise (to lift; see *raze*)
rai·sin
ral·ly (ral·lies)
ram·ble

ram·bunc·tious
ram·i·fi·ca·tion
ram·i·fy
ram·page
ram·pant
ram·part
ram·rod
ram·shack·le
ran·cor·ous
ran·dom
rang·er
ran·sack
ran·som
ra·pid
ra·pi·er
rap·ine
rap·port
rar·efy
rar·i·ty (–ties)
ras·cal·i·ty (–ties)
rasp·ber·ry
raspy
ratch·et
rate
rat·i·fy
ra·tio
ra·tion
ra·tio·nal (relating to reason; see *rationale*)
ra·tio·nale (underlying reason; see *rational*)
ra·tio·nal·ize
rat·tan
rat·tle
rau·cous
raun·chy
rav·age
rav·en·ous
ra·vine
rav·i·o·li
ray·on
raze (destroy to the ground; see *raise*)
raz·zle-daz·zle
reach·able
re·ac·tion
re·ac·tion·ary
re·ac·ti·vate
re·ac·tor
read·able
readi·ly
re·align
re·al·is·tic

re·al·iz·a·tion
re·al·ly
realm
re·al·i·ty
re·al·ty
ream
re·ap·por·tion
re·arm
rea·son·able
re·as·sur·ance
re·bate
re·bel·lious
re·bound
re·buff
re·buke
re·but·tal
re·cal·ci·trance
re·ca·pit·u·late
re·cede
re·ceipt
re·ceiv·able
re·ceiv·er
re·cent·ly
re·cep·ta·cle
re·cep·tion·ist
re·cep·tive
re·cess
re·ces·sion
re·cid·i·vist
re·cip·ro·cate
rec·i·proc·i·ty (–ties)
re·cit·al
rec·i·ta·tive
reck·oned
rec·la·ma·tion
re·cluse
rec·og·ni·tion
re·cog·ni·zance
re·col·lect
rec·om·mend
rec·om·men·da·tion
rec·om·pense
rec·on·cil·able
re·con·nais·sance
re·con·sti·tute
re·con·struc·tion
re·con·vert
re·cord·er
re·coup
re·course
re·cov·er·able
rec·re·ant
rec·re·ation

re·crim·i·nate
re·cru·des·cence
re·cruit
rect·an·gu·lar
rec·ti·fy
rec·ti·tude
rec·tor
re·cum·bent
re·cu·per·ate
re·cur·rent
re·cy·cla·ble
re·cy·cle
red·den
re·deem·er
re·demp·tive
re·de·sign
re·dis·trict
red·o·lent
re·dou·ble
re·dound
re·duc·ible
re·duc·tion
re·dun·dan·cy (–cies)
re·elec·tion
re·en·act
re·en·try
re·fec·to·ry (–ries)
re·fer·able
ref·er·ee
ref·er·ence
ref·er·en·dum
re·fer·ral
re·fi·nance
re·fine·ment
re·flec·tion
re·flec·tor
re·flex
ref·or·ma·tion
re·for·ma·to·ry (–ries)
re·frac·to·ry (–ries)
re·frain
re·fresh·ment
re·frig·er·a·tor
ref·u·gee
re·fund
re·fur·bish
re·fus·al
ref·u·ta·tion
re·gal (royal; see *regale*)
re·gale (to give pleasure; see *regal*)
re·ga·lia
re·gard·less

re·gat·ta
re·gen·cy (–cies)
re·gen·er·ate
re·gent
re·gime, ré·gime
reg·i·men (systematic plan; see *regiment*)
reg·i·ment (military unit; see *regimen*)
re·gion·al
reg·is·ter (to enroll formally; see *registrar*)
reg·is·trar (keeper of records; see *register*)
reg·is·try (–tries)
re·gres·sion
re·gres·sive
re·gret·ta·bly
reg·u·lar·i·ty (–ties)
reg·u·la·to·ry
re·gur·gi·tate
re·ha·bil·i·tate
re·hears·al
reign (sovereignty; see *rain, rein*)
re·im·burse
rein (part of a bridle; stop or check; see *rain, reign*)
rein·deer
re·in·force
re·in·vest·ment
re·is·sue
re·it·er·ate
re·jec·tion
re·join·der
re·ju·ve·nate
re·lapse
re·la·tion
rel·a·tive
rel·a·tiv·i·ty (–ties)
re·lax·ation
re·lay
re·lease
rel·e·gate
re·lent·less
rel·e·van·cy
rel·e·vant
re·li·abil·i·ty
re·li·ance
rel·ic
re·lied
re·lief
re·lieve
re·li·gious

re·lo·cate
re·luc·tant
re·main
re·main·der
re·mark·able
re·me·di·a·ble
re·me·di·al
rem·e·dy (–dies)
re·mem·brance
rem·i·nis·cence
re·mis·sion
re·mit·tance
rem·nant
re·mon·strate
re·morse·ful
re·mote
re·mov·able
re·mu·ner·ate
re·nais·sance, re·na·scence
ren·der
ren·dez·vous
ren·di·tion
ren·e·gade
re·nege
re·ne·go·ti·ate
re·new·al
re·nounce
ren·o·vate
rent·al
re·nun·ci·a·tion
re·open
re·or·ga·ni·za·tion
re·pair·able
rep·a·ra·tion
rep·ar·tee
re·pa·tri·ate
re·peal
re·peat·ed·ly
re·pel·lent, re·pel·lant
re·pen·tance
re·per·cus·sion
rep·er·toire
rep·er·to·ry (–ries)
rep·e·ti·tious
re·place·able
re·plen·ish
re·plete
rep·li·ca
rep·li·cate
re·port·able
re·pose
re·pos·i·to·ry (–ries)
re·pos·sess

rep·re·hend
rep·re·hen·si·ble
rep·re·sen·ta·tive
re·pres·sion
re·prieve
re·pri·sal
re·prise
re·proach
rep·ro·bate
re·pro·duc·tion
rep·tile
re·pub·lic
re·pu·di·ate
re·pug·nance
re·pul·sive
rep·u·ta·ble
re·pute
re·quest
re·qui·em
re·quire·ment
req·ui·site
req·ui·si·tion
re·scind
res·cue
re·search
re·sem·blance
re·sent·ful
res·er·va·tion
res·er·voir
re·shuf·fle
res·i·dence
res·i·den·tial
re·sid·u·al
res·i·due
res·ig·na·tion
re·sis·tance
re·sist·er (one who opposes; see *resistor*)
re·sis·tor (electrical device; see *resister*)
res·o·lute
re·solve
res·o·nance
res·o·nate
res·o·na·tor
re·sound
re·source·ful
re·spect·abil·i·ty (–ties)
re·spec·tive·ly
res·pi·ra·tion
res·pi·ra·tor
re·splen·dent
re·spon·dent

re·spon·si·bil·i·ty (–ties)
re·spon·sive
re·spon·so·ry (–ries)
re·state·ment
res·tau·rant
res·ti·tu·tion
res·to·ra·tion
re·strain
re·stric·tion
re·struc·ture
re·sult
re·sume (to begin again; see
    resumé)
re·su·mé (short account of
    career; see resume)
re·sump·tion
re·sur·gence
res·ur·rec·tion
re·sus·ci·tate
re·tail·ing
re·tain·er
re·tal·i·ate
re·tar·da·tion
re·ten·tive
ret·i·cence
ret·i·nue
re·tire·ment
re·tract
re·trench
ret·ri·bu·tion
re·triev·al
ret·ro·ac·tive
ret·ro·grade
re·tro·spect
re·turn·able
re·unite
re·us·able
re·veal
rev·e·la·tion
rev·el·er, rev·el·ler
rev·el·ry (–ries)
re·venge·ful
rev·e·nue
re·ver·ber·ate
rev·er·ence
rev·er·ie, rev·ery (rev·er·ies)
re·ver·sal
re·vers·ible
re·vert·ible
re·view (to see again; see revue)
re·vile
re·vi·sion
re·vi·tal·ize

re·viv·al
re·vive
re·vo·ca·ble
re·voke
re·volt
rev·o·lu·tion
rev·o·lu·tion·ize
re·volv·er
re·vue (theatrical production; see
    review)
re·vul·sion
re·ward
re·write
rhap·so·dy (–dies)
rheo·stat
rhet·o·ric
rheu·mat·ic
rhi·noc·er·os (rhi·noc·er·os·es or
    rhi·noc·eros or rhi·noc·eri)
rhu·barb
rhyme
rhythm
rhyth·mic
rib·ald
rib·bon
rick·ety
rid·dance
rid·dle
ridge
ri·dic·u·lous
ri·fle
rift
rig·ging
right (correct; see rite)
righ·teous
ri·gid·i·ty (–ties)
rig·ma·role
rig·or·ous
ring·er
rins·ing
ri·ot·ous
ri·par·i·an
rip·ple
risky
ris·qué (French: off·color)
rite (a ceremonial act; see right)
rit·u·al
ri·val·ry (–ries)
riv·er·side
riv·et
roach
roam
roast

rob·bery (rob·ber·ies)
ro·bot
ro·bust
rock·et
ro·co·co
ro·dent
ro·deo (ro·de·os)
rogue
rogu·ish
rol·lick·ing
ro·man·ti·cize
roomy
roost·er
ro·sette
ros·ter
ros·trum
ro·ta·ry (–ries)
ro·ta·tion
rote
ro·tund
ro·tun·da
rouge
rough
rou·lette
rouse
route
rou·tine
rov·ing
row·dy
roy·al·ist
roy·al·ty (–ties)
rub·bery
rub·bish
rub·ble
ru·bric
rud·der
ru·di·men·ta·ry
ruf·fi·an
ruf·fle
rug·by
rug·ged
ru·in·ous
rul·ing
rum·ba
rum·ble
ru·mi·nate
rum·mage
ru·mor
run·ner
rup·ture
ru·ral
ruse
rus·set

rus·tic
rus·ti·cate
rust·i·ness
rus·tle
ru·ta·ba·ga
ruth·less
rye

S

sab·bat·i·cal
sa·ber, sa·bre
sa·ble
sab·o·tage
sab·o·teur
sac·cha·rine
sa·chet
sac·ra·ment
sa·cred
sac·ri·fice
sac·ri·fi·cial
sac·ro·sanct
sad·den
sad·dle
sa·fa·ri
safe·ty (safeties)
saf·flow·er
sa·ga
sa·ga·cious
sage
sail (canvas used to propel ship;
    see *sale*)
sail·or
sal·able, sale·able
sal·ad
sal·a·ry (—ries)
sale (act of selling; see *sail*)
sales check
sales·clerk
sales tax
sa·lient
sa·line
sa·li·va
sal·i·vate
sal·low
salm·on (salm·on *or* salm·ons)
sa·lon (elegant living room; see
    saloon)
sa·loon (place selling alcoholic
    drinks; see *salon*)
sal·u·tary
sa·lu·ta·to·ri·an
sa·lute

sal·vage
sal·va·tion
salve
sam·ple
san·a·to·ri·um
sanc·ti·mo·nious
sanc·tion
sanc·tu·ary (—ar·ies)
san·dal
sand·wich (—es)
san·i·tary
san·i·ta·tion
sap·ling
sap·phire
sar·casm
sar·cas·ti·cal·ly
sar·dine (sar·dines *or* sar·dine)
sar·don·ic
sa·ri, sa·ree (Sanskrit: woman's
    Hindu garment)
sar·sa·pa·ril·la
sar·to·ri·al
sas·sa·fras
satch·el
sa·teen
sat·el·lite
sa·ti·ate
sa·ti·ety
sat·in
sat·ire
sat·is·fac·tion
sat·u·rate
sat·u·ra·tion
sat·ur·nine
sa·tyr
saucy
sau·er·kraut
sau·na
saun·ter
sau·sage
sau·té
sav·age·ly
sa·van·na, sa·van·nah
sa·vant
sav·ior, sav·iour
sa·voir faire (French: sureness in
    social behavior)
sa·vory, sa·voury
sax·o·phone
scab·bard
sca·brous
scaf·fold
scald·ing
scal·lion

scal·lop
scalp·er
scan·dal
scan·dal·ous
scan·ner
scanty
scape·goat
scap·u·lar
scar·ci·ty (—ties)
scarf (scarves)
scary, scar·ey
scath·ing
scat·o·log·i·cal
scat·ter
scav·enge
sce·nar·io
sce·nar·ist
scen·ery (—er·ies)
sce·nic
scent·ed
scep·ter, scep·tre
sched·ule
sche·mat·ic
scheme
schism
schizo·phre·nia
schnau·zer
schol·ar·ly
scho·las·tic
school
schoo·ner
schwa
sci·at·ic
sci·ence
sci·en·tif·ic
scin·til·late
scis·sors
scle·ro·sis
scoff·law
scone
scope
scorch
scor·ing
scorn·ful
scor·pi·on
scoun·drel
scour
scourge
scram·ble
scrap·ing (grate harshly; see
    scrapping)
scrap·ping (quarreling, converting
    to scrap; see *scraping*)
scratch

scraw·ny
scream
screech
screen
screen·play
screw
scrib·ble
scrim·mage
scrim·shaw
script
scrip·ture
scrounge
scruff
scru·ple
scru·pu·lous
scru·ti·nize
scru·ti·ny
scu·ba
scuff
scuf·fle
sculp·tor
sculp·ture
scur·ri·lous
scut·tle
scythe
sea (body of water; see *see*)
seamy
sé·ance (French: a session to receive spirit communications)
search
sea·shore
sea·son·al
seat
se·cede
se·ces·sion
se·clu·sion
sec·ond·ary
se·cre·cy (–cies)
secret
sec·re·tar·i·at
sec·re·tary (–tar·ies)
se·crete
se·cre·tive
sect
sec·tar·i·an
sec·tion·al
sec·tor
sec·u·lar
se·cu·ri·ty (–ties)
se·dan
se·date
sed·a·tive
sed·en·tary
se·der

sedge
sed·i·ment
se·di·tion
se·duce
se·duc·tive
sed·u·lous
see (perceive by eye; see *sea*)
seed·ling
seem·ing·ly
seep·age
seer·suck·er
see·saw
seethe
seg·ment
seg·re·gate
seg·re·ga·tion
se·gue
seine
seis·mic
seis·mo·graph
seize
sei·zure
sel·dom
se·lec·tion
se·lec·tive
self-con·scious
self-de·fense
self-por·trait
sell (to exact a price for; see *cell*)
sell·er (one who offers for sale; see *cellar*)
se·man·tics
sema·phore
sem·blance
se·mes·ter
semi·an·nu·al
sem·i·nal
sem·i·nar
sem·i·nary (–nar·ies)
semi·pro·fes·sion·al
sem·pi·ter·nal
sen·a·to·ri·al
se·nes·cence
se·nile
se·nil·i·ty
se·nior·i·ty
sen·sa·tion
sense
sense·less
sen·si·bil·i·ty (–ties)
sen·si·tive
sen·si·tiv·i·ty
sen·so·ry
sen·su·al

sen·su·ous
sent (past of *send*; see *cent*)
sen·tence
sen·ten·tious
sen·tient
sen·ti·men·tal
sen·ti·nel
sen·try (sentries)
sep·a·ra·ble
sep·a·rate
sep·a·ra·tion
sep·ul·cher, sep·ul·chre
se·quel
se·quence
se·quen·tial
se·ques·ter
se·quoia
ser·e·nade
se·ren·i·ty
serge
ser·geant
se·ri·al (arranged in series; see *cereal*)
se·ries (plural also series)
se·ri·ous
ser·mon
ser·pent
ser·rat·ed
se·rum
ser·vant
serv·er
ser·vice
ser·vice·able
ser·vi·tude
ses·a·me
ses·sion
ses·tet
set·tle
set·tle·ment
sev·enth
sev·er·al
sev·er·ance
se·ver·i·ty
sew·age
sew·ing
sex·ism
sex·tant
sex·ton
sex·u·al
sexy
shab·by
shack·le
shad·ing
shad·owy

shaft

shag·gy

shaky

shale

shal·low

sham·ble

shame·ful

sham·poo

sham·rock

shank

shan·ty (shanties)

shape

shard

share·crop·per

shark

sharp·en

shat·ter

shav·ing

sheaf (sheaves)

shear (cut off; see *sheer*)

sheath (case for a blade; see
   sheathe)

sheathe (to put into a sheath; see
   sheath)

sheer (transparent; see *shear*)

sheet

sheikh, sheik

shelf (shelves)

shel·lac

shel·ter

she·nan·i·gan

shep·herd

sher·bet

sher·iff

sher·ry (sherries)

shib·bo·leth

shield

shifty

shin·gle

shin·ing

shiny

ship·ment

shirk·er

shirt·sleeve

shish ke·bab

shiv·er

shoal

shock

shoe

shop

shor·ing

short·age

short·en·ing

short·hand

short·term

should

shoul·der

shout

shove

shov·el

show·case

show·er

showy

shrap·nel

shrewd

shriek

shrine

shrink

shriv·el

shroud

shrub·bery

shrug

shud·der

shuf·fle

shut·ter

shut·tle

shy

sib·i·lant

sick·le

sick·ly

sick·ness

side·line

si·de·re·al

siege

sieve

sigh

sight·ly

sign

sig·nal

sig·na·to·ry (–ries)

sig·na·ture

sig·nif·i·cant

si·lent

sil·hou·ette

sil·i·con

silky

silver·ware

sil·very

sim·i·an

sim·i·lar

sim·i·lar·i·ty (–ties)

sim·i·le

si·mil·i·tude

sim·per

sim·ple

sim·pli·fy

sim·u·la·tion

si·mul·ta·neous

sin·cere·ly

si·ne·cure

sin·ew

singe

singe·ing

sin·gle

sin·gly

sin·gu·lar·i·ty (–ties)

sin·is·ter

sin·u·ous

si·nus

si·phon

si·ren

sis·ter·ly

site (place; see *cite*)

sit·u·at·ed

sit·u·a·tion

six·ty (sixties)

size

siz·zle

skein, skean, skeane

skel·e·ton

skep·ti·cal

sketchy

skied

ski·ing

skil·let

skill·ful, skil·ful

skim·ming

skimpy

skip·per

skirl

skir·mish

skit·tish

skul·dug·gery, skull·dug·gery
   (–ger·ies)

skulk

sky

slack·en

slack·er

sla·lom

slan·der·ous

slaugh·ter

slav·ery

slea·zy

sledge

sledge·ham·mer

sleek

sleeve

sleigh

slen·der·ize

sleuth
slic·ing
slick·er
slide
slight·ing·ly
slime
slip·pery
slip·shod
slith·er
sliv·er
slob·ber
sloe (fruit; see *slow*)
slo·gan
sloop
slope
slop·ing
slop·py
sloth·ful
slouch
slough
slov·en·ly
slow (not hasty; see *sloe*)
sludge
slug·gish
sluice
slum·ber
slushy
sly
small
smart
smat·ter·ing
smear
smelly
smid·gen, smid·geon, smid·gin
smile
smirk
smith·er·eens
smoke
smol·der, smoul·der
smooth
smor·gas·bord
smudge
snail
snake
sneak·er
sneer
sneeze
snif·ter
snip·er
snob·bery
snor·kel
snow·flake
snow·mo·bile

snug·gle
soap opera
soapy
soar·ing
so·ber·ly
so·bri·ety
soc·cer
so·cia·bil·i·ty (–ties)
so·cial·ism
so·cial·ize
so·ci·etal
so·ci·ety (–et·ies)
so·cio·eco·nom·ic
so·ci·ol·o·gy
sod·den
soft·ware
sog·gy
soil
soi·rée, soi·ree (French: evening
   party)
so·journ
so·lace
so·lar
sol·der
sol·dier
sole (fish or bottom of foot; see
   soul)
so·le·cism
sol·emn
so·lem·ni·ty (–ties)
so·le·noid
so·lic·it
so·lic·i·tor
so·lic·i·tous
so·lic·i·tude
sol·i·dar·i·ty
so·lid·i·fy
so·lil·o·quize
sol·i·taire
sol·i·tary
sol·i·tude
so·lo·ist
sol·u·ble
so·lu·tion
solv·able
sol·ven·cy
som·ber
son (male child; see *sun*)
so·nar
son·ic
son·net
so·no·rous
soothe

sooty
so·phis·ti·cat·ed
soph·ist·ry
soph·o·more
so·po·rif·ic
so·pra·no (–nos)
sor·cer·er
sor·did
so·ror·i·ty (–ties)
sor·row·ful
soul (spiritual essence; see *sole*)
sought
sound
soup du jour (French: soup of the
   day)
sour
source
south·ern
sou·ve·nir
sov·er·eign
soy·bean
space
spa·cial
spa·cious
spa·ghet·ti
span·gled
span·iel
spar·ing·ly
spar·kle
spar·row
sparse
spasm
spas·mod·ic
spas·tic
spa·tial
spat·u·la
spay
speak·er
spe·cial
spe·cial·ty (–ties)
spe·cies
spe·cif·ic
spec·i·fic·ca·tion
spec·i·fic·i·ty
spec·i·men
spec·ta·cle
spec·tac·u·lar
spec·ta·tor
spec·tral
spec·trum
spec·u·late
spec·u·la·tion
speech·less

spell·check, spell·check·er
spend·thrift
sperm
sphere
spher·i·cal
sphinx (sphinx·es *or* sphin·ges)
spice
spic·ing
spig·ot
spill·age
spin·ach
spin·dle
spin·dly
spin·et
spin·ster
spi·ral
spir·i·tu·al
spite·ful
splashy
splen·dor
splice
splin·ter
splut·ter
spoil·age
spokes·man
spo·li·a·tion
spon·dee
sponge
spongy
spon·sor
spon·ta·ne·ity
spon·ta·ne·ous
spooky
spoon·ful (spoon·fuls *or* spoons·ful)
spo·rad·ic
spore
sport·ive
sporty
spot·light
spot·ty
spouse
spright·ly
spring·time
springy
sprin·kling
sprock·et
sprout
spry
spunky
spu·ri·ous
spurred
spu·tum
spy (spies)

squab·ble
squad·ron
squal·id
squa·lor
squan·der
square
squash
squat·ted
squat·ter
squawk
squeaky
squeal
squea·mish
squeeze
squelch
squint
squire
squirm
squir·rel (squir·rels *or* squir·rel)
squirt
sta·bil·i·ty (–ties)
sta·ble
stac·ca·to
stacked
sta·di·um (sta·dia *or* sta·di·ums)
staff
stage
stag·ing
stag·nant
staid
stair·case
stake (pointed post; see *steak*)
sta·lac·tite
sta·lag·mite
stale·mate
stalk
stal·lion
stal·wart
stam·i·na
stam·mer
stam·pede
stance
stan·chion
stan·dard·ize
stand·by
stan·za
sta·ple
starchy
star·ry
star·tle
star·va·tion
stash
state
state·ment

stat·ic
sta·tion
sta·tion·ary (immobile; see *stationery*)
sta·tio·nery (materials for writing; see *stationary*)
stat·is·ti·cian
sta·tis·tics
stat·ue
stat·ure
sta·tus
stat·u·to·ry
staunch
stead·fast
steak (slice of meat; see *stake*)
steal (to take the property of another; see *steel*)
stealthy
steel (a metal; see *steal*)
stee·ple
steer·age
stein
stel·lar
sten·cil
ste·nog·ra·pher
sten·to·ri·an
step (an advance of a foot; see *steppe*)
steppe (treeless plain; see *step*)
ste·reo·type
ste·reo·typ·i·cal
ster·ile
ster·ling
ste·ve·dore
stew·ard
stick·ler
sticky
sti·fle
stig·ma·tize
sti·let·to
stim·u·late
stim·u·lus
stin·gy
sti·pend
stip·u·late
stir·rup
stitch
stock·ade
stock·bro·ker
stodgy
stol·id
stom·ach·ache
stop·page
stor·age

sto·ried
stow·age
strad·dle
strag·gle
straight (free from curves; see *strait*)
straight·en
strait (a narrow passageway between two bodies of water; see *straight*)
strang·er
stran·gle
stran·gu·late
strat·a·gem
stra·te·gic
strat·e·gy (–gies)
strat·i·fy
strato·sphere
stra·tum (stra·ta)
streaky
stream·line
strength
stren·u·ous
stress·ful
stretch·er
stri·at·ed
strick·en
stric·ture
stri·dent
strike
strin·gent
strobe
stroll
strong
struc·tu·ral
struc·ture
strug·gle
strych·nine
stub·ble
stub·by
stuc·co
stu·dent
stu·dio
stu·di·ous
study
stul·ti·fy
stum·bling
stu·pe·fy
stu·pen·dous
stur·dy
stur·geon
stut·ter
sty, stye (sties *or* styes)
style

styl·ish
styl·ized
sty·lus (sty·li *or* sty·lus·es)
suave
sub·com·mit·tee
sub·con·scious
sub·di·vi·sion
sub·due
sub·ject (noun), sub·ject (verb)
sub·ju·gate
sub·lime
sub·lim·i·nal
sub·ma·rine
sub·merge
sub·mis·sion
sub·or·di·nate
sub·orn
sub·poe·na
sub·scribe
sub·scrip·tion
sub·se·quent
sub·ser·vi·ent
sub·side
sub·sid·iary
sub·si·dize
sub·si·dy (–dies)
sub·sis·tence
sub·stance
sub·stan·tial
sub·stan·tive
sub·sti·tute
sub·sume
sub·ter·fuge
sub·tle
sub·trac·tion
sub·ur·bia
sub·ver·sion
suc·ceed
suc·cess·ful
suc·ces·sion
suc·ces·sor
suc·cinct
suc·co·tash
suc·cu·lent
suc·cumb
suck·le
suc·tion
sud·den
sudsy
sue
suede, suède
suf·fer·ance
suf·fice
suf·fi·cient

suf·fo·cate
suf·frage
suf·fuse
sug·ar
sug·ges·tion
sui·cid·al
suit·able
suite
suit·or
sulky
sul·phur, sul·fur
sul·try
sum·ma·ry (abridgment of discourse; see *summery*)
sum·mer·time
sum·mery (like summer; see *summary*)
sum·mit
sum·mon
sump·tu·ous
sun (celestial body; see *son*)
su·per·an·nu·ate
su·perb
su·per·cil·ious
su·per·fi·cial
su·per·flu·ity (–ities)
su·per·flu·ous
su·per·high·way
su·per·in·ten·dent
su·pe·ri·or
su·per·la·tive
su·per·nat·u·ral
su·per·sede
su·per·sti·tious
su·per·vi·sion
su·per·vi·so·ry
su·pine
sup·plant
sup·ple
sup·ple·men·ta·ry
sup·pli·ant
sup·pli·cate
supply (supplies)
sup·port·ive
sup·po·si·tion
sup·pos·i·to·ry (–ries)
sup·pres·sion
sup·pu·rate
su·prem·a·cy (–cies)
sur·cease
sur·charge
sure·ty (–ties)
sur·face
sur·feit

sur·fer
surge
sur·geon
sur·gery
sur·gi·cal
sur·mise
sur·name
sur·plice
sur·plus
sur·re·al·ism
sur·ren·der
sur·ro·gate
sur·round·ings
sur·tax
sur·veil·lance
sur·vey (noun), sur·vey (verb)
sur·viv·al
sus·cep·ti·bil·i·ty (—ties)
sus·cep·ti·ble
sus·pect
sus·pense
sus·pi·cious
sus·te·nance
su·ture
svelte
swad·dling
swag·ger
swampy
swank
swar·thy
swash·buck·ler
swath, swathe
swear
sweaty
sweet·ened
swel·ter
swept
swerve
swin·dle
swing
swirl
swish
switch
swiv·el
swol·len
sword
syc·a·more
sy·co·phant
syl·lab·ic
syl·lab·i·fy
syl·la·bus (—bi *or* ·bus·es)
syl·lo·gism
sylph

syl·van
sym·bol·ic
sym·met·ri·cal, sym·met·ric
sym·me·try (—tries)
sym·pa·thet·ic
sym·phon·ic
sym·po·sium
symp·tom
syn·chro·nize
syn·di·cate
syn·onym
syn·op·sis
syn·op·tic
syn·tax
syn·the·size
syn·thet·ic, syn·thet·i·cal
syph·i·lis
sy·ringe
syr·upy
sys·tem·at·ic, sys·tem·at·i·cal
sys·tem·atize
sys·tem·ic

T

Ta·bas·co
tab·by
tab·er·na·cle
tab·la·ture
ta·bling
ta·ble·spoon·ful (ta·ble·spoon·fuls *or* ta·ble·spoons·ful)
tab·let
tab·loid
ta·boo, ta·bu
tab·o·ret, tab·ou·ret (French: type of seat or stand)
tab·u·lar
tab·u·late
tab·u·la·tor
ta·chom·e·ter
tac·it
tac·i·turn
tack·le
tacky
tact·ful
tac·tic·al
tac·tile
tad·pole
taf·fe·ta
taff·rail
taf·fy

tai·chi
tail (rear end; see *tale*)
tai·lored
taint
tak·ing
talc
tal·cum
tale (story: see *tail*)
tal·ent
tales·man (juror; see *talisman*)
tal·is·man (charm: see *talesman*)
talk·ative
talk·ie (sound motion picture; see *talky*)
talky (too much talk; see *talkie*)
tall·ish
tal·low
tal·ly (tal·lies)
tal·on
ta·ma·le
tam·a·rack
tam·bou·rine
tam·ing
tam·per
tan·a·ger
tan·dem
tan·ge·lo
tan·gent
tan·gen·tial
tan·ger·ine
tan·gi·ble
tan·gling
tan·gled
tan·go (tan·gos)
tangy
tan·kard
tan·nery (—ner·ies)
tan·ning
tan·ta·lize
tan·ta·mount
tan·trum
tape
ta·per
tap·es·tried
tap·es·try (—tries)
tap·i·o·ca
tar·an·tel·la
ta·ran·tu·la
tar·di·ly
tar·dy
tare (weed; see *tear*)
tar·get
tar·iff

tar·mac
tar·nish
tar·ot
tar·pau·lin
tar·pon
tar·ra·gon
tar·ry
tar·tan
tar·tar
task
tas·sel
taste·ful
tasty
tat·tered
tat·too
taught
taunt
taupe
taut
tav·ern
taw·dry
taw·ny
tax·a·tion
tax·ex·empt
taxi·der·my
tax·ied
taxi·ing
tax·on·o·my (–mies)
tax·pay·er
teach·able
tea·ket·tle
teak·wood
team (group; see *teem*)
team·ster
tear (damage from being torn;
    see *tare*)
teas·ing
teat
tech·ni·cal
tech·ni·cian
tech·nique
tech·no·log·i·cal, tech·no·log·ic
tech·no·lo·gy
tech·no·phile
te·dious
te·di·um
teem (filled to overflowing; see
    team)
teen·age
tee·ter
teethe
tee·to·tal·er, tee·to·tal·ler
tele·cast

tele·com·mu·ni·ca·tion
tele·com·mu·ni·cate
tele·con·fer·ence
tele·gram
tele·graph
tele·mar·ket·er
te·lep·a·thy
tele·pho·to
tele·scope
tele·vise
te·mer·i·ty (–ties)
tem·per·a·ment
tem·per·ate
tem·per·a·ture
tem·pered
tem·pes·tu·ous
tem·plate
tem·ple
tem·po (tem·pi *or* tem·pos)
tem·po·ral
tem·po·rar·i·ly
tem·po·rize
tempt
temp·ta·tion
tem·pu·ra
ten·a·ble
te·na·cious
te·nac·i·ty
ten·ant
ten·den·cy (–cies)
ten·den·tious, ten·den·cious
ten·der·ize
ten·der·loin
ten·der·ly
ten·don
ten·dril
ten·e·ment
te·net
ten·or
tense
ten·sile
ten·sion
ten·ta·cle
ten·ta·tive
ten·ter·hook
ten·u·ous
ten·ure
te·pee
tep·id
ter·gi·ver·sa·tion
ter·i·ya·ki (Japanese: spicy meat
    or shelfish dish)
ter·ma·gant

ter·mi·nal
ter·mi·nate
ter·mi·na·tion
ter·mi·nol·o·gy (–gies)
ter·mi·nus (–ni *or* –nuses)
ter·mite
ter·race
ter·ra-cot·ta
ter·rain, ter·rane
ter·rar·i·um (ter·rar·ia *or*
    ter·rar·i·ums)
ter·res·tri·al
ter·ri·ble
ter·ri·er
ter·rif·ic
ter·ri·fy
ter·ri·to·ri·al
ter·ri·to·ry (–ries)
ter·ror·ize
ter·ry
terse
ter·tia·ry
tes·sel·tate
tes·ta·ment
tes·ta·tor
test·ed
tes·ti·cle
tes·ti·fy
tes·ti·mo·ni·al
tes·ti·mo·ny (–nies)
tes·ty
tet·a·nus
tête-à-tête (French: private con-
    versation between two people)
teth·er
tet·ra·chlo·ride
te·tram·e·ter
text·book
tex·tile
tex·ture
thank·ful
thatch
the·atre, the·ater
the·at·ri·cal
theft
their (relating to them; see *there*)
the·ism
the·mat·ic
theme
thence
the·oc·ra·cy (–cies)
theo·lo·gian
the·ol·o·gy (–gies)

the·o·rem
the·o·ret·i·cal
the·o·rist
the·o·ry (–ries)
the·os·o·phy
ther·a·peu·tic
ther·a·pist
ther·a·py (–pies)
there (in that place; see *their*)
ther·mal
ther·mom·e·ter
ther·mo·stat
the·sau·rus (the·sau·ri *or* the·sau·rus·es)
the·sis
thes·pi·an
thew
they
thick·en·ing
thick·et
thief
thiev·ery (–er·ies)
thigh
thim·ble·ful
think·able
thin·ner
third
thirsty
thir·teenth
this·tle
thith·er
thong
tho·rac·ic
thorny
thor·ough
thor·ough·bred
thor·ough·fare
though
thought
thought·ful
thou·sand
thrash
thread·bare
threat·en
three-di·men·sion·al
thren·o·dy (–dies)
thresh·old
thrift
thrive
throat
throe
throm·bo·sis (–bo·ses)
throne

thronged
throt·tle
through
through·out
thru·way
thug
thumb
thump
thun·der·ous
thwart
thyme
thy·roid
ti·ara
tick·et
tick·ing
tick·le
tid·al
tid·ings
ti·di·ness
tier
tight·rope
tile
till·age
tim·ber (wood; see *timbre*)
tim·bre (quality of sound; see *timber*)
time·ly
time·table
tim·id
tim·ing
tim·o·rous
tim·pa·nist
tinc·ture
tin·der
tinge
tin·gle
tin·kle
tin·ny
tin·sel
tint·ing
tip·sy
ti·rade
tire
tis·sue
tithe
tit·il·late
tit·i·vate, tit·ti·vate
ti·tled
tit·tle
toasty
to·bac·co
to·bog·gan
toc·sin

tod·dle
to·ga
to·geth·er·ness
tog·gle
toil
toile (French: type of fabric)
toil·worn
to·ken·ism
tole
tol·er·a·ble
tol·er·ance
toll
tom·a·hawk
to·ma·to (–toes)
tomb
to·mor·row
to·nal·i·ty (–ties)
tongue
tongu·ing
to·nic·i·ty
to·night
ton·nage
ton·sil·lec·to·my (–mies)
ton·sil·li·tis
ton·so·ri·al
ton·sure
tool·box
tooth·some
to·paz
top·i·cal
to·pog·ra·phy
to·pol·o·gy (–gies)
top·ple
top·sy-tur·vy
toque
to·re·ador (Spanish: bullfighter)
tor·men·tor
tor·na·do (–dos *or* –does)
tor·pe·do (–does)
tor·pid
tor·por
torque
tor·ren·tial
tor·rid·ly
tor·sion
tor·so (tor·sos *or* tor·si)
tor·ti·lla
tor·toise
tor·tu·ous
tor·ture
to·tal·ing
to·tal·i·tar·i·an
to·tal·i·ty (–ties)

to·tal·ly
to·tem
touch
touchy
tough·en
tou·pee (French: wig)
tour de force (French: a feat of
    strength, skill, or ingenuity)
tour·ism
tour·na·ment
tour·ney
tour·ni·quet
tou·sle
to·ward
tow·el·ing, tow·el·ling
tow·er·ing
tow·head
town house
tox·ic
tox·ic·i·ty
tox·in
tra·chea (tra·che·ae or tra·che·as)
trac·ing
trac·ta·ble
trac·tion
trac·tor
trade·mark
trad·er
tra·di·tion
traf·fic
trag·e·dy (—dies)
trail
train·ing
trai·tor
trai·tor·ous
tra·jec·to·ry (—ries)
tram·mel
tram·ple
tram·po·line
trance
tran·quil
tran·quil·ize, tran·quil·lize
tran·quil·li·ty, tran·quil·i·ty
trans·ac·tion
trans·at·lan·tic
tran·scen·dence
trans·scen·den·tal
tran·con·ti·nen·tal
tran·scribe
trans·script
tran·sect
tran·sept
trans·fer·al

trans·fer·ence
trans·for·ma·tion
trans·fu·sion
trans·gres·sion
tran·sience
tran·sient
tran·sis·tor
tran·sit
tran·si·tion
tran·si·to·ry
trans·la·tion
trans·lu·cent
trans·mis·si·ble
trans·mit·tance
trans·mute
tran·som
trans·par·en·cy (—cies)
tran·spire
trans·port·able
trans·pose
trans·verse
tra·peze
trashy
trau·ma
tra·vail
trav·eled, trav·elled
trav·el·er, trav·el·ler
trav·el·ing, trav·el·ling
trav·el·ogue, trav·el·og
tra·verse
trav·es·ty (—ties)
trawl·er
treach·er·ous
trea·cle
trea·dle
trea·son·able
trea·sur·er
trea·tise
trea·ty
treble
trek·king
trel·lis
trem·ble
tre·men·dous
trem·or
trem·u·lous
tren·chant
trep·i·da·tion
tres·pass
tres·tle
tri·an·gle
tri·bal
trib·u·la·tion

tri·bu·nal
trib·u·tary
trick·ery
tri·col·or
tri·cy·cle
tri·dent
tri·fling
trig·ger
tril·o·gy (—gies)
tri·mes·ter
trin·ket
trio
tri·ple
trip·let
trip·li·cate
trip·tych
trite
tri·umph
tri·um·vir·ate
triv·et
triv·i·al
trol·ley, trol·ly (trol·leys or trol·lies)
trom·bone
tro·phy (trophies)
trop·i·cal
trou·ba·dour
trou·bling
trough
troupe
trou·sers
trow·el
tru·an·cy (—cies)
tru·cu·lence
true
tru·ism
tru·ly
trum·pet·er
trun·cat·ed
trun·cheon
trun·dle
truss
trust·ee
truth·ful
try
tryst
tsu·na·mi
tu·ba
tu·ber·cu·lar
tu·ber·cu·lo·sis
tu·ber·ous
tu·bu·lar
tu·ition
tum·brel, tum·bril

tu·mes·cent
tu·mor
tu·mul·tu·ous
tun·dra
tung·sten
tu·nic
tun·nel·ing, tun·nel·ling
tur·ban
tur·bine
tur·bo·jet
tur·bu·lence
tu·reen
tur·moil
tur·pen·tine
tur·quoise, tur·quois
tur·tle
tus·sle
tus·sock
tu·te·lage
tu·te·lary
tu·to·ri·al
tut·ti-frut·ti
tux·e·do (–dos or –does)
twain
tweak
tweed
twee·zers
twelfth
twen·ti·eth
twi·light
twill
twine
twinge
twin·kling
twirl
twist
twitch
twit·ter
two·fer
ty·coon
ty·ing, tie·ing
type·script
type·writ·er
ty·phoid
ty·phoon
ty·phus
typ·i·cal
typ·i·fy
ty·pog·ra·phy
ty·ran·ni·cal, ty·ran·nic
tyr·an·nize
tyr·an·nous
tyr·an·ny (–nies)

U

ubiq·ui·tous
ubiq·ui·ty
ud·der (contains a cow's
    mammary glands; see *utter*)
ug·li·ness
uku·le·le
ul·cer
ul·cer·ous
ul·te·ri·or
ul·ti·mate
ul·ti·ma·tum (–tums or –ta)
ul·tra
ul·tra·vi·o·let
um·ber
um·bil·i·cal
um·brage
um·brel·la
um·laut
um·pire
un·abat·ed
un·able
un·abridged
un·ac·cept·able
un·ac·com·pa·nied
un·ac·count·able
un·ac·cus·tomed
un·adorned
un·adul·ter·at·ed
un·af·fect·ed
un·aid·ed
un·alien·able
un·aligned
un·al·ter·able
un·am·big·u·ous
una·nim·i·ty
unan·i·mous
un·an·tic·i·pat·ed
un·ap·peal·ing
un·ap·pe·tiz·ing
un·ap·proach·able
un·armed
un·ashamed
un·asked
un·as·sail·able
un·as·sist·ed
un·at·trac·tive
un·avail·able
un·avoid·able
un·awares
un·bal·anced

un·be·com·ing
un·be·known
un·be·liev·able
un·bi·ased
un·bri·dled
un·budg·ing
un·can·ny
un·cer·tain·ty (–ties)
un·change·able
un·char·i·ta·ble
un·cle
un·com·fort·able
un·com·mu·ni·ca·tive
un·com·pli·men·ta·ry
un·con·di·tion·al
un·con·scio·na·ble
un·con·scious
un·con·trol·la·ble
un·couth
un·de·bat·able
un·dem·o·crat·ic
un·de·ni·able
un·der·achiev·er
un·der·gird
un·der·grad·u·ate
un·der·priv·i·leged
un·der·signed
un·der·stand
un·der·state·ment
un·der·tak·er
un·de·sir·able
un·de·vi·at·ing
un·due
un·du·lant
un·dy·ing
un·easy
un·em·ployed
un·en·dur·able
un·equiv·o·cal
un·err·ing
un·fa·mil·iar
un·fash·ion·able
un·fa·vor·able
un·flag·ging
un·flat·ter·ing
un·flinch·ing
un·for·get·ta·ble
un·for·tu·nate·ly
un·fre·quent·ed
un·gain·ly
un·glued
un·gov·ern·able
un·gra·cious

un·gram·mat·i·cal
un·guard·ed
un·hes·i·tat·ing
un·hinged
uni·corn
uni·di·rec·tion·al
uni·fi·ca·tion
uni·for·mi·ty (–ties)
uni·fy
uni·lat·er·al
un·imag·in·able
un·im·pas·sioned
un·im·peach·able
un·in·hib·it·ed
un·in·tel·li·gi·ble
un·in·ten·tion·al
un·in·ter·rupt·ed
union
unique
uni·sex
uni·son
unit
uni·tary
unite
uni·ver·sal
uni·ver·si·ty (–ties)
un·kempt
un·know·able
un·known
un·law·ful
un·less
un·lim·it·ed
un·man·ner·ly
un·men·tion·able
un·mis·tak·able
un·mit·i·gat·ed
un·nec·es·sary
un·oc·cu·pied
un·of·fi·cial
un·or·tho·dox
un·pal·at·able
un·par·al·leled
un·par·lia·men·ta·ry
un·pleas·ant
un·plumbed
un·prec·e·dent·ed
un·pre·dict·able
un·prej·u·diced
un·pre·ten·tious
un·prof·it·able
un·qual·i·fied
un·ques·tion·ing
un·rav·el

un·re·al·is·tic
un·rea·son·able
un·re·lent·ing
un·re·spon·sive
un·re·strained
un·ri·valed, un·ri·valled
un·ruly
un·sad·dle
un·safe
un·sat·u·rat·ed
un·saved
un·sa·vory
un·scathed
un·sci·en·tif·ic
un·scram·ble
un·scru·pu·lous
un·sea·son·able
un·seat
un·seem·ly
un·seg·re·gat·ed
un·se·lect·ed
un·self·ish
un·set·tle
un·shack·le
un·sheathe
un·shod
un·sight·ly
un·skill·ful
un·snap
un·snarl
un·so·cia·ble
un·so·phis·ti·cat·ed
un·sought
un·sound
un·spar·ing
un·speak·able
un·sports·man·like
un·spot·ted
un·sta·ble
un·steady
un·stop·pa·ble
un·stressed
un·struc·tured
un·stud·ied
un·sub·stan·tial
un·suc·cess·ful
un·suit·able
un·swerv·ing
un·tan·gle
un·tapped
un·taught
un·ten·a·ble
un·think·able

un·ti·dy
un·tie
un·til
un·time·ly
un·ti·tled
un·touch·abil·i·ty
un·touch·able
un·trod·den
un·truth·ful
un·tu·tored
un·twine
un·used
un·usu·al
un·ut·ter·able
un·var·nished
un·veil
un·ver·bal·ized
un·voiced
un·war·rant·able
un·wary
un·whole·some
un·wieldy
un·wise
un·wit·ting
un·wor·thi·ness
un·wound
un·writ·ten
un·yield·ing
un·yoke
un·zip
up·beat
up·braid
up·bring·ing
up·com·ing
up·date
up·grade
up·heav·al
up·hol·ster
up·lift
up·load
up·on
up·right·ness
up·ris·ing
up·roar·i·ous
up·set
up·side down
up·stage
up·stand·ing
up·surge
up·swept
up·tight
up·turn
up·ward, up·wards

up·wind
ura·ni·um
ur·ban (relating to a city; see
    urbane)
ur·bane (suave; see *urban*)
ur·ban·ite
ur·chin
ure·mia
ure·ter
ure·thra
urging
ur·gen·cy (–cies)
uric
uri·nal
uri·nary
urine
urn
us·able, use·able
us·age
use·ful
use·ful·ness
ush·er
usu·al
usu·al·ly
usu·fruct
usu·rer
usu·ri·ous
usurp
usu·ry
uten·sil
uter·ine
uter·us (uteri *or* –us·es)
util·i·tar·i·an
util·i·ty (–ties)
ut·most
uto·pi·an
ut·ter
ut·ter·ance
ut·ter·most
uvu·la (–las *or* –lae)

V

va·can·cy (–cies)
va·cant
va·cate
va·ca·tion·ing
vac·ci·nate
vac·cine
vac·il·late
vac·il·la·tion
va·cu·ity (–ities)

vac·u·ole
vac·u·ous
vac·u·um
va·ga·bond
va·ga·ry (–ries)
va·gran·cy (–cies)
va·grant
vague
vain (worthless; see *vane*)
va·lance (drapery: see *valence*)
vale·dic·tion
vale·dic·to·ri·an
vale·dic·to·ry (–ries)
va·lence (combining power or
    chemical element; see
    valance)
val·en·tine
va·le·ri·an
va·let
val·iant
val·id
val·i·date
va·lid·i·ty
val·late
val·ley (valleys)
val·or
valse
valu·able
val·u·ate
val·u·a·tor
val·ue
val·ued
val·ue·less
valve
val·vu·lar
va·moose
vam·pire
va·na·di·um
van·dal·ism
van·dal·ize
vane (weathercock; see *vain*)
van·guard
va·nil·la
van·ish
van·i·ty (–ties)
van·quish
van·tage
va·pid·i·ty (–ties)
va·por
va·por·iza·tion
va·por·iz·er
va·por·ous
vari·abil·i·ty

vari·able
vari·ance
vari·ant
vari·a·tion
var·i·cose
var·i·cos·i·ty (–ties)
var·ied
va·ri·ety (–et·ies)
var·i·ous
var·mint
var·nish
var·si·ty (–ties)
vary
vas·cu·lar
vase
va·sec·to·my (–mies)
Vas·e·line
vast·ly
vaude·ville
vaude·vil·lian
vault
vaunt
veal
vec·tor
veer
ve·gan
veg·e·ta·ble
veg·e·tar·i·an
veg·e·tar·i·an·ism
veg·e·tate
veg·e·ta·tive
ve·he·mence
ve·hi·cle
ve·hic·u·lar
veiled
veined
vel·lum (leather binding; see
    velum)
ve·loc·i·ty (–ties)
ve·lour, ve·lours (plural also
    ve·lours)
ve·lum (part of soft palate; see
    vellum)
vel·vet
vel·vety
ve·nal
vend
ven·der, ven·dor
ven·det·ta
ve·neer
ven·er·a·ble
ven·er·ate
ven·er·a·tor

ve·ne·re·al
ven·ery
ve·ne·tian blind
ven·geance
venge·ful
ven·i·son
ven·om
ven·om·ous
vent
ven·ti·late
ven·ti·la·tor
ven·tral
ven·tri·cle
ven·tril·o·quist
ven·ture
ven·ture·some
ven·tur·ous
ven·ue
ve·ra·cious
ve·rac·i·ty (–ties)
ve·ran·da, ve·ran·dah
ver·bal·ly
ver·ba·tim
ver·be·na
ver·biage
ver·bose
ver·dict
verge
verg·ing
ve·rid·i·cal
ver·i·fi·able
ver·i·fi·ca·tion
ver·i·fy
ver·i·ly
veri·si·mil·i·tude
ver·i·ta·ble
ver·i·ty (–ties)
ver·mi·cel·li
ver·mil·ion, ver·mil·lion
ver·min
ver·min·ous
ver·mouth
ver·nac·u·lar
ver·nal
ver·ni·er
ver·sa·til·i·ty
verse
ver·si·cle
ver·si·fi·ca·tion
ver·si·fi·er
ver·sion
ver·sus
ver·te·bra

ver·te·brate
ver·tex
ver·ti·cal
ver·tig·i·nous
ver·ti·go
verve
very
ves·sel
ves·ti·bule
ves·tige
vest·ment
ves·try (–tries)
ves·ture
vetch
vet·er·an
vet·er·i·nar·i·an
vet·er·i·nary
ve·to (–toes)
vex·a·tion
vex·a·tious
vi·a·ble
via·duct
vi·al (small container; see *vile*)
vi·and
vi·at·i·cum (–cums *or* –ca)
vibes
vi·brant
vi·brate
vi·bra·tor
vi·bur·num
vi·car·i·ous
vi·chys·soise
vic·i·nage
vi·cin·i·ty (–ties)
vi·cious
vi·cis·si·tude
vic·tim·ize
vic·to·ri·ous
vic·to·ry (–ries)
vict·ual
vid·eo·tape
view·ing
vig·i·lance
vig·i·lan·te
vi·gnette
vig·or·ous
vile
vil·i·fi·ca·tion
vil·i·fy
vil·lag·er
vil·lain
vil·lainy (–lain·ies)
vil·los·i·ty (–ties)

vin·ci·ble
vin·cu·lum (–lums *or* –la)
vin·di·cate
vin·dic·tive
vin·e·gar
vin·ery (–er·ies)
vin·tage
vi·nyl
vi·o·la
vi·o·la·ble
vi·o·late
vi·o·lence
vi·o·let
vi·o·lin
vi·per
vir·gin·al
vir·gin·i·ty (–ties)
vir·i·des·cent
vi·rid·i·ty
vir·tu·al
vir·tu·al·ly
vir·tue
vir·tu·os·i·ty (–ties)
vir·tu·o·so (–sos *or* –si)
vir·tu·ous
vir·u·lence
vi·rus
vis·age
vis-à-vis (French: face to face
  with)
vis·cer·al
vis·cos·i·ty (–ties)
vis·count
vis·cous
vis·i·bil·i·ty (–ties)
vis·i·ble
vi·sion·ary
vis·i·ta·tion
vis·i·tor
vi·sor
vis·ta
vi·su·al
vi·su·al·ize
vi·su·al·i·za·tion
vi·tal
vi·tal·i·ty (–ties)
vi·ta·min
vi·ti·ate
vit·re·ous
vi·va·cious
viv·id
viv·i·fy
vi·vip·a·rous

vivi·sec·tion
vix·en
vo·cab·u·lary (–lar·ies)
vo·cal·ist
vo·ca·tion
voc·a·tive
vo·cif·er·ate
vo·cif·er·ous
vod·ka
vogue
voice
void
vol·a·tile
vol·ca·nic
vol·ca·no (–noes or –nos)
vo·li·tion
vol·ley (vol·leys)
volt·age
vol·ta·ic
vol·u·ble
vol·ume
vo·lu·mi·nous
vol·un·tary
vol·un·ta·rism
vol·un·teer
vo·lup·tuous
voo·doo
vo·ra·cious
vo·rac·i·ty
vor·tex (vor·ti·ces or vor·tex·es)
vo·ta·ry (–ries)
vo·tive
vouch
vouch·safe
vow·el
voy·age
voy·eur
vul·gar
vul·gar·ism
vul·ner·a·ble
vul·ture
vy·ing

W

wacky
wad·ding (soft mass; see wading)
wad·dle
wad·ing (step through water; see wadding)
wa·fer
waf·fle
waft

wage
wag·ging (to be in motion; see waging)
wag·gle
wag·ing (to engage in; see wagging)
wag·on
waif
wail
waist (narrowed part of body above hips; see waste)
wait·er
wait·ress
waive (relinquish voluntarily; see wave)
wak·ened
walk·ie-talk·ie
wal·let
wal·lop
wal·low
wall·pa·per
wal·nut
wal·rus
waltz
wan·dered
wan·der·lust
wan·ing
wan·ton
war·bled
war·den
ward·robe
ware·house
war·fare
wari·ly
war·mon·ger
warmth
warn
warp
war·rant
war·ran·tee (person to whom warranty is made; see warranty)
war·ran·tor
war·ran·ty (–ties) (written guarantee; see warrantee)
war·ren
war·ring
war·rior
wash·able
wast·age
waste (refuse from human habitations; see waist)
waste·land
watch·dog

watch·ful
wa·ter·proof
wa·tery
watt·age
wat·tle
wave (moving swell on sea surface; see waive)
wave·length
wavy
wax·en
waxy
way·far·er
way·lay
way·side
way·ward
weak·ened
wealthy
wean
weap·on
wear·able
wea·ried
wea·sel (–sels)
weath·er (state of atmosphere; see whether)
weave
web·bing
web page, web·page
web site, web·site
web·cam
web·cast
web·master
wed·ding
wedg·ing
wed·lock
weedy
weep·ing
wee·vil
weigh
weighty
weir
weird
weird·ly
wel·com·ing
weld·er
wel·fare
well·ness
welsh
welt
wel·ter
were·wolf
west·ern
west·ward
whack
whale

wham·my (–mies)
wharf (wharves *or* wharfs)
what·so·ev·er
wheel·ing
wheeze
whelp
whence
when·ev·er
where·abouts
where·as
where·fore
where·so·ev·er
wher·ev·er
wheth·er (alternative condition;
    see *weather*)
whey
which·ev·er
whiff
while
whim·per
whim·si·cal
whim·sy, whim·sey (whim·sies *or*
    whim·seys)
whine
whin·ny
whip·pet
whirl·ing
whirl·wind
whis·ker
whis·key, whis·ky (whis·keys *or*
    whis·kies)
whis·pered
whis·tle
whis·tling
whit·en·er
whith·er
whit·tle
whoa
whole·sal·er
whole·some
whol·ly
whoop
whose
why
wick·er
wide·awake
wid·ow·er
width
wield
wie·ner
wife (wives)
wig·gle
wig·wam

wil·der·ness
wile
will·ful
wil·lies
wil·lowy
wim·ple
wince
winch
wind·ing
wind·lass
win·dow
wind·swept
windy
wine
wined
wing·span
win·ner
win·now
win·some
win·ter·rize
win·ter·time
win·try
winy
wip·ing
wire·less
wir·ing
wiry
wis·dom
wise
wish·ful
wishy-washy
wispy
wist·ful
witch·ery (–er·ies)
with·al
with·drawn
with·er
with·hold
with·out
wit
wit·less
wit·ness
wit·ti·cism
wit·ty
wiz·ard
wiz·ened
wob·ble
woe·be·gone
woe·ful, wo·ful
wolf (wolves)
wolf·ish
wom·an·ish
womb

won·der·ful
won·drous
wont (habit; see *won't*)
won't (will not; see *wont*)
wood·en
woody
woof·er
wool·en, wool·len
woo·zy
wordy
work·able
work·a·day
work·man·ship
world·ly
world·wide
wormy
wor·ri·some
wor·ry (wor·ries)
wors·en
wor·ship
worst
wor·thy
would
wound·ed
wrack
wran·gle
wrap·per
wrath·ful
wreak
wreath (wreaths)
wreathe
wreck·age
wrench
wres·tle
wretch·ed
wrig·gle
wrist·watch
wring
wrin·kle
writ
writhe
writ·ing
wronged
wrought
wry

X

xe·non
xe·no·phile
xe·no·pho·bia
xe·rox

X-ray
xy·lo·phone

Y

yacht
ya·hoo
yak
yak·king
yam
Yan·kee
yap·ping
yard·age
yar·mul·ke, yar·mel·ke
yar·row
yawn·ing
yawp, yaup
year·ling
year·ly
yearn
yeasty
yel·low·ish
yelp·er
yes·ter·day
yield
yip·pee
yo·del

yo·ga
yo·gurt, yo·ghurt
yoke (wooden bar; see *yolk*)
yo·kel
yolk (yellow portion of egg; see
    yoke)
yon·der
yoo·hoo
yore
you
young
young·ster
your (relating to you; see *you're*)
you're (you are; see *your*)
your·self (your·selves)
youth·ful
youth·ful·ness
you've
yowl
yo-yo
yuc·ca
yum·my

Z

zag·ging
za·ny (—nies)

zapped
zeal·ot
zeal·ous
ze·bra
ze·nith
zeph·yr
zep·pe·lin
ze·ro (ze·ros *or* ze·roes)
zesty
zig·zag
zilch
zil·lion
zinc
zin·nia
Zi·on·ism
zip code
zip·per
zir·con
zith·er
zo·di·ac
zom·bie, zom·bi
zone
zonked
zoo (zoos)
zoo·log·i·cal, zoo·log·ic
zo·ol·o·gy
zoom